Gleanings: Columns from the Peterborough Examiner 2018-2021

Rosemary Ganley is a gift to Peterborough. She is a social justice warrior, a raconteur, a feminist. Tireless in challenging institutions and shining a light on inequalities, she has a curious mind, full heart and fierce conviction. She reminds us all to go deeper, get political, disrupt our comfort, and rail against systems that are leaving more and more people behind.
Jim Russell, Executive Director, United Way of Peterborough

From local politics to the state of the world, Rosemary Ganley always seems to write with such thought and generous wisdom that readers are struck with how much beauty and hope she sees, despite everything. How full of kind-heartedness she is, as a writer, thinker and fellow citizen.
Jonathan Bennett, Author and Founder of Laridae Communications

I look forward to Rosemary Ganley's second collection of essays published in the Peterborough Examiner from 2018 to 2021. Her writing is highly personal, critically informed and highly entertaining. She continues to challenge us to look deeply at issues. Her first collection, "Positive Community" highlighted community profiles and events. This new book moves to broader concerns affecting us all: climate, Covid-19, cannabis, politics, control of the media and much more. They are always lively, thoughtful and fearless.
Nan Williamson, Author and Artist

One can grab onto her red cloak and spend pleasant hours reading her latest book: backwards or forwards or start in the middle of these stunning columns. Rosemary may not appear serious, but she has serious intents: to inform, to entertain and to change attitudes. Here is a bouquet of anecdotes about life in Peterborough and beyond. They reflect the human kindliness to be discovered in the murky depths of the present moment.
Sandra Burri, Teacher and Librarian

Gleanings

Columns from the Peterborough Examiner
2018-2021

ROSEMARY GANLEY

YELLOW DRAGONFLY PRESS

Peterborough, Ontario, Canada

Gleanings:
Columns from the Peterborough Examiner 2018-2021
Copyright ©2021 Rosemary Ganley

Published by *Yellow Dragonfly Press*
www.yellowdragonflypress.ca

Photo Credits
Page 13 - Rosemary Ganley © Jessica Melnick for the Red Pashmina Campaign

Editorial & Book Design by Pegi Eyers, Stone Circle Press **www.stonecirclepress.com**

Disclaimer: Any errors and shortcomings in this discourse are my own.
Some columns may not have complete attribution, for which I apologize.

Library and Archives Canada Cataloguing in Publication

Ganley, Rosemary
Gleanings: Columns from the Peterborough Examiner 2018-2021
ISBN-13: 978-1-7774245-0-3

On The Cover ~ Rosemary Ganley at the United Nations Plaza, East River, New York City, March 2018. She was a civil society delegate from Canada to the 62nd Annual Session of the UN Commission on the Status of Women, and also participated in the 2021 conference online. The UN Plaza is marked by a large metal sculpture of our wounded Earth.

Contents

Columns 2019

Columns 2020

Columns 2021

Foreword

Cathy Bolan and Peter Laurie

The reader who first encounters the writing of Rosemary Ganley is in for a treat.

Stimulating, warm and insightful pieces, which first appeared in the Peterborough Examiner over the past four years, these essays are deceptively simple. They seem prosaic - people, groups and issues - but each one contains a universal truth about courage, goodness and simplicity.

Regardless of whether the arena is national politics, culture, or religion, Ganley takes on issues that appear vast and unsolvable, while maintaining the hope that spurs action.

She has found her voice and distilled her wisdom in the simplest of formats, the newspaper column. We are the richer for it.

Cathy Bolan is a senior arts policy analyst, and Peter Laurie is a post-secondary educator.

Introduction

Thank you for opening this new collection of mine.

The time is early 2021, and we are still partially locked down, coping with the global pandemic of COVID-19.

It is a year now, and has taken a tragic toll worldwide. But at home in Peterborough Ontario, and bolstered by good health and regular contact - though virtual - with friends and family, I have been able to continue to write a weekly column for the Peterborough Examiner.

When the number of my columns passed 100, I decided it was time to ask author and editor Pegi Eyers to put them together and publish. Digital is good, but it does not supplant a hard copy.

This book, called "Gleanings," consists of 128 columns written since June 2018. They range from stories of admirable personalities in my community, to larger questions of national politics, culture and religion.

I hope you enjoy the articles!

My website is www.yellowdragonfly press.ca

Rosemary Ganley
April 1, 2021
Peterborough, Ontario

The Columns

March On: Strong, Brave Women Are Doing it Again
January 25, 2018

As a global feminist, with the same revulsion towards and worry about Trumpocracy as so many other Canadians, I can't let the week of January 25 go by without a crow of joy.

Just look at the marches - the staying power: thousands and thousands on the streets, walking not only against the appalling public ethos emanating from the White House, which infects the airwaves, and foments bitter divides in the States, but the firm announcing by feet on the ground that things are indeed connected.

When the movement grasps, as it is beginning to do, new intersections: misogyny, the absence of women in decision-making, runaway climate change, nasty deportations, growing isolationism, racism and obscene wealth, we are moving forward. We are not going away. There were 20 percent more participants than last year. They say five million.

Seventy-six percent of Canadians report they are aghast at the state of American politics. It is an unruly state of affairs. Worrisome, therefore. The craven Republicans can't seem to haul the president in.

But one constitutional right our neighbours have and are using, is freedom of assembly. The signs were wildly witty. I saw a photo of a small boy on his father's shoulders saying, "I'm not allowed to act like the President." Nor speak presumably the trash talk this man used last week in describing several poor black countries. Unforgivable. Thuglike.

These peaceful demonstrations of resistance, a year after the first mass public show on January 21, 2017 got barely a mention beforehand in the mainstream media, but they were quietly organized by determined women everywhere, Not just LA and New York and Chicago but in in Texas and North Carolina and in 30 Canadian communities: Halifax, Victoria, Toronto, Sudbury.

Do see the one in Sandy Cove, Nova Scotia, which drew double last year's number for a total of 32. Oh Canada.

There is an important American thinker, Robert Reich, well worth keeping tabs on. He speaks in an understandable way of the seven signs of a tyrant: making everyone an enemy, disparaging the free press, scapegoating such groups as immigrants, and worst of all, calling down divine blessing on it all.

In the Toronto March, MP Maryam Monsef, in her bright red parka, took heart from the strength of women's support to renew her commitment to Canadian women's equality. It will have to include economic equality, and that is why she is with eight other Canadian cabinet ministers in Davos, Switzerland this week at the World Economic Forum.

So much confidence has this government in Peterborough's youthful member, smart, quick as a whip to learn, personable, committed, genuine, and community-based. Monsef will have a leading role in this year's G7 meeting in Canada.

Are we on the cusp of a major change in world values and governance? Have the women massively awoken? Can they sustain their activity, get along with each other, show male colleagues that everyone stands to benefit? Indeed to survive?

The thing about Peterborough is we are never far behind .and sometimes we are ahead, on our analysis and our activism.

On March 8, International Women's Day, A Day of Resistance will be organized at Seeds of Change from 5 to 8 pm.

Same themes as the global march. Shape the agenda, share solidarity, build bridges.

Worthy life goals.

Haroon Akram-Lodhi is Peterborough's Public Intellectual
April 26, 2018

I moved to Peterborough from Montreal in 1969. Trent university, the "Oxford on the Otonabee," had started up in 1964. You could say we developed together. My involvement with Trent was largely athletic. But there was also a stimulating course on Canadian literature to which the professor, K.P Stich, persuaded writer Margaret Laurence to come and speak.

In the 1980's, I offered courses through Trent Continuing Education in feminist theology at the Bata Library to 30 adult community members. Two of my three sons graduated from Trent, heavy into rowing. To this day they insist I pick up a beer mug for each from the Head of the Trent regatta.

The culmination for Trent and me was the invitation, engineered I am sure, by Prof. Marg Hobbs, that I deliver the 22nd annual Margaret Laurence lecture in 2011 on "Feminist Theologies Challenge Patriarchy."

But to some extent I've always felt that Trent and Peterborough operated in two silos. Many professors live elsewhere and commute to Trent. They are unable to serve, as I think would be desirable, given their brains and the level of their education, on local civic organizations.

There have been notable exceptions, of course. T.H.B. Symons was on the Peterborough Police Board, Jim Struthers on the Social Planning Council, Alan Slavin and Stephen Hill into Sustainable Peterborough, David Morrison on the board of Horizons of Friendship, Julia Harrison helping Reframe Film Festival and Cathy Bruce with Jamaican Self Help. But overall.....

Today, I take my griping back. With my new assignment on the Gender Equality Advisory Council to the oncoming G7 meetings, I am dependent on the scholarship of and dedication to global goals of Haroon Akram-Lodhi, eminent professor of international development studies at Trent and generous consultant to me. To say nothing of his serving the women of the world by advising the United Nations Development Program since 2011 with the design of modules for online learning, on such issues as gender-aware poverty analysis, agriculture and women's unpaid labour. I knew he would be impressive when I learned he grew up in Thunder Bay. Leaving home at age 15, he worked in food service to save money and travel, first off to North Africa. He started post-secondary education in England at the School of Oriental and African Studies, then earned a Master's at Cambridge and returned to Canada for PhD studies at the University of Manitoba. His dissertation was on Gender and Rural Development in Pakistan.

Married in 1998 to Catherine from Ireland, Haroon and his wife have two teenage children and live in Toronto. He travels to speak, give workshops, and provide policy advice to UN agencies, mostly in Asia and Africa, about three months a year.

At Trent since 2006, after some years of teaching in London and The Hague, Akram-Lodhi, with his sharply-honed gender lens, is a powerful ally in the struggle for equality. Editor of the "Canadian Journal of Development Studies," he is author of five books on agriculture, food insecurity, and rural women.

He belongs to the International Association for Feminist Economists and has brought to Peterborough many world-known scholars, including Diane Elson of the University of Essex. Elson coined the term "gender-based budgeting" (She is with me on the council).

Who better to advise me for this work than a passionate Canadian intellectual and advocate for women who moves in international circles of thinkers? And can meet me right here in town at Natas? The grass is definitely not greener elsewhere.

Vastly popular with students, Akram-Lodhi won the Trent Prize for research in 2015. He in turn admires the 20-year-olds in front of him. "In one sense," he says "I have no worries about the future.

"These mostly Canadian students are open, liberally-minded, inclusive and concerned. They are the best one can have."

Teaching is a vocation, and Haroon Akram-Lodhi, my consultor, powerfully embodies this vocation.

Melinda, Malala and Me: a Peterborough Activist's Adventures with the Gender Council
May 10, 2018

When I looked out the Greyhound bus window as we pulled in to the Ottawa bus station, and saw a neatly dressed man standing beside a fine car, holding a sign with my name on it in neat letters, I knew for sure I had arrived at big-shot status.

We 19 members of the Gender Equality Advisory council for the G7 meetings in Quebec in June were gathering for three days face-to-face for the first time. Aside from the civil servants who live in Ottawa, I think I was travelling the shortest distance of the 19, who come from the U.K., Africa and Asia.

My friend Pat Parnall told me I really should have arrived at the Chateau Laurier Hotel by bike. My son's teenage students in B.C. were wowed at my ascendant position, and said "That is really dope!" (I offer you a new word which is replacing "cool" in young people's vocabulary.)

In consideration of the expenditure of taxpayer money, my senior bus fare was $60 return. In my suitcase were five copies of Malala Yousafzai's autobiography brought to me by little girls wo had studied her life. In exchange, since all things must be mutual, I asked them for a photograph of themselves doing some activity such as soccer or school work or volunteering so that Malala could enjoy seeing whom she is inspiring. Somebody had urged me to go on Netflix and see David Letterman's funny and insightful interview with Malala at Oxford University in England where she is a student. She is a smart, articulate 20-year-old, whose Malala Fund raised $6 million last year for her dedicated cause: the education of girls. Her goal is that every girl in the world reach Grade 12.

Also in my suitcase was an impressive explanation of an invention, a painless, disposable needle from retired engineer and global thinker Dick Crawford of Lakefield. He was hoping I'd have an opportunity to pitch it to co-chair of our Council, Melinda Gates of the Gates Foundation, for her worldwide inoculation program for children. I did find an assistant who took it and promised to send to the vaccination department.

But good manners dictated I decline the humorous suggestion from a few friends that I tell Melinda they don't like Windows 10. In a good exchange with Ms. Gates, who clearly spends a lot of time sitting on a straw mat in the global south listening to women's dilemmas, she and I chatted about the inspiration we each got from the Fourth United Nations Conference on Women in Beijing in 1995.

We had memorable sessions with Prime Minister Justin Trudeau who has set all this in motion. He may be the most gender-sensitive man I have ever met. There was an unforgettable panel discussion he affably chaired, featuring Leyma Gbowee, a feisty Liberian Nobel winner, Roberta Jamieson, former ombudswoman of Ontario and Order of Canada member ("Don't mess with a Mohawk!"), Lieut-Gen Christine Whitecross, a Canadian who head the NATO College in Rome, Melinda Gates, and the head of UN Women, Phumzile Mlambo-Ngcuka of South Africa.

There were bureaucrats in the room who actually wept as that conversation continued.

Mme. Gregoire-Trudeau came to breakfast with us, telling us her four-year-old was refusing to go to school that day, so she "left them all with my husband."

We could relate.

We had lunch with a dynamic group of progressive, grassroots women who work with CSOs (Civil Society Organizations), such as Oxfam, Inter Pares, MATCH International and Climate Action Group.

There I met a Syrian liberation activist-in-exile. She was in deep conversation with our Canadian diplomat Peter Boehm, who has the heavy task of carrying all our ideas forward to his counterparts who accompany their leaders to Charlevoix in June.

Peterborough-Kawartha was definitely there, participating. Hope we make a difference for the marginalized all over the world.

A Peterborough Priest in
"An Age of Great Transition"
May 17, 2018

About two years ago, one Saturday night, a neighbor of mine came over in deep distress.

Her elderly mother, recently arrived in Peterborough, was in hospital in the final stages of life. Unaffiliated with any church or temple, she was very apprehensive and agitated about death.

My neighbour just wondered if I knew anyone who might comfort her mother.

I did.

Then I called my friend of 50 years, Fr. Leo Coughlin, age 86, at home. He is the most open and available person I know to anyone who calls. Regardless of faith (or no faith), age, background, condition of life, familiar or unknown to him, he responds with a heart full of love and acceptance.

He is also a Roman Catholic priest of 60 years, thoroughly ecumenical, well-read, progressive and up-to-date on modern dilemmas.

Leo went to see Alice that very night and in the next few days, dropped by several times. "I didn't talk God to her," he told me. "I just held her hand and told her she was going home. The images of her childhood home, a farm up near Owen Sound, seemed to bring her peace. I am happy I was able to know her."

That is the pastor to people Leo Coughlin has become in his senior years. From an Irish Catholic farm family in Norwood, he was one of 10 siblings born to Charles and Agnes Coughlin.

After a public school education, he worked a year, mulling over the Catholic priesthood and finally entered St. Augustine's Seminary in Scarborough, being ordained in 1958. "I had a lot of friends, and I played sports, especially hockey, and it seemed right."

Fr. Leo went to Parry Sound and, "it was there I came to realize that the questions people were asking weren't being answered by my education in traditional Catholic doctrine."

He came to Peterborough to Sacred Heart parish, reading and thinking critically, and seeing the gap between what he calls "elevator theology" and the newer ideas around the divine spirit being found in nature and all things.

"There is so much beauty and goodness all around in people," he says. "I feel pain when traditional Catholic teaching refuses to include people, drives them away with rules."

He went to Ottawa to study counselling and then spent 10 years listening to and encouraging clients to believe in their intuition and their own goodness. These days Leo Coughlin lives with both heart disease and cancer, but he is joyful and thankful. In 2013 he was inducted into the Peterborough Pathway of Fame.

On May 27 at 11 a.m. at Sacred Heart church there will be a thanksgiving service for his 60 years of priesthood, to which the public is invited.

He leads a Tuesday book club for 20 people, writings by mystics and social justice activists of any faith. There is a public meeting once a month at the Mount Community Centre on such topics as "Dance as Prayer," "Faith and Feminism" and "The Inclusion of LGBTQ People."

"We are in an age of great transition," he says, "and the institutional churches are very slow to get aboard."

I asked him about conflict with the institutional church he is in. "I am under the radar," he says with a smile. "I visit homes, the sick and dying, sometimes six in a day." Yes, I see him tooling around in a small red convertible.

His own inner life is formed by walks in Jackson Park, where he says he feels at one with the world. "Creation is the first scripture," he says. "I am the thinking part of Jackson Park."

Fr. Leo's favorite song is Josh Groban's "You Raise Me Up." For him, that is true of the Lord he believes in and of the multitude of friends he has in Peterborough.

Running Scared from a Doug Ford Government
May 24, 2018

This column is frankly political. My Examiner columns, all 108 of them so far, are usually mildly political, the small-p kind, about communities and volunteers, and the need to define ourselves differently from the malignant regime south of us.

The majority of Canadians sit to the centre-left of the political spectrum. But elections can be strange. So this time around, I am pulling out the stops to alert readers to the dangers coming down the track: a possible Doug Ford premiership. In Ontario, of all places, the sophisticated and multicultural province, and one of the country's economic engines.

I object to Mr. Ford because of his record, his policies and his personality, that's all. The defender of his out-of-control brother, the late Toronto Mayor Rob Ford, who so embarrassed the city of Toronto nationally and internationally with his bullying, drug use, chauvinism and overall lack of competence.

If this is what a protest vote gets us, let's try protesting another way.

I challenge Doug Ford and his dangerous brand of politics, because his far-right, neo-conservative, and vague policies and many of his candidates will pull Ontario backwards. This Doug Ford was put into leadership by the religious zealot Tanya Granic Allen, who favours therapy to 'cure' LGBTQ people and wanted to ban the enlightened sex ed curriculum in our schools. She once decribed burka-wearing Muslim women as "ninjas." Not my kind of feminist.

Even though he recently ditched Ms. Granic Allen as candidate in Mississauga, he is beholden to her supporters who put him over Christine Elliott in the leadership race. Ford, I fear, will signal to his base that he will sidle over to some of these views. Maybe on a woman's right to choose.

I fear he will divide and embitter public discourse. Surely one Ford has been enough, and one Trump too. Recently in TV debates, he patronized Premier Kathleen Wynne with the remark, "You have a nice smile." We women are very wary of such an approach and the men behind it.

Ford recently demonstrated his ignorance of green policy by threatening to open up green space around Toronto for development. Does the man know anything about water supply and healthy food sources?

His practice of restricting media access to his campaign is frightening. He will not allow legitimate reporters on his bus and has hired a onetime "journalist" to do Ford-friendly videos for social media.

Of the 124 seats in the Ontario legislature, he has appointed the Conservative candidates in 11. No public nomination. One is Andrew Layton for London West. Layton has said that climate science is junk. He was once suspended from his Radio 950 AM job for homophobic remarks.

The PC's may be in the lead, but pollsters also say it's anyone's election to win. It's our game now: the reasonable, the conscientious, the concerned, the middle-of-the-roaders.

I don't know why our present premier attracts such disdain. No one has told me a reason, apart from our high provincial debt. It worries me too, but not enough to vote Ford. Employment is up; the unemployment rate is 5.5 percent. We stand to have a minimum wage of $15 an hour. Ontario's cap-and-trade (which is a form of carbon pricing) is beginning to cut emissions.

Facts should matter to voters. Voting Ford on a vague feeling of "time for a change" is not sufficient cause to usher in a Trump-lite government for this province.

The sitting government has announced more money for mental health, for child and senior prescriptions, for child care and post-secondary education. These programs are at serious risk in a Ford government.

I've been embarrassed in the past by a national leader and by a local member of Parliament. I'm not embarrassed by Kathleen Wynne, I'm proud. Proud too of our local Liberal candidate, the honest and hardworking Jeff Leal. A lot is at stake as the June 7 election approaches. Kindly resolve to vote, and drive the percentage who do, above 60 percent.

To the G7 in Quebec
June 7, 2018

Our 19-member GEAC received a last-minute but nonetheless exciting invitation from the Prime Minister's office on May 13. We had been working pretty hard, thinking deeply about the status of girls and women worldwide in our fragile world, and researching the data (there is not enough of it, disaggregated by gender) and responding to many policy papers which are being prepared for the G7 leaders to sign during their two-day meeting in Charlevoix PQ, June 7-9, 2018.

Assisted by some very competent civil servants at Global Affairs Canada, (talking to you, Nell Stewart and you, Sherry Hornung and you, Suzanne Cooper), we had edited our bold ideas into a powerful 48 pages. Around 16,000 words.

I can only guess that our work has been valued and has had an impact, because we are invited to come to Quebec City on June 7 and meet with the G7 leaders at breakfast on June 9.

I have to pinch myself.

What do I say to British Prime Minister Theresa May, over croissants? Can I comment on Brexit? Can I get to tell France's President how delighted I was to see the Mali man, Mamadou Gassama, scramble like Spiderman up a four-story apartment block in Paris and rescue a four-year-old toddler hanging off a balcony? Quick off the mark, President Macron had him in to chat and presented him with French citizenship. Can I express to Chancellor Angela Merkel my gratitude for her long, enlightened leadership in Germany? She, the daughter of a Lutheran pastor, has a doctorate in chemistry.

I do wish I spoke more than one-and-a-half languages.

And then there is the President of the United States of America. There is no certainty he will come to the G7, but if he does and if he comes to breakfast, and if he has a moment for me, what, dear readers, do I do or say?

Is what I am rehearsing OK?

"Welcome to my country, Mr President. I have not been able to agree with a single thing you have done or said since taking office. But I know you have the power to do immense good."

If he makes a beeline for Melinda Gates or Christine Lagarde of the IMF, or Malala Yousafzai, I'll try to eavesdrop, Kawartha-style, and let you know.

If even for a minute I should doubt the importance of this work for us all, I am reminded every day. Today in the bank lineup, I spoke to a woman whose daughter, abused by her boyfriend, has fled back home, broken and confused. On the weekend I spoke with Toronto women starting a civil society organization called HART, to provide succor and support to young women being trafficked into Canada for coercive sex.

When one sees that Toronto van careening down Yonge Street sidewalks, killing eight women and two men, and learns its driver was a man linked to online groups preaching hatred of women, one knows the struggle must continue.

How long will it take for humanity to banish misogyny?

Our Council is demanding conditions in which girls and women are safe, educated, healthy and heard, that's all.

Thirteen years ago, leaders of the advanced nations delivered a bold promise to "make poverty history." The goal hasn't been fully achieved by any means, but life for the world's poorest people has improved by almost every measure.

I dared to suggest to the Council, half-playfully, that we print T shirts with the slogan "Make Misogyny History" for the G7. To my delight the idea was endorsed by one of Britain's brightest scholars, Professor Diane Elson.

It was a rueful suggestion, not really G7-style.

For 22 years, my basic feminist manifesto has been the final statement of the Beijing Women's Conference, the "Platform for Action." Now this G7 declaration from our Council updates and makes more relevant, powerful and do-able the policies to deliver progress for all.

Over to you, G7!

CanWaCH Puts its Focus on Women's Health in Peterborough and Around the World
June 14, 2018

Diviya Leonard is a 16-year-old youth advocate who was honoured for promoting women's and children's health rights worldwide. CanWaCH gave her the Gender Equality Award for her years of dedication to the cause, through active participation in various Plan International Canada initiatives.

I have long been curious about the phenomenon of virtual offices. These are instruments of organization and action that operate with maximum use of technology to link up employees and volunteers without their ever having to leave their homes. Virtual offices are particularly suited to these times, since they leave little carbon footprint, eliminate commuting time, can be managed across time zones and, when it is made intentional, can foster collaboration that often physical presence in an office cubicle does not.

They are also of course empowering for a person in the global south, anyone with a computer and internet and basic skills. Hence the virtual office suits a Peterborough-based civil society organization called CanWaCH to a T.

CanWaCH, is a 94-member coalition of Canadian organizations: health-profession organizations, research institutes, and non-governmental organizations, all with deep involvement in women's and children's health around the world. Formed in 2010, it is headed by Dr Helen Scott, an epidemiologist, and Julia Anderson, an experienced international development practitioner whose former work included Jamaican Self-Help and Trent University in human rights activity.

In 2010, the G7 countries, which was then the G8 (Russia being expelled a couple of years later because it invaded Ukraine), met in Muskoka. The member nations pledged $5 billion over five years in support of maternal and child health around the world.

I remember at the time being both pleased and suspicious, suspicious because it absolutely did not include reproductive health services. Touchy subject then and still, though a little less touchy today. (Witness Ireland's overwhelming vote to repeal its abortion ban, just two weeks ago.) A mechanism was needed to disburse this money effectively through new partnerships, while gathering data on the state of female health, and sharing insights and best practices among Canadians already involved.

CanWaCH, the Canadian Partnership for Women and Children's Health, was incorporated in 2015. Its focus is first of all on collecting good data about the state of affairs for women and children. In my recent work with the Gender Equality Advisory Council, I have noticed that all initiatives around the status of women lament a scarcity of good data on which to base decisions.

"Canada has a very good reputation as an international leader in global health," says Anderson. "We intend to build on it. We work with researchers developing innovative programs such as the one by Dr Stanley Zlotkin, of Sick Kids Global Health. He originated 'sprinkles,' a child nutrient. We also support work in Haiti." Member groups of CanWaCH include Horizons of Friendship in Cobourg, UNICEF, the Red Cross, and other major Canadian hospitals with medical schools. Fees to belong are high, from $500 to $1,000, but for small groups they are waived.

The office hours of CanWaCH are 10 a.m. to 3 p.m. across Canada, and each employee (there are 13) works an eight-hour day. The software that enables this work to be done is called GLIP.

When a lay person thinks of health around the world, one thinks of malnutrition, vaccinations, and the risks of Ebola and dengue fever through travel. CanWaCH also encourages us to think of women's fertility control and of newborn babies' chances of survival in what are now called "fragile situations" (such as refugee camps.)

In a side note, Anderson told me about the impressive project of Hayley Wickenheiser, a Canadian Olympic heroine, who is starting medical school in Calgary at age 39. Called WICKFEST, it is a biennial project for 12-14-year-old girls who play hockey anywhere in the world. They are brought to Calgary to compete, but more than that, they are offered four days of leadership training, along with their parents, siblings and coaches. It is an international program that will influence a generation and a community. Readers can call up the CanWaCH website (www.CanWaCH.ca) and get the newsletter. And be proud that its work and its vibes are here among us.

"Orange Man" Doesn't Slow G7 Gender Meeting Enthusiasm
June 21, 2018

There was a cheeky text from son Jim: "Mother, you go to your first-ever G7 meeting, and all hell breaks loose!"

That's true. I was there and I was in the room, with about 20 others, seated for the breakfast meeting with the G7 leaders. I saw the offensive behaviour of the Orange Man, plunking himself down three seats from me, as the clicking cameras of the world press drowned out the remarks of our Gender Council chair, Isabelle Hudon. He was late and disdainful; he greeted no one; gender equality is not his favourite subject.

How did I get to be there? Here is how it happened. In January, I had a delightful phone call from the Prime Minister telling me of his creative plan to appoint 18 internationally-known feminist thinkers and leaders to form an advisory committee on the status of girls and women around the world. Then to write a report, "bold and strong," he said, which he could present to the G7 leaders when they came to Quebec in June.

The job was temporary and unpaid, for 2018, which is the duration of Canada's presidency of the G7. When I saw the list of women who had agreed, I swooned: Phumzile Mlambo, head of UN Women, Winnie Byanyima, head of OXFAM International, Melinda Gates of the Gates Foundation, Malala Yousafzai of the Malala Fund, Christine Lagarde of the IMF, Lieutenant-General Christine Whitecross of NATO College, Rome.

And me. It seems Peterborough, Ontario rocks.

We set to work, mostly virtually, once in person. We produced a 36-page document, a call to action for the G7 countries, called "Make Gender Inequality History." It is, if I can say so, a worthy successor to the much-heralded statement that came out of the UN Conference on Women in Beijing in 1995, the "Platform for Action," which has been my feminist manifesto for 23 years.

We were invited to come to Quebec and meet with the leaders on June 9. We spent a day deciding who of the eleven of us who had come to Quebec would speak if called on.

I was ready with my pitch on women's movements and organizing. I also had my prepared remarks for President Trump should he stop by to shake my hand.

They were, "Welcome to my country. I have not been able to agree with one thing you have said or done since being elected, sir, but I know you have the power to do immense good."

He shook hands with no one, made small talk with no one, and looked scornful when not fiddling with the translation system in front of him.

He is a very large man at 6'2", and rotund. Threatening.

But you would have been proud of the Canadian leadership around that table: Chrystia Freeland, the Prime Minister, Maryam Monsef, and chair Isabelle Hudon. Their poise and their determination not to be provoked or derailed was a model of civility.

Five of our council members spoke succinctly, on health, violence, poverty, education and the clear economic benefit of equality. The G7 leaders listened intently. Our African members and our Indigenous Canadian member wore striking traditional dress.

We drove back to Quebec City in quiet contemplation, and then heard the joyful news that six of the G7 countries, the World Bank and others had committed new money, $3 billion, to "quality, gender-sensitive" education of girls in the global south in the next five years.

I came home to find Peterburians fully informed about the drama of the weekend: I mean, people at fitness class and the watch repair and the dentist.

"You wanna talk tariffs?" said one woman as we practiced our balance. "All the facts that have eluded the Orange Man all these weeks?"

Wow.

Next column, I'll tell stories about the unique lives of the women I have worked with for six months.

And, for citizens' groups in Peterborough, if you'll invite me, I'd like to come talk about this event and its meaning for us all.

The Good and the Noble on the G7 Weekend
June 27, 2018

Turning away from that noxious president, who continues daily to charge through the world like a raging bull in a china shop, wreaking havoc and disdain, seemingly impossible to stop by cowardly politicians in the Republican Party and by his misled, poorly-educated constituents, I'd like to point to some fine achievements from the meeting made by the democratic countries of the west (and Japan) in early June.

Gender equality made it firmly and likely permanently on to future agendas of the coalition. France will be next to host, and M. and Mme. Macron will be reliable leaders. Their Advisory Council, should they establish another one for their G6(7), I look forward to seeing. Europe brims with women of distinction: the Nordic countries, the older European countries and the new NATO ones. For example, a woman from Croatia came close to being elected Secretary General of the United Nations this year. Spain has just appointed more women to its cabinet than men (16-13).

Secondly, new money, a lot of money, was pledged by the G6 and the World Bank for "quality, gender-sensitive education of girls" in the global south. This is Malala's one and only cause: education of girls everywhere to grade 12. The difference one young woman can and did make!

It's really astonishing to sit beside someone who has just said, "We're in for $140 million."

Other moments I'll remember: the bus ride from Quebec City in the early morning of June 9, as we Council members went for breakfast to Charlevoix. I sat beside Winne Byanyima of Uganda, eminent head of Oxfam International. I had my pink blazer on, but it dimmed next to her African traditional dress. As women do, we talked about our families. Winnie's mother was orphaned at age 5 and raised by a group of French Canadian nuns from Chicoutimi! Winnie intends to make a pilgrimage to Chicoutimi to pay her respects.

At age 20, her mother told the Sisters she'd like to enter the convent. They told her to go see the world first. She did, and married and had six children.

After a silence, Winnie said to me, "You had a Catholic childhood, didn't you?" "Yes," I said. "Well then, let's pray."

So we did. "Come Holy Spirit, fill the hearts of the faithful; enkindle in them the fire of your love. Send forth your spirit and they shall be created and you shall renew the face of the earth."

Whatever power there was, Winnie embodied it in her passionate plea to the leaders at breakfast to absorb the suffering of women and girls, especially in the parts of the world where OXFAM works.

As we were ushered out of the Chateau Richelieu by the ever-smiling and efficient Ian of Global Affairs Canada, we ran into Mme. Gregoire-Trudeau with her group of G7 spouses. There was Mr. May, a huge cheerleader for his wife, Mrs. Shinzu Abe who speaks no English, but enthusiastically admires every flower and plant, Mme. Macron, and the spouse of EU representative Donald Tusk, Mme. Malgorzata Sochacka, who is Polish.

We stopped to be introduced and someone said, "Oh Mme. Trudeau, you are making history!"

Sophie's eyes widened. "Oh, I am not trying to make history," she said, "just to allow the good to flourish, if I can."

Now that's a fridge magnet.

The sunshine, the wide river, the image of the Minister of Status of Women enjoying an apple, the glorious sky and the sense of promise drove out foreboding. Apart from too many American flags and grim-faced security talking into their headsets, all was well.

If even briefly I doubt the importance of this work, I am reminded every day.

In the bank lineup, I speak to a woman whose daughter, badly abused by her boyfriend, has fled back home. A Toronto van careens down Yonge Street sidewalks killing eight women and two men, its driver a man linked to online groups spreading hatred of women.

How long will it take for humanity to really banish misogyny?

Bach Takes Peterborough
to New Musical Heights
July 5, 2018

It often happens that just around the corner in this town is a fantastic surprise or opportunity.

To wit: I recently read about a series of organ concerts: live, free and of agreeable length (one hour, more or less) to be staged at on Sunday afternoons at Sacred Heart Church on Romaine Street in Peterborough.

The announcement had such a sense of creativity and fun. "In honour of J.S. Bach's 333rd anniversary of birth" (who knew?), four Sunday afternoon organ concerts, entitled "Bach@Three," would be presented by the talented and knowledgeable Randy Mills of Cobourg, who is choir master at Trinity College School (with 60 kids in the choir) and organist at St Mark's Anglican Church in Port Hope.

I am at the stage of wanting to hear more and learn more about the great classics of Western culture and was intrigued by the opportunity. The organ had been my mother's favorite instrument.

So many questions. Why here in Peterborough, in a south-end church, one I had to confess I had never been in.

The link is especially interesting. Sacred Heart Church now has a priest, a classically-trained tenor who has come here from Argentina, Fr. Andrew Ayala.

(No, he's not generally available during certain World Cup games!)

Fr. Ayala is also a scholar, having recently earned his PhD in theology from St. Michael's College in the University of Toronto. Naturally, he was determined to renew fine music at Sacred Heart.

The organ, a Casavant from 1914, was originally donated to the church by the McManus family. It is, Randy Mills tells me, worth a million dollars today.

"It is a stunning piece of work in an outstanding classical Italian church with a great interior vault similar to those of the Renaissance," Mills says.

He himself has been in the Cobourg area for 25 years, having grown up in London, Ontario to a musical family with European roots, and obtaining his Bachelor of Music of the University of Western Ontario followed by studies at Concordia Lutheran University in Chicago.

Randy Mills is currently chapel organist at Trinity College School, Port Hope, Organist at St. Mark's Anglican Church, Port Hope and now director of the Sacred Heart Children's Choir and Bellringers.

Parents are thrilled with the results.

Witty and knowledgeable about all things Bach, often described as the greatest of all composers, Mills plays fugues, cantatas and preludes and offers informative commentary between songs from the choir loft.

Fr. Ayala sang Bach-Gounod's "Ave Maria" and the scholars sang "Jesu, Joy of Man's Desiring."

In this age of the immigration crisis along the Mexican-U.S. border, it could hardly be missed that one the church's brilliant stained glass windows depicts Jesus seated, welcoming the children.

The season of public performance concludes on July 11 when Sacred Heart Church hosts a 45-voice Boys Choir from Bordeaux, France in concert at 7 pm.

"There is a remarkable upsurge in choral music," says Mills, "especially in France and in Quebec. The director from Bordeaux came here some months ago, loved the acoustics and asked if they could perform. We a billeting the boys. The concert will be free, with donations towards expenses."

I suspect it will be beautiful, and will catapult our city and this musical collaboration to new heights.

UK Roasts Trump as Peterborough Neighbourhood Fires Up the Grills
July 19, 2018

"Trump Baby Blimp" lifts off, Parliament Square London
LUKE MACGREGOR/BLOOMBERG

We can think big and we should, but the truth is we live our lives at the local level, and here we have the modern challenge: to resist what is happening under Trumpism in its many forms, and stand up to it by building a clear alternative society.

We have to leave it to the equally shocked and appalled Americans to bring him and what he is promoting to heel. Sooner, we all hope, than later.

Just to recap: 250,000 Brits demonstrated against his visit to London, saying he does not respond to moral indignation or reason, so they satirize him. Did you see the orange blimp?

Canadians are just as shocked, fed up and frightened by the man, the movements and the tweets. So contradictory, self-aggrandizing and deceptive are they, we have to guard against addiction to the bad.

I follow the posts of Robert Reich, former Secretary of Labour in the Obama administration, and Prof. Timothy Snyder, a Yale historian. The creeping fascism analysis. Then, there's the essential, exasperated, late-night comic, Stephen Colbert.

It's bad, but we must not be enervated. While Mr. Trump damns the torpedoes, turns on every ally, praises his own faulty thinking, cosies up to tyrants and nudges his society towards fascism, we have to shake ourselves off and plan a wily campaign of resistance.

I think it begins with neighbourhood barbecues, myself.

On June 24, Manning Avenue, just north of Parkhill, had its second annual community picnic. The 65 people who came brought everything needed: burgers, buns, chairs, coolers, beer, hockey nets and balls. They clamoured for it to become an annual event, so we are setting aside the last Sunday in June as the permanent date.

One friend, a teacher at Kenner, reads lots of books. "This," he crowed, "is building social capital!" Whatever it is, it gets us knowing each other, recognizing the growing kids, finding out who does pedicures, and counting the number of dogs on one block: 16. Not a cent changed hands. It took four women 20 minutes of organizing: make a little flyer announcing the event, and dragoon kids into delivering one to every door for five blocks around.

Sheila Harrington offered her good, wide double driveway. Ever co-operative neighbours Des Hickie and Mary Ten Doeschate wheeled their barbecue in. The new family from Chile was introduced, the rain held off and the single men prided themselves in presenting their casseroles. Marty from Benson Avenue won chef of the day with his huge platter of ribs. There was chocolate cake with a Canadian flag, and the national anthem in both languages.

All over the country in all manner of ways, we Canadians are doing similar things. It's a middle-class thing, true, but Peterborough is 70 percent middle class. I learned at the housing summit on July 12 that we are a really poor city, economically. Do you know our average income is 22 percent lower than anywhere else in Ontario? That we need 2,000 geared-to-income homes?

But everybody who lives here also knows our wealth: each other, voluntarism, good health care and education, safe streets, music and theatre, and above all, the natural environment. Mighty wealthy.

Hence we aren't so prone to extremism, to targeting media, to scapegoating certain groups, to believing lies and propaganda, to the cultivation of dreadful manners, to hatred of women, even I dare to claim, to the wiles of greed. We haven't let big money dominate our politics (i.e. the Koch Brothers' zillions) or private media (Fox News, Rupert Murdoch) mislead our people. We've made some smart decisions here in little old Canada.

So can we resist trumpism? My modest suggestion for neighbourhood barbecues is that City Hall set up a small fund for groups of at least four citizens, on application, to receive $100 for a gathering of their neighbours, as long as it's all-inclusive and free. Next week more ideas for resistance garnered from a lively meeting at New Canadians Centre, July 12.

Canadian Reaction to U.S. Politics Takes Shape in Peterborough
July 26, 2018

John Fewings Cartoon

Let's put everyone with a sense of humour in front of the line of this rag-tag, unorganized, grassroots movement being born in Peterborough, "The Anti trump Resistance" in Canada. (We don't capitalize the man's name, because it is more than just him).

Leading the parade will be the likes of political cartoonist Michael de Adder and his colleague, Bruce MacKinnon of the Halifax Chronicle Herald, who have an uncanny finger on our national pulse. Today's cartoon by de Adder, who is a New Brunswicker with a degree from Mount Allison, shows a pudgy Canadian in a ball cap offering a pint can to two astonished Americans with heavy-duty guns. "This is open-carry in Canada," he says.

Where, oh where is Rick Mercer when we most need him? This summer of discontent and rising nonsense, ripe for the satirist's plucking. Jokesters must be favoured in the first rank of our movement, since, as de Adder says, "We all have a reason to be stressed." Everybody I meet is stressed. Around the globe, news is made and re-made by a man whom conservative columnist George Will describes in the Washington Post, as "a sad, embarrassing wreck of a man."

My tongue-in-cheek column last week recommended the neighbourhood barbecue as a powerful, subversive activity meant to build social capital and solidarity. This week, brighter minds than mine have sent me the following wisdom. "For heaven's sake, strengthen the study of Canadian history in our schools! Do you know that a high school grad needs only one course in Canada's history? One! How can we know and value and defend liberal democracy with such puny exposure?"

Yes, let's really get all of us expert on Canada's past: the glorious and the inglorious, the heroic and the racist, the slow walk, without a civil war, to independence, finally sealed in 1982. (Seems a very sensible pace, now.) Absorb our inspired Charter of Rights and Freedoms, which, to their communal detriment, the Americans do not have. Learn about our costly internationalism through two world wars.

"For social solidarity and to prevent widening the gap between rich and poor, we need political decisions of an enlightened kind, such things as a decent guaranteed income, and single-payer health and education," another wrote. Private philanthropy, on which so many Americans depend, is not the answer. Social sharing, the redistribution of wealth through fair taxation, is. Ideas kept coming. "Psychologically, people need to belong to the community. A doctor told me that that loneliness is next to heart disease as an ailment of the aged."

"Don't let up on pressure to preserve what has been gained in sexual and reproductive rights in Canada."

"Challenge the talented retirees moving to Peterborough to lend their skills: on boards, with civic and volunteer associations. There is no retiring from life or from the need to be useful."

"Practise meeting one newcomer a week: At the NCC or in the neighborhood or at work or at the doctor's office. Maybe take a rebuff or two, but go at it again."

"Make Peterborough's slogan 'You're welcome here.'" (In Africa, they would add, "now pick up a hoe.")

"Take the heart, the emotions, the feelings of a people into account more fully, tell the stories of human goodness. They have a multiplying effect."

"Dire predictions about climate disaster fuel fear. Show that successful efforts are being made here and everywhere to reduce carbon emissions, and must be speeded up." Many of these resisters turned up on July 21 for an important run at civil engagement - protesting Premier Doug Ford's repeal of the progressive 2015 Sex Education curriculum.

"Keep and increase public spaces, playgrounds, community gardens, DIY hockey and skating pads, picnic tables everywhere, so citizens (and don't call us 'taxpayers,' please) can engage and meet one another."

"Get us weaned off the automobile with good bus service, widespread cyclepaths, and a change in driver attitudes."

I can see the movement gathering steam.

Charmaine Magumbe Pursues Peterborough City Council Seat
August 9, 2018

Charmaine Magumbe was the recipient of the 2017 YMCA Peace Medal at a ceremony on Friday November 24, 2017 at the YMCA in Peterborough. Magumbe is an advocate for racial justice who has organized numerous peace rallies, and is also the chair of the Community Race Relations Committee.   CLIFFORD SKARSTEDT/EXAMINER

Both are women of accomplishment. Both were born elsewhere but are thoroughly Canadian. Both are "women of colour," to use an awkward but understandable term. And both are on the younger side of the field, articulate and positive about the city, its assets and its challenges. I would be confident in either were they to win office. Both represent the future of Peterborough. And I imagine both would be formidable opponents to the Ontario Tory government with its rolling series of backward policies. Charmaine Magumbe and Kemi Akapo, Charmaine in Monaghan Ward and Kemi in Town Ward, have launched vigorous campaigns for municipal council for the election of October 22. This week I will profile Charmaine Magumbe, and in two weeks' time, Kemi Akapo.

Magumbe rides up on her bike to greet me with a wide smile at a bistro downtown. She is 53, a mother of five and grandmother of one, living with her youngest child and her mother. She is happily employed as International Students' Advisor at Fleming College in Lindsay.

Her ward has the largest population of the five wards, 16,000 people. Her opponents will be current councilors Don Vassiliadis and Henry Clarke. Twenty percent in the ward are senior citizens. "But my ward has only one seniors' centre," she says. "Mapleridge."

Magumbe has an extensive resume. She does occasional stand-up comedy at the Red Dog Tavern. She enjoys music and plays violin in the

Kawartha Community Orchestra. Her Christian faith is important to her, she tells me, though she is not bound to a traditional church right now.

Upfront about race, Magumbe says she came to Canada from Jamaica when she was four years old and grew up in all-white communities. "This election is not about race," she says, "but about passion, ideas and the future." She is refreshingly frank and even-tempered on this topic. "What I have experienced, race-wise, is invisibility. In some white circles, I am simply not seen. But I assert myself, I am not hostile nor resentful. I just want to get on with the project or job we have undertaken. If I can open doors for other young people of colour, so much the better."

Growing up in Sudbury, Magumbe earned a B.A. in psychology and lived in a "great social housing project called Unicorn Non-Profit Homes. There were market-rent, geared-to-income and senior and disability apartments," she said. "It was well-integrated and we were hardly aware of which group our neighbours came from." While at Laurentian, she met a fellow student from Zimbabwe, a metallurgist. They married and returned to Zimbabwe for seven years, where four children were born. When the family came back to Canada, the marriage ended and Magumbe became a single mother, determined to provide good education for her children. Three now have university degrees.

I recall personally about 10 years ago speaking with Charmaine Magumbe about her family and learning that, when racist graffiti was scrawled on the walls of her daughters' elementary school, the teachers hastened to remove it. Magumbe decided to make it an issue of education for all at the school. She coached the principal into having a reconciliation session with the young perpetrator and his family, and her daughters.

Always alert and active in the community, she is now Chair of the Community and Race Relations Committee, and recently co-organised two large public rallies: Last year's Solidarity Weekend against Nazism, and later a Black Lives Matter gathering to protest police violence against young black males, widely reported in the States and not unknown in Canada.

She was honoured last year by the YMCA as Peacemaker of the Year. What I see her contributing to Peterborough City Council is a very honest assessment of life from all sides, and a way of encouraging frank speech without hostility. To say that more female voices are needed at council is a truism. We currently have two out of eleven women in governance: a record that should, this time, be shattered.

Every Canadian Diocese
Must Come Clean on Abuse
August 23, 2018

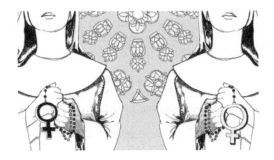

In my four years as columnist in this space, and as a critical thinker, most often appreciatively critical, I have on a few occasions written about the institutional Catholic Church with deep indignation.

I was taught critical thinking first by my parents, then my studies in philosophy and theology at a Catholic college in Toronto, then as a writer and editor, watching this Church for many years. In what Italian journalist Massimo Faggioli has called the "greatest crisis since the Reformation 500 years ago," even more grievous than that one because it is written on the backs of children and the vulnerable, new data is pouring out of a Pennsylvania Grand Jury investigation that took two years, heard 500 witnesses and unearthed thousands of pages of incriminating documents. Even though we have for 50 years been uncovering clerical sex abuse....ours in St John's, Newfoundland at Mount Cashel orphanage in 1990, then in London, Ontario with offender Charles Sylvestre, and Peterborough not immune in the 1980's.

For the same number of years, feminist Catholics have been calling for deep restructuring of this church and they do so again today: build an egalitarian church at last, and do away utterly with the clergy-lay division. Call Constitutional congresses in every diocese; all options open; divest the all-male, celibate College of Cardinals and all their inappropriate decision-making processes. Look at modern forms of leadership: temporary posts, elected, inclusive of all members.

Dare I say democratic? I do. Build in accountability, financial and moral.

Radical? Perhaps. But people are reeling in horror at the release of this report on seventy years of child molestation and ecclesial cover-up in six of the eight Pennsylvania dioceses (Canada has 61 dioceses). Three thousand American Catholics have demanded in a powerful letter, dated August 20, that all bishops, guilty and innocent, resign, since this is systemic sin.

This necessary excision of past and recent history, shocking and dismaying, must lead to some conclusions about systemic dysfunction, even corruption. The investigation found 1,000 cases of child abuse by 300 priests, living and dead. By legal means, 24 names have been blacked out. The rest appear.

I follow several American reform groups. One of them, the Women's Ordination Conference said, "For many of us, those earlier stories were happening somewhere else: now we know it happened everywhere."

The grand jury described a "criminally and morally reprehensible betrayal of trust that robbed survivors of their dignity and their faith. The priesthood was treated like a ruling class in a failed experiment, with horrible ramifications for children."

This is all happening 20 years after the Spotlight crisis in Boston, where the newspaper rooted out evidence of widespread abuse by clergy and cover-up. The jury recommended that statutes of limitations for prosecution, both civil and criminal, be lifted. It described church behaviour as a "playbook for concealing the truth. We have had to pry information from a church that has placed its reputation as a holy institution above the pain of helpless victims."

All 61 dioceses in Canada must come clean. Now. Open files, reveal financial settlements and report the movements of perpetrators. Clarify penalties for failure to report child abuse. Globally, do away with the clergy class.

Empower the people to elect leaders. End mandatory celibacy. Withdraw harmful, outdated sexual teachings. Said Marianne Duddy-Burke of Dignity, a group of LGBT Catholics, "No official in the Catholic church has a shred of credibility when speaking of issues of sexuality, gender or relationships. They do not deserve to be consulted by public policy-making bodies."

Patriarchal gender stereotypes are falling apart everywhere, and the patriarchal priesthood must go with it. It is a moment of truth for the institution.

Concrete action is demanded. Whether leadership, existing in an echo chamber of its own supporters in Rome, and headquartered in docile chanceries around the world, can muster the daring is a question for the next few months.

Kemi Akapo:
Potentially the "Toast of the Town"
August 30, 2018

Kemi Akapo could well become the toast of Town Ward this coming election. With its population of 10,000 people, the area comprises the downtown streets, stately old homes, student digs, performance sites, businesses, restaurants, the waterfront and cultural centres. In fact, she chose Market Hall for her campaign launch August 1. She will face Jane Davidson, Jenny Lanciault, Dean Pappas and Jim Russell.

Kemi's own background has prepared her for leadership roles. She was born into the Yoruba tribe in Lagos, Nigeria, to a family of professional parents, and spent some for her childhood in the city of Ouagadougou, Burkina Faso. She grew up speaking English. She recalls a childhood of social service led by her mother who took her on weekly visits to an orphanage.

After following her older brother (she has three of these) to Trent in 2005 - 2009, she studied English literature and international development. Following graduation, Kemi was scooped up by Trent to work in the Office of Student Affairs where she worked for five years until becoming Coordinator of Settlement Services for the New Canadians' Centre four years ago. She continued to take courses in women's and gender studies.

She makes visits to her parents, now in Montreal. Kemi says, "I have behind me 14 years of living here, and four years observing Council closely. Monday night for me is devoted to City Council, in person or by video."

The first priority in her ward is housing. "I want to work towards ensuring everyone has safe and affordable housing. In addition, financial accountability is crucial. I have experience in good stewardship of public funds, always spending considerable time drawing up proposals and then accounting to funders for the disbursement of money."

This, I expect will be a useful skill on Council.

She is an expert in the resettlement of newcomers, and finds great joy in it. "It connects me to community services, businesses and employers."

Another of her important concerns is mental health, especially for the young. "A city that is inclusive is better for all citizens," she says. "We have a way to go in this area."

Speaking face-to-face to people is her preferred method of communication.

"I have begun door knocking between four and eight p.m. letting people know I am running and hearing from them about their concerns. So far, I am hearing about the condition of our roads, the shortage of accommodation and the official plan."

"I will be using a website and literature, but I know that nothing is as effective as a personal call. I have a great team of volunteers and supporters."

A concern shared by all election observers is that the percentage of those who vote has been dropping slowly, down to almost 40 percent in the last election four years ago. At the same time, online voting is up, suggesting it suits many: the home-bound, students, busy workers and those with disabilities.

The opening day of advance and online voting for this election is Oct 9. The voter must be on the Voters List and should check that so as to get a pin number for online voting. A voter can still register on the day of the election if they are not on the list. Many people still prefer to walk to a poll and put their paper ballot in the box.

Kemi Akapo is a follower of the arts and well-known among Peterborough students, artists and social justice advocates. She has volunteered for three years at the Warming Room overnight shelter.

She has a strong green consciousness and a steady, listening presence.

"I have energy, time and a strong sense of civic responsibility," she says. She also has a measured and careful approach to issues, which suggests she could be very valuable on Council.

(My apologies to two candidates in Monaghan Ward whom I didn't mention in my article on candidate Charmaine Magumbe: Jeff Westlake and Dave McGowan.)

Ultimate: There's a Sense of Spirit in this Team Sport Played in Peterborough
September 6, 2018

Flying discs i.e. by Frisbee are used
in the growing sport Ultimate.

I've been searching the culture for small, almost hidden, ways we are resisting Trumpism and Fordism. This week I have seen the resistance clearly, not on the streets or in the press, but in sport; in a game. Ultimate frisbee, better known as Ultimate.

Twenty-five years ago, our middle son met the woman he was to marry, a social worker from Moncton, while they were playing Ultimate Frisbee on the Halifax Commons. Their favorite wedding gift was an antiqued disc from their friends, which hangs today on their living room wall.

So I have had a soft spot for this game, the most democratic and alternative team sport I've ever seen. Seven players a side, usually four men and three women, throwing a 175-gram plastic disc, short or long distances, with huge curves, unexpected trajectories and soft landings.

The Ultimate thing persists for that son and his wife, now with three teenagers who all play, and I seek to more fully understand its appeal.

Two weeks ago, I felt some of it in Brampton as I trudged in the heat around a play field, Sandalwood Park, which has 20 spaces big enough for an Ultimate game. I was at the National Championships, where, for three days, 2000 teenagers from all provinces, and later hundreds of older folks, threw their hearts out. There was a march-in and a welcome banquet, and a heartfelt farewell one, too.

Then I made my way to Holy Cross field here in Peterborough to take in a PUL (Peterborough Ultimate League) game the following Tuesday.

All I saw was joy of movement, laughter and smiles, body types of all heights and sizes and great cardio fitness. And small kids playing along the sidelines.

It is the ethic and the behaviour of competitors that so impress one. Shouts of "nice try" and "good throw" and "well done" resound. Opposing players' hands stretch out to give an opposing player a hand-up. Everyone gets to play equal time. It is co-ed, non-contact, social and affordable.

"All you need is some green space, a disc and some friends," says my grandson.

"Oh yeah," said my neighbor, "Ultimate, that's the hippie game!" Actually, it was founded on a college campus, Amherst College in Massachusetts in 1968 and came to Canada in 1979. In Peterborough, the league was started in 2004 by Stephanie Ogilvy-King, and has grown steadily, now up to about 200 people, mostly ages 20-45. High schools and even elementary schools here are quickly taking it up.

Who plays Ultimate in the PUL? Teachers, mechanics, political staffers, salespeople, my physiotherapist, an emergency-room physician, long-haul drivers, young mothers. It's a sport that is highly participatory, low-organization and low-tension. Summer league games are scheduled three nights a week, and in winter, the Spiplex, an air-supported dome near Fowlers Corners, is home.

Peterborough has developed an original idea called the "carbon flip" that is spreading across the region. If you have arrived at the playfield by bike or car pool, you have earned the right to pick which end of the field you start on. That's the flip.

Counter-cultural to its core, Ultimate has no referees: you just sort out, as reasonable people, what just happened: if the disc went out-of-bounds or you took too long to launch it, or bumped someone too vigorously. Talk it over, decide quickly, and if all else fails, take it back to where the play began.

There is an explicit SOTG, "Spirit of the Game" in Ultimate, which includes these qualities.

At game's end, originally, the losing team had to compose an honour song for the winning team and go over and sing it to them. That nice touch seems to have been supplanted by a circle of all players, arms linked, and a discussion of the many incidents of spirit shown during the game.

Hardly mentioned in the sports pages, I nonetheless maintain that the virtues of Ultimate are the ones needed for our future.

Peterborough Council Candidate Kim Zippel Brings Passion, Knowledge to Otonabee Ward
September 13, 2018

Green Party leader Mike Schreiner with Kim Zippel, co-founder and chair of Harper Park Stewardship Initiative.
CLIFFORD SKARSTEDT/EXAMINER

It was impressive to note how carefully Kim Zippel, candidate for council for Otonabee Ward, prepared for our conversation. I can imagine that this woman of high intelligence and sense of organization will be a great addition to city governance.

She knows she has 6,000 doors to knock on before election day. She has spoken with citizens at 1,407 doors. That means 600 a week. I found that fact daunting, remembering running in Northcrest, unsuccessfully, in 2010, and flagging, after 20 or so encounters with strangers. "I am clearing my work calendar," she says "and giving my all to speak to people. I enjoy it. Each door brings a different viewpoint. I avoid mealtimes and I sometimes drop literature with a handwritten message, but I really enjoy speaking with constituents."

"It is my second time running. I have a great team of volunteers. Walking the ward gives me an opportunity to assess our housing needs for people of all socioeconomic groups. We don't have enough housing, especially in the West End when many students come to Fleming."

Kim Zippel's campaign is allowed to spend $13,848 by provincial electoral law. "I have a donation page on my website," she says. "Some supporters are giving to me at the door." Her passion for the natural world and her expert environmental grasp have been formed by her studies and by active membership in the Peterborough Field Naturalists. "We have to look at the environment from a global perspective; climate knows no boundaries," she says, "but take action locally."

Zippel was prominent in the Save Harper Park effort as the casino discussion took place. "Smart business respects the environment. Wetlands lessen the impact of flooding which is critically important for people in the south end who are downstream of the casino." I felt myself hoping Kim is a voice on our council as we stagger to the end of a searing summer and a record-breaking forest fire season.

What has disappointed her in the present council is "the divisiveness with police, with Cavan Monaghan township over annexation, and with the province over the Parkway. These have been distracting," she says.

Born in London, Ontario to a bank manager and a nurse, Kim moved around a lot, and was living in Walkerton when the polluted drinking water episode occurred. It made her vigilant about water resources. She attended the Centralia College of Technology in Guelph, followed by bio-chemistry at the Trent University. Kim worked for many years at Darlington Nuclear Plant, working for Ontario Hydro as the first woman licensed by the Canadian Nuclear Safety Commission as a control room operator.

I'd say that qualifies as pressure.

She and her husband Mark now own a business on Water Street providing project management to large industrial installations. Their son Keith is with the Canadian Forces, deployed in Latvia.

"I advocate for green space. I follow city politics and planning on storm water. I am a fact-based decision-maker. We must apply our understanding of development under climate change," she says.

"I live in the ward. It is very a strong and proud area. People take care of each other. Otonabee ward has an exceptional history of industry and sports but has retained its natural beauty. We have Fleming College, the Wellness Centre, the Exhibition, 20 parks, schools, churches, and sports. At the same time, we in our ward are often overlooked. We don't have a single piece of public art. Yet we aren't primarily industrial any more."

Public art? That kind of thinking impresses me: A political figure conscious of the elevation of the spirit through surroundings?

"I am interested in better planning, more transparency from Council and in ensuring citizen engagement. We won't any longer be the left-out ward." There is a lot of interest in Otonabee Ward: six candidates in all - Brock Grills, Bob Hall, Lesley Parnell, Jason Wallwork and Ryan Waudby.

Kim Zippel seems to stand out.

Jim Russell Would Be a Mediator for Peterborough City Council

September 20, 2018

Since our city council has so consistently come to decisions with a 6-5 vote, and a certain ideological split has become apparent between the corporate and business-minded councilors and the social/environmental/change-oriented ones, I think it may be time for Jim Russell to take his place at that table.

Jim, who is running in Town Ward and lives along Little Lake with his partner Tammy, has been in Peterborough seven years; having long hoped for an opening so he could come from Toronto and live here. Jim was a close friend of the well-known writer Charles Foran and his wife Mary, and frequently visited them.

He came to sense something unique about our place: The size, the composition, the location, the arts, the social conscience and the liveability.

So when the position of executive director of United Way came open, Jim quickly applied and was selected. And anyway, the city lost the Forans to Toronto! Jim has over 30 years of front line work and senior leadership in the not-for-profit sector. He has bachelor's and master's degrees in social work from Ryerson and the University of Toronto. He grew up in a politically aware family.

"My siblings," he muses, "include one socialist, one Conservative, one Liberal and one not-really-interested in party politics."

"I chose the municipal level because I am fairly distrustful of party loyalties and herd thinking which often prevails at the federal and provincial levels. I disdain partisanship."

He smiles. "I would invite 15 pro-Parkway and 15 anti-Parkway enthusiasts to meet in a room. I'd give them bread and water, and only let them out when a solution, a compromise of some kind, had been reached."

He has obviously thought deeply about our community context. "What are really to be valued is not alignments, but principles. One needs enough healthy ego to change one's mind at times. The question is, what is better for poor people in this situation and fifty years down the road?" Looking at our downtown population and our shelters, I think Jim Russell's social justice voice is needed at the table.

"The city belongs to those who choose to live here. You will notice many of the candidates this time are from away. That is healthy for the possibilities of politics. The quickest way to change people's lives is by the stroke of a pen at the social policy level and that is why it matters when it comes to political leaders we choose," he says.

"We should elect councilors for their good judgment. All should have the desire to drive towards consensus. I thought long and hard about running. My motto has always been: listen, and then lead. People are mentioning to me that at council there is a party of six and a party of five. Not the best for good governance."

Interestingly, Jim Russell spent five years at Daybreak in Richmond Hill at the Jean Vanier-inspired L'Arche community, where the differently-abled live with assistants in a mutual relationship. He was then in his 20's, influenced by a Canadian priest we discovered we both knew: the late Fr. Brian Massie, S.J. with whom I worked in Kingston, Jamaica in a campaign against capital punishment.

Jim would like to see more animation downtown, not more police. He urges more understanding and compassion for those with mental health and addiction problems. "There are broken people," he says. "For most, it is not character flaws that have brought them to a low point, but lack of opportunity. The first response from individuals should be sympathy, and council should respond too."

I look forward to a walk downtown led by Jim Russell, as he models approaches to those seated on the sidewalks with begging bowls.

"Our level of homelessness is unacceptably high," he says. "We need a five-year housing strategy, accelerated."

"Consider what this community looks like to young people," he says. "Are we a phoenix rising, or a city in decline?" I'd rather like to see Mr. Russell providing this thinking at City Hall.

Visit www.jimrussell.ca

Candidate Stephen Wright Brings Financial Know-How to Peterborough City Council Campaign
September 27, 2018

If Stephen Wright, candidate for Northcrest Ward in the city election of October 22, knocks on your door and you mistake him for Olympic gold medal sprinter Donovan Bailey, that's understandable. Both have Jamaican roots and the likeness is uncanny, though Stephen's roots go back some generations. His grandparents came first to New Brunswick and then to Manitoba. He grew up in Calgary and earned a degree in political science at the University of Manitoba.

What he brings to the table, in his second bid for a Northcrest seat, are 15 years in the city, and long experience in the field of taxation, which would be a very helpful quality for the financial fate of citizens and taxpayers.

Full disclosure of my bias here. I lived and thrived in Jamaica for three years and came to treasure the literature, the music, the cuisine, the sports, the sense of humour and the gregariousness.

Wright worked for the Canadian Federation of Independent Business, known as a "big voice for small business." He can tell me that property taxes here have risen 28 percent over 15 years. "Property taxes have increased at a faster rate than income has increased," he says.

Since his work has largely taken him out of Peterborough and has involved lobbying policy-makers at all levels, he is aware that our council has never mounted a mission to the province for economic development as a municipality.

He wants to add more vigour to that aspect of governance. Municipal governments can't, by law, deficit-finance their budgets, nor surplus-finance them. This means that what council decides to fund, it must take from taxes. Really judicious decisions are needed.

Wright also hopes to improve the traffic flow from south to north but protect Jackson Park. "Why would you destroy a natural asset like that when you have it?" he asks. His constituents have long been worried about traffic, both cottage traffic and other, using residential streets because there is no wider thoroughfare. Long-term planning should develop Chemong Road and County Road 19 by means of road widening and some appropriations as needed.

He smiles as he says, "I would give every member of council a map of Peterborough and county and urge them to think about possible future scenarios, especially amalgamations. We need public engagement; there are many smart ideas out there."

"Growth is coming, it is actually here, with housing developments. Developers fees are way too low," he says. His ward has 11,000 voters and 25 polls. There are three senior's homes in Northcrest so senior's issues concern him. Ease of transportation and good access to health care are among them.

The father of six, who works from home and is advised in this campaign by respected political veteran Peter Adams, is concerned about youth unemployment. New green technologies interest him. There is also the issue of the sale of PDI.

"Despite overwhelming opposition to the sale of PDI, council decision to move ahead with the sale, irrespective of the wishes of residents. That raises a number of questions for me."

"In the fiscal year 2019-2020, where will we get the lost revenue from it? Will Hydro One cover a portion of the costs of maintaining the Riverview Park and Zoo? Will there be two separate utility bills coming to the home, one from Peterborough Utilities for water, and one from Hydro One for electrical distribution? Or will the PUC continue to bill for both corporations, adding an administration fee?"

Wright adds, "There is now an opportunity to reverse the decision as the Ontario Energy Board is reviewing it." He concludes our conversation by pondering public service. "I think public service is the rent we pay for the space we occupy on this planet."

Learn more at www.electstephenwright.ca.

Peterborough Mayoral Candidate Diane Therrien - Youthful, Experienced and Progressive
October 4, 2018

I was late for my appointment with mayoral candidate Diane Therrien. Couldn't find my keys: the result of distraction. I looked in the freezer and in the fridge. Then I thought to pray to St. Anthony, and there they were, in the cutlery drawer. It didn't matter to her: while waiting, she met up with DBIA executive director Terry Guiel and there is always lots to discuss.

Diane came to Peterborough, as a student, as so much of our new talent does, from out-of-town: from Hamilton in this case, to go to Trent. She earned her master's degree in Canadian and Indigenous studies while a grad student at Traill College. She then began working for the Poverty Reduction Network, and then at the YWCA. In 2016, she received the Trent University Alumni Young Leaders award, which recognizes alumni who have shown outstanding leadership in the first 10 years since graduating. Diane is now 32. For recreation, Diane walks her two dogs, which were acquired from the Humane Society, and plays slo-pitch softball.

Being downtown and actively involved in community issues, she got a feel for the city, ran for city council in 2014 in Town Ward and was successful. After a four-year term on council, during which she served on the DBIA committee and the art gallery board, she was persuaded to run for mayor this time around, against incumbent Mayor Daryl Bennett.

She announced her candidacy on May 3 and opened a George Street campaign office.

I can't help noticing Mr. Bennett has no campaign office. She has been full-time campaigning, speaking to "thousands of residents" and visiting all wards. After announcing her 39-point policy platform in September she received 400 "likes" online and many calls, emails and "shares." It confirmed for her that the city is ready and keen for new leadership, more transparency and more consultation. "People are ready for a new voice," she says, "And I believe I am that voice."

Therrien's slogan is "Expect More." I asked her what this entailed. Ride-sharing for one thing, given that taxi fares are rising, bike-sharing and expansion of trails, a green bin program, ranked ballots for the next election, a multi-purpose convention centre and reducing driving speeds on residential streets to 40 km/hr.

The allowed expenditure for a mayoral campaign in this size community is $50,000. Therrien is proud of the number of small donors who are giving. I remember running in 2010 for a seat in Northcrest.

My expenditures were $5,000 (signs and printing) and I raised $5,010, from 110 people. I was pleased to present my financial report promptly after the election to the city clerk because it showed that an unwealthy person, with support, can run for office, and it demonstrated approval from many sectors. Plus, I had $10 over and above, too!

A fundraiser for Diane Therrien's campaign has been organized for October 11 at the Red Dog Tavern. Tickets are $20 and the show, from 7 to 10 p.m. will feature Kate Suhr, Linda Kash and Dub Trinity.

For me, a revealing piece of political literature called the "City Report Card" is in circulation, the research by local environmental groups. It shows how each Peterborough councillor voted on four "green" issues during the last term: the casino vote, the parkway vote, the sale of PDI to Hydro One and environment decisions in general, including approving subdivisions, and providing parking and roads for the casino and an adjacent hotel.

Therrien has a perfect score on her voting, all green across the board.

All-red scores are attached to the names of David Haacke, Andrew Beamer, Dan McWilliams and Lesley Parnell in addition to Mr. Bennett. The report is available at v4sp.ca (Vote for Sustainable Peterborough).

If we citizens still need any motivation to help a planet in jeopardy as a priority, we need not look further than Drew Monkman's brilliant and readable two-part series in the Examiner September 14 and September 21, 2018.

Visit www.dianetherrien.ca for more information about the candidate.

Catholic Schools and Human Rights: A Deep Contradiction
October 11, 2018

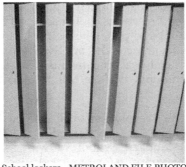

School lockers - METROLAND FILE PHOTO

There is a deep contradiction in the governance of schools in three provinces in Canada, the three last provinces to publicly fund Catholic schools: Ontario, Alberta and Saskatchewan. The clash is too seldom aired and discussed, but the Trent University Teacher Education department and Prof. Karleen Jimenez performed this public service last week with a talk by Prof. Tonya Callaghan of the University of Calgary.

Callaghan presented her findings, the result of research done for her PhD at the University of Toronto, to a full crowd, at Trent, and sold out her book, *Homophobia in the Hallways: Heterosexism and Transphobia in Canadian Catholic Schools*. It was exactly the right place and time, and Prof. Callaghan adopted exactly the right tone: sober, calm and well-documented.

"In some Catholic schools in Canada," she said, "there are human rights violations because some teachers and students are told that canon law trumps civil and constitutional law." She cited section 15 of the Charter of Rights and Freedoms (1982). prohibiting discrimination based on gender and sexual identity. The clash comes with official Catholic church teaching on all manner of sexual issues but particularly homosexuality.

Rather than challenging the harmful words of Canon law in the Catechism of the Catholic Church (1993), where homosexuality is described as "intrinsically disordered" and "contrary to natural law," many Catholic schools adopt a pastoral tone of "hate the sin but love the sinner." This is scant progress over the recent past of condemning homosexuals outright.

Catholic sexual teaching is characterized by a condemnation of contraception, abortion, masturbation and divorce. Despite the work of Catholic feminists and theologians to persuade the church to rescind offensive phrases and bring church teaching into the 21st century, the condemnations remain. For anyone who cares about words and their impact, this is very troubling. Publicly-funded schools are required to have elected boards and elections, but many will tell you the ultimate authority for curriculum and policy lies with the bishop of the diocese. Conscientious teachers are caught on the horns of a dilemma. To disagree with the official teaching means risking their jobs. But to abandon their gay students takes a toll too. So a certain hypocrisy prevails.

Callaghan believes the "revolution" will be led by the young. For example, Leanne Iskander, 16, was denied a gay-straight alliance in St Joseph's Catholic Secondary School in Mississauga in 2011. Her campaign involving youthful supporters led to province-wide legislation that publicly-funded schools must have such clubs and call them this, not "Equity Clubs."

In 2002, 17-year-old Marc Hall of Oshawa, with the support of his family, won a court ruling against the Durham Catholic Board that he could indeed bring his same-sex boyfriend to the school prom. The ruling came on May 10, the very night of the dance. But Callaghan also discovered flagrant abuses of human rights. In one case, a teaching assistant in Alberta was fired for attempting to have a child with her same-sex partner (2008), and another teacher was fired for transitioning from female to male. Heterosexual allies have also been subject to penalties. One straight ally was fired for putting up a supportive poster.

There is, in some Catholic schools, the referral of homosexual youth to a "reparative" program called Courage International, a conversion therapy denounced by psychologists. Remarks and taunts are heard in many schools. "That's so gay," is one. One teacher said that the aggressive boys in her class often quoted the church's exclusion of women in defense of their misogynistic views. "The Vatican," Callaghan said, "exercises a hegemonic force within Catholic schools."

When I heard about this lecture, I alerted the Roman Catholic bishop of Peterborough, the Catholic board trustees and the Director of Education as interested parties. But only two Catholic teachers, who advise Gay Straight Alliances in Peterborough's two Catholic Secondary schools, attended. "Shouldn't educational institutions scrupulously respect the constitution of the land?" Callaghan concluded. It was an honest and important discussion, entered in to by teacher-trainees of great goodwill.

Don't Let Toxic American Political Culture Seep North
October 18, 2018

Supreme Court nominee Judge Brett Kavanaugh opening statement Senate Judiciary Committee Capitol Hill. SAUL LOEB/AP FILE PHOTO

We Canadians are bruised and battered after watching with shock the machinations in Washington around the confirmation of Brett Kavanaugh to the Supreme Court of the United States, a lifetime appointment. We watched, some of us for hours, since we really do seek to know what is going on in the world, as the Senate Judiciary Committee approved by the slimmest of margins his nomination, and it went on to the full Senate for endorsement.

All that, in spite of the searing and sincere testimony of Prof. Christine Blasey-Ford of Palo Alto University in California about her recollection of being sexually assaulted by Kavanaugh when they were in high school in the 1980s. Then there was his whingeing defence of himself, his overweening sense of entitlement and his extreme partisanship, all of which undermine any claim of his to being impartial once on the bench.

His nomination was opposed by the American Bar Association, by 2,000 law professors, by Yale's former president, by the Jesuit magazine America, and by the largest coalition of American churches ever assembled. But no, those elderly, mostly white, men and one woman, many of whom were around to dismiss Anita Hill's similar testimony against Justice Clarence Thomas 27 years ago, forged on to guarantee another extreme right-wing voice on the court. It was the triumph of patriarchy again in America.

In an interesting twist, people on Facebook were circulating an insightful quote from Elon Musk's first wife, Justine Taylor Musk, who was born in 1972 in Peterborough!

Musk, a novelist said, "The enemy of feminism isn't men, it is patriarchy. Patriarchy is not men, it's a system. Women can support the system of patriarchy just as men can support the fight for gender equality."

That's certainly what I have experienced.

So toxic is the atmosphere in American politics today, fostered by a demonic president who knows no truth, former Canadian Prime Minister Jean Chretien, a sharp observer, just wrote, "I fear that Hillary Clinton's defeat in November, 2016 and the arrival of the fanatical Trump mark the true end of the American Empire." Chretien was writing in his new book *My Stories, My Time*.

Writing the book, he says, has helped him recover his serenity, when he got too tired of observing the "surrealist vagaries of President Trump and listening to his nonsense."

"It has been very sad to observe the monumental error our neighbours to the south made in November 2016. We have much better institutions but we must not backslide when it comes to social values."

For me, regaining my serenity has taken me to even deeper meditation and then to activism on behalf of women as I go about telling groups in my community about my G7 experience on the Gender Equality Advisory Council. I've taken heart by looking at the TIME magazine cover of October 5 showing Blasey Ford's face and hair covered with her words. I tried to reach her with a message of support, but so threatening are her critics, her email has been erased and she has not even returned to her home.

I've also taken heart from reading the great Quaker thinker in Philadelphia, Parker Palmer, who writes, "I watched the president of the United States use the massive power of his office to vilify a private citizen. It was a chilling sight. I could not shake off images of the Roman Coliseum, where mobs relished blood sport while a Mad Emperor egged them on. It should have been an impeachable offense, but in these twisted times, it's a ploy to grab headlines and mobilize the base."

The Atlantic magazine examined the cruelty that it saw. "Trump and supporters find community by rejoicing in the suffering of those they hate and fear. Malice has been made a virtue." And the court, the editors said, is headed back to the 19th century.

One grabs on to such progressive American voices. Then one redoubles efforts to be fair, civil, non-violent and inclusive. To be human.

Sister Ruth Hennessey and the Hospitality of Peterborough's Casa Maria Homes
October 25, 2018

Refugee families find safe haven and community support at Casa Maria homes located in Peterborough, Ontario. RICHARD LAUTENS/TORONTO STAR

I thought I had a hospitable home, it being for many years called "Potluck Central," until I recently visited Sister Ruth Hennessey, CSJ over on Downie Street. Ruth gives new meaning to the word "hospitality," having been the founder and present director of Casa Maria House, a tidy, brick home, where for 25 years, she another Sister and many volunteers have given temporary shelter to some 200 refugees from 45 countries, people fleeing persecution in their homeland. The house has three "apartments," each with a kitchen, but it feels like a family home.

"The work has been fully supported by my religious congregation, the Sisters of St. Joseph of Peterborough. We have an advisory board, and many donors, including some who have lived here in the past as refugees themselves," Ruth says.

A highly personal, grassroots welcome awaits the refugees at Casa Maria and two other homes in Peterborough, one in East City (Medaille House) and one on Donegal Street (Joseph House). The day I called, the three houses held 18 refugees. Usually they are families, the first being from Burundi in 1994. "All three children from this family are grown now," Ruth says with some pride, "and professionals in their work lives."

In 1994, the Peterborough Sisters had a call from Fort Erie, Ontario, where some local Sisters had relatives. Among the members of a small prayer group there was a border official. He told his group about desperate arrivals with nowhere to go. His group put some people up in motels, and became hosts to others. The Fort Erie group sought assistance from the Peterborough community of nuns.

Ruth Hennessey had just retired from 35 years of teaching small children in local elementary schools. She felt the call to volunteer.

The Sisters run the houses and pay the taxes. They fundraise, quietly, having had a successful annual bazaar for 15 years. Former residents often donate. "Yesterday," Ruth tells me, "I received a generous check from someone I taught in Grade 1."

The paperwork is tremendous.

"Our immigration lawyers are in Toronto. Refugees are given two weeks to start the process of entering Canada. I am overwhelmed at the generosity of people. Dentists, doctors , schoolteachers, social workers, neighbours: there is so much good will."

I can't help thinking it was such a place as Casa Maria that prepared our city to successfully integrate 300 Syrians in the recent crisis. The Roman Catholic diocese of Peterborough became the ultimate sponsoring organisation for the Syrian arrivals.

The day I visited, a young man from Haiti, upgrading his training as a nurse had arrived. I tried out my French, but Ruth advised me to switch to English. "Speaking English is crucial for people to adjust to life here," she said.

Only three nights before, a Colombian family had left, and Ruth's friend Helen McFadden had come to help change bed linen and make two apple pies. It felt not at all like an institution, but like a home. Ruth's space is on the third floor.

"People in Peterborough want to do good and are grateful for their Canadian citizenship," she says. "We welcome refugees regardless of race, social status, religious or cultural traditions. An important goal for us is deepening local public support and awareness of the plight of refugees."

The United Nations Convention, 1951, describes a refugee as a person, "who, owing to a well-founded fear of being persecuted for reasons of race, religion, nationality, or political opinion, is outside the country of his nationality and is unable, or, owing to such fear, unwilling to avail himself of the protection of that country."

Casa Maria homes are committed to "safeguard the dignity and rights of those forced to flee their homeland."

It is real, brave and faithful service.

The Parliament of the World's Religions in Toronto
October 31, 2018

This week I will get myself to the bus and head to Toronto, and then to the Metro Convention Centre, for the 10,000-person-strong Parliament of the World's Religions. It's the first time in Canada for such a great assembly, organized by the non-profit organization in Chicago, a global meeting of religious leaders, theologians, writers, artists and activists held every four or six years somewhere in the world.

The very first PWR was in 1893 in Chicago. Then 100 years elapsed. The Parliaments resumed in 1993, and have been held in Capetown, Barcelona, Salt Lake City, Melbourne and now Toronto. There will be representatives of 200 religions! For a week, all will forge ahead with workshops, plenary sessions, worship services of every kind, including pagan rites, art exhibits, yoga, concerts, meditation, gardens: all in search of peace, reconciliation, and understanding.

And maybe there will be more political activism on behalf of the vulnerable and the earth. In 1997, Father Hans Kung, the Swiss-German Roman Catholic thinker, and a profound ecumenist, said, "There will be no peace until there is peace among the religions."

Modern history proves that assertion is correct. He drafted a powerful 16-page declaration. "Towards a Global Ethic." It begins with the words, "The world is in agony."

I have, all my life been interested in the power, influence, teachings and errors of the world religions. When I heard in March this conference was happening as close as Toronto, I determined to go. The organizers were asking for proposals. I approached Peterborough-Kawartha MP, Hon. Maryam Monsef and suggested we two offer a workshop entitled, "Faith and Feminism: A Muslim and Christian Work Together for Women's Advancement."

She readily agreed. The organizers accepted our idea, no doubt because of her international accomplishments, not so much mine!

A meeting such as this has to keep 10,000 people busy all day and evening for six days, so our session is scheduled for November 2 at 6 pm. We are to turn up at the Speakers Ready Room an hour early. We won't need technology, I think, just storytelling.

One day is devoted to Indigenous issues and spirituality. I notice that Alice Williams of Curve Lake will present, as will writer Pegi Eyers. Among my circles there is some buzz growing about the PWR. Reverend Julie Stoneberg of the Unitarians will be there. However, participation is not cheap: $450 for the week.

It may yet garner some media attention. Among the luminaries to speak are the Dalai Lama, Jim Wallis of Sojourners magazine, historian Karen Armstrong, and former Canadian PM Kim Campbell.

Writer Jack Jenkins of the US Religious News Service has said, "Questions about religion can paralyze some politicians." He was interviewing Senator Cory Booker, an African-American former mayor of Newark who, in contrast, loves talking about the influence of religion. Booker has said, "Before you tell me about your religion first show it to me in how you treat other people."

The religious "left" is making a big mistake ceding territory to the religious "right." Being multifaith, LGBT-inclusive, liberation theology-influenced, and social justice-focused, progressive religion is often drowned out by the well-organized and financed religious "right."

As I wander the halls of the Parliament, I'm going to be watching for signs that religious leaders are tackling the big and urgent questions. Nothing bland, self-satisfied or soporific, please. How about Israel in Palestine, Sunni-Shia hatred in Turkey and other parts of the Middle East, Christian fundamentalism in the United States, inaction on the environment, and the thorny topic of global population control.

I am going to be watching for the presence of Roman Catholic leadership. I know they are busy with scandals and synods in Rome, but still.

Religions usually cruise under the radar of attention. But with this congress they will be seeking attention.

As for our workshop, I will consider it a success only if the Dalai Lama comes. More next week. Visit www.parliamentofreligions.org for more information.

Infinite Variety, Infinite Possibilities at Parliament of Religions
November 14, 2018

Self-esteem is often based on what one has accomplished all by oneself. Just ask my granddaughter, age 6.

I went to the Big Smoke for five days with one backpack and several senior TTC tickets. No taxis for me, no extraneous possessions, no hotel reservations. Couch-surf in friends' homes, and take public transportation. Mastered.

Then there was the Metro Convention Centre on Front Street. First of all, it has no sign hanging outside, as one might find in Peterborough, and the main doors are a devil to find. Once inside, have fun. The architects are playing a major joke on you. The North Building has four floors (100, 200, 300 and 400), all connected by numerous escalators, and then one passes across an artistically carpeted "bridge" to the South Building, where the numbers resume, but downwards. The 600, 700 and 800 floors are under one another. Go DOWN to 800!

But lots of smiling volunteer guides were about, in purple T-shirts. I met Peterborough's Janice Keil and other familiar faces, such as John and Lorna Devan and Gayl Hutchison. And truth to be told, there were glories inside that Convention Centre, day after day.

The Parliament of World Religions was one part love-in, one part Sikh hospitality, one part illuminating talks at the post-grad level, one part singing and circle dancing, and another part meditating in the "Red Tent."

The organizers wisely chose the themes for each day: Indigenous wisdom, the rising of women, the crisis of the environment, and the scourge of violence. The whole point, then, is whether and how quickly the religions can absorb and respond to these signs of the times. I had a shock when I approached the registration desk. Programs, the size of an Eaton's catalogue, holding descriptions of over 400 talks, events, services and workshops, cost $50. "Oh no," I said, "I can't afford that!"

"Well, if you had pre-ordered, it would have been $15." Drat. "And you can download (dread word) the App."

I did that, with help, but then I decided to mostly forego technology and just go wherever my steps and my goodwill would take me. I do have an eye for faces, and these are a few of the faces I encountered and spoke with: Gen. Romeo Dallaire, Green Party leader Elizabeth May, Harvard Business School dissenter David Korten who wrote "When Corporations Rule the World," African feminist theologian Teresia Hinga, and Indian ecologian Vandana Shiva. The latter has been called by Forbes magazine one of the seven most important thinkers in the world.

For me, there was yet another part, a warm personal reunion of longtime Vatican II Catholic reformers, such as Joanna Manning, now an Anglican priest, Heather Eaton, now an eco-feminist theologian at St. Paul's University in Ottawa, and Bishop Marie Bouclin of the Women Priests Movement.

My presentation with Hon. Maryam Monsef was scheduled for 6 p.m. November 2. It was entitled "Faith and Feminism: a Muslim and a Christian Work for Women's Advancement."

The minister had had one heck of a week: Status of Women Canada was elevated to a full government department. This means it cannot easily be downgraded in future by another government. Also, the YWCA of Canada, replete in white scarves, had spent that very day on Parliament Hill lobbying successfully for new money from her department for its long and effective work with girls and women at risk. So she had taken Porter Air from Ottawa to Toronto late Friday afternoon and arrived in our meeting room with 10 whole minutes to spare, as serene and focused as I was scattered.

"Why don't we just put these chairs in a circle," she suggested to the 50 or so diverse men and women who had turned up.

There followed a rich and revealing dialogue among us all about our various faiths, and none, and how they motivated us to undertake justice work. It ended in a shared song of peace.

Catholics Play a Key Role at Parliament of Religions in Toronto
November 22, 2018

St. Basil's Catholic Church is one of Toronto's oldest churches. The city recently hosted the Parliament of the World's Religions. RICK MADONIK/TORONTO STAR

Readers have been asking for some more detail about that great gathering in Toronto last week, the Parliament of the World's Religions. Let me describe three. In one airy hall, there was a beautiful installation: hundreds of colourful, fluttering ribbons tied to rows and rows of string. It was the Climate Ribbon Project, and everyone stopped to participate. On a nearby table, were markers and foot-long ribbons, each about three inches wide. We were asked to answer the question, "What do you love and hope to never lose in climate chaos?" and write it on a ribbon.

The answer came readily to me, "The well-being of my grandchildren." I wrote, and silently attached it. Then we were invited to write the same hope on a second ribbon and tie it to our wrists for the duration of the conference, and beyond, if we like.

It could be done anywhere by any group. Marian, who was standing nearby, said to me, "The tying of names and hopes to a living tree is an ancient ritual that has been practiced across diverse human cultures for thousands of years."

I also promised to "cover" Catholic presence at the Parliament. The choirs of the internationally renowned St. Michael's Choir School on Bond Street offered a free performance of Gabriel Faure's "Requiem Mass in D Minor" with orchestral accompaniment. Also on this program was "De Profundis" by Arvo Part, Psalm 130, "Out of the Depths, I Cry to You, O Lord."

There were influential individual Catholics, usually not identified, but some in monastic garb. The important writer Mathew Fox, a former Dominican priest who years ago criticized the idea of original sin and wrote "Original Blessing," for which he was tossed from the Church, celebrated a "cosmic mass."

Jesuit Robert Allore from Vancouver gave a session on the 2016 letter of Pope Francis on the environment, "Laudato Si." That letter was widely praised at the assembly. I chatted with Fr. Thomas Ryan, a Paulist priest from New York who has visited Canada several times. He told me he was "relieved" to be back. He is director for interfaith relations for his community and a well-known yoga instructor who has written 11 books on the subject of bodily spirituality. I ordered one for my son, the coach, called *Wellness, Spirituality and Sports*.

Then I went to a session sponsored by the Archdiocese of Toronto entitled "Catholic Women on the Front Lines." Three panelists, two of whom teach in seminaries, defended the official church bio-ethical principle. I had to utter a respectful word of dissent. The teaching is that life is sacred from the moment of conception to the moment of natural death (declared in 1869). This rather limits one's bio-ethical thinking. Modern Canada has legislation about both ends of this spectrum, with which I agree, and which challenge this idea.

The Margaret Atwood session drew one thousand people into a big hall for a lively interview with the great writer, now age 79. Ever sardonic, Atwood started by saying her friends were amazed she had accepted to be at a gathering of religions. "You are a skeptic," they reminded her.

But to me, her work shows a holy concern: women (*The Handmaid's Tale*) and the earth (*The Year of the Flood*).

Ever a scientist, she spoke of "ooho," a container for water which can itself be eaten. Even though she has written powerfully about dystopian societies, Atwood now writes a blog of hope. "We are moving to a culture of renewables and a culture of stewardship." Of course, not without problems.

"Religion is misused in service of totalitarianism and fundamentalism," she said, "yet there is a new realization that unless people of faith get involved in mending the planet, it's not going to happen. Differences among denominations, even great religions, seem irrelevant with what we face now."

It was time for some circle-dancing with the wiccans, to awaken the right side of my brain.

Parliament of World Religions:
of Compassion, Crones and Chappatis
November 28, 2018

Rosemary Ganley at Parliament with
Prof Heather Eaton, Ottawa University

What makes a compassionate city? Could we declare Peterborough to be one? In 2009, Karen Armstrong, the famous British historian of religion, and a former nun, led the launch of the "Charter of Compassion," a four-paragraph document calling on humans to "work tirelessly to alleviate the suffering of our fellow creatures, dethrone ourselves from the centre of our world and put another there, and treat everybody with absolute justice, equality and respect."

It continued, "To speak or act violently out of spite, chauvinism or self-interest or to incite hatred by denigrating others is a denial of our common humanity." The Charter didn't spare the religions. "Any interpretation of scripture that breeds violence, hatred or disdain is illegitimate."

Thousands of individuals, groups and organizations signed on. Now there is an NGO based in Washington State which has 11 employees, working to expand the reach of the Charter and increase the number of signatories.

Four hundred and eleven cities from all over the world have declared themselves to be compassionate communities, committed to social change and development. To move towards this, a steering committee identifies "discomforts" in the community, discovers already-existing programs and builds on them. It chooses a focus, creates a plan, shares it with local government and works for a public affirmation of the "Charter of Compassion."

Then there is a kickoff event. Progress can also be measured against the United Nations Sustainable Development Goals (there are 17), for 2030.

I realize this work is all aspirational, but inspiring words, as history shows, have immense power for good. Learning about the existence of the "Charter of Compassion," reading it, possibly critiquing it, and signing on to it can all be positive, educational and action-oriented.

Karen Armstrong spoke several times at the Parliament of the World's Religions. I was recently in a school where the student leaders took it on. I have a Charter lapel pin for our new mayor, and will present it to her at the first opportunity!

There are restaurants of all kinds along Simcoe Street, but I was drawn daily to the "langar" (Punjabi word for "the Guru's Kitchen"), within the Metro Convention Centre. It occupied the space of two gymnasiums, and there the Sikhs of Toronto undertook to cook lentils, rice, chappatis and beans to serve 4,000 people each day.

We entered, took off our shoes, washed our hands and sat down, as Sikh women tied orange bandanas on our heads. Then we took our places side by side along a wide ribbon of cloth, and assumed, as best we could, the cross-legged position on the floor, to be served what was a delicious lunch by the men. I learned later they had arranged with the Convention Centre to have any leftover food taken nightly to Toronto's homeless shelters.

"It is sharing, not charity," said one smiling man to me. "That is a Sikh value."

Now you will certainly want to know about the ritual crafted by the "Circle Sanctuary" pagan presenters in which I participated. It is "croning," at which older women (54 is the minimum age to become a crone, or for men, a sage) develop a short ceremony, individual or in a group, to accept and welcome their aging. A kind of rite of passage, with enthusiastic chants and a leader, in our case Selena Fox of Wisconsin, who asked us cheerily, "What is better than aged wine? Aged cheese?"

Altogether it was a counter-cultural experience. No bad jokes about getting old, either self-inflicted jokes or those uttered by others. Links were made with St. Brigid of Kildare in the sixth century, who was a powerful abbess of a religious community, practiced folklore coming from an earlier time, and had a magic cloak she hung on a sunbeam.

With the cloak, I conclude these tales of the Parliament of the World's Religions, Toronto, 2018. Don't miss the next one.

Discovering NIA, a New, Fun Way to Keep Fit
December 6, 2018

NIA teacher Elizabeth Kiser shares her passion for the fitness progam with local participants each week.
METROLAND FILE PHOTO

This fitness thing is always on our minds. As the evidence piles up that longevity and vitality are closely connected to our moving our bodies in a lifelong commitment, our sense of guilt and unease often increase. The bad news: one third of Canadians are overly heavy and only 20 percent do the recommended 150 minutes of exercise a week.

I don't have numbers, but I think seniors may be among the least of the participants. I was typical. A modest athlete in high school and college, I entered family life with the attitude that working out is not "ladylike," and I gave up intentional exercise for 30 years. Then, as new knowledge surfaced that we should be active forever, I took up going to a gym.

Now in 2018, in comes NIA for me. Out at the Trent Athletic Centre every morning, as at the other two wellness centres, there are various opportunities for community members (should I say crones and sages) to do something physical. I appear there at any hour that suits me, generally later rather than earlier. There are yoga, treadmills, bikes, strength training, swimming, or just wandering among the machines, taking a quick glance at what the students are doing. (Better, of course to have a personal fitness person teach you.)

One is surrounded by students, who have taken seriously the admonition that exams are best taken and depression is warded off when one is fit. They hardly blink at us white-headed athletes. They hold doors, say "good morning," make small talk. Are they thinking "Grandma among the lions?"

As they probably would say, "Get over yourself." The main obstacle to our joining in is our vanity.

So I was curious about this NIA offering on the calendar, twice a week at noon. The lively and encouraging leader, the only NIA teacher in town, is Elizabeth Kiser, who comes from Port Hope.

Started in 1983 by a couple in San Francisco, NIA is a heady combination of martial arts, (yeah to inner aggression!), dance and yoga. It is aerobic without one being conscious of it, so busy is the mind on the rhythms of the music and the dance steps. Lots of attention is given to the hips, a good strategy, since so many of us seem to come into the hip replacement stage. Everything, from warm-up on is to music: pop, jazz, Latin, Indian and hip hop.

The initials NIA stand for neurological integrative action, or moving in your body's way, both sides equally involved.

Elizabeth has been practising NIA for 18 years, beginning in Virginia, and giving classes in the area for 12. Qualified in yoga and pilates, she has earned her black belt in NIA, and is articulate about its philosophy and benefits.

"It has gone international," she says, "in its ability to help people create new neurological pathways."

I'm not so good at exercising in silence. With NIA, I'm getting more up-to-date on modern tunes. Every few weeks we take on a new routine, basically much of the old with a few twists. We move in front of a mirror, but we are hardly conscious of the person beside us. We move for 55 minutes and are exhilarated. Every level of skill can be seen.

(I am usually a half-a-step behind.)

It is fascinating to see the range of people who come. Since NIA is neurological in nature, at least two of our class members are people with Parkinson's. You can see them enjoy and benefit.

Elizabeth Kiser tells me there are just 52 moves in NIA. Her classes at Trent are increasing in number, every age and body type. In her spare time, she hosts a weekly radio program on public radio in Port Hope; an interview show, called "Happy Hour," Tuesday evenings at 7, on Northumberland's Truly Local radio, FM 89.7.

It is more, I think, than the fitness flavor of the month. Plus, everybody loves to dance.

Let's Leave This Bad Year Behind and Move Forward With Hope
December 13, 2018

President Trump and Prime Minister Trudeau attend the Group of Seven Summit (G7) in Charlevoix, Quebec. EVAN VUCCI/ASSOCIATED PRESS

I feel the need, and as I read my culture, so does my community, to refill my hope chest these days. It's been a bruising year, psychologically, and, for the Earth, physically. There is hardly any need to recite the pressures: the shock and dread we've been undergoing: global climate reports ever more dire, even as we in our region live blessedly immune from, but emotionally fixated on, the misery of forest fires on our continent, and the sight of thousands of climate refugees on the move from drought-ridden areas in other parts of the world.

To be dreary, 60 percent of living mammals, birds and fish, which were alive in 1960, are extinct today. We plunge headlong into a hothouse of a world where many will not survive. Psychiatrists have identified eco-anxiety as a serious depressive condition and are empowered to write prescriptions for people to get outside in nature.

In the liberal democracies, we have seen deep vulnerability as strong men rise to power (the U.S., the Philippines, Egypt, Brazil, Russia, Saudi Arabia). We have seen America eat its young, betray its values, cling to an intemperate and ignorant man as its leader, a man and his cronies who lust for continuing power and run roughshod over historically hard-won systems of justice and honesty.

It has been woeful and disturbing. I saw him up close at Charlevoix in June at the G7 summit. I shuddered. Until the United States comes to its senses and gets a new government, the rest of us must go on without them as much as possible, quarantining them in their illness.

I am indebted to writer Rebecca Solnit, an editor at Vanity Fair, for her little book *Hope in the Dark* (2016). "It is a nightmarish time," she writes. "It is a time of hideous economic inequality and climate chaos faster and more devastating than all our predictions."

For Solnit, hope doesn't mean denying anything. It means facing reality, not with the belief that everything will be fine, but with a steady look at "the possibilities that invite or demand that we act."

"Complexities have openings," she says. While rooted in grief and rage, we don't know what will happen, and what we have is "the spaciousness of uncertainty." Her "faith" is grounded in a knowledge of history.

I am also strengthened by the great Quaker, Parker Palmer, who says, "When we feel certain that the human soul is no longer at work in the world, it's time to make sure that ours is visible to someone, somewhere."

My third spiritual mentor has become Timothy Snyder of Yale University. "Believe in truth," he says. "To abandon facts is to abandon freedom. If nothing is true, then no one can criticize power. If nothing is true, then all is spectacle."

Hope is a gift you don't have to surrender. But it's not naive optimism. Nor is it cynicism. It should be, says John Berger, a "detonator of energy for action today." An antidote to despair.

My cup personally right now runneth over. I think of the memorable ceremony at the YMCA on November 27, at which I received the 2018 Peace Medallion. Such a good time, thanks to Cindy Mytruk of the Y, and to my nominators Sheila Nabigon Howlett, Cath D'Amico, Cam Douglas, Anne Orfald and Julie Stoneberg, who wrote sufficient material for my obit, when such is necessary.

Unprompted, granddaughter Emma, age 9, leapt to the mike and recited the Girl Guide pledge. Anyone remember it?

I'm pondering two responses: have I not been sufficiently combative that I should receive a peace prize? And though I'm not given to quoting Christian scriptures in public discourse, a passage from Luke 6 (26) jumps to mind. It admonishes one not to take pride in "praise from men."

All the great faiths have resources to strengthen hope. One has to go deeper than the glitz and the banal "Baby Jesus" message, not to mention separating oneself from the Consumer-in-Chief, Santa Claus, and false cheer. More next week.

Peterborough Aglow With Hope For the Holidays
December 19, 2018

The holiday season and last days of the year are a time to reflect. ANDREW WALLACE/TORONTO STAR

Now, in late December, there is earlier dark, more silence and snow; slower driving. I am reading some books I have longed to get to, and using Kindle to do it. Books, such as Miriam Toews' *Women Talking* and Brenda Baker and Andrew Harvey's *Savage Grace*. My doctor recommended the Baker/Harvey.

We're coming to a year-end, tending to reflect. I'm paying more attention to my inner life, paying scant attention to Facebook, except for witty cartoons, such as the one where a harassed radio host assures his listeners that indeed mommy gave her informed consent before being kissed under the mistletoe. I'm moving towards vegetarianism. Am I on track for minimalism?

Advocacy work is so visible in the month of December, one can avoid all the excess of the consumerist society. Not to be Scrooge or anything, one can still arrange a gift for one's loved ones. (I just bought the gift of a car wash, and for another, a Reframe Film festival pass).

On Dec. 6, there was a moving vigil in front of the orange-lit City Hall as we again remembered the murder of women engineering students in 1989 at Ecole Polytechnique, and all gender-based violence.

On December 9 and 10, Amnesty International Group 46 organized letter writing for 10 women human rights defenders in such countries as Ukraine, Iran, Morocco and the U.S. I have learned over many years that Amnesty data is to be trusted. One can grab a case study and know it is not exaggerated. It is beholden to no authority but truth.

There were three opportunities in our city for people to take 15 minutes and put one's name to an appeal for a woman who is detained, and maybe worse, for non-violently speaking out for human rights.

At Emmanuel East United Church on December 9, there were scores of signers and writers after service. At Whistlestop Cafe on December 10, more conscientious citizens of Peterborough, aware of the plight of the oppressed somewhere else in the world, came to write. Total 175 letters. On December 13 at Kenner Collegiate, 100 students, organized by Lydia Etherington, brought together classmates for an earnest letter-writing session. I was moved by a lad, scarcely literate but very sincere, who wrote his letter to some tyrant with just the words, "Please don't be so bad."

Moreover, social justice work and the arts are inextricably linked. This city can hold its head high in this regard. The arts provide cries of pain which are indelible. "Cottagers and Indians," the powerful play by Curve Lake playwright Drew Hayden Taylor, drew overflow crowds to Market Hall. Infused with compassion for the two parties in conflict, Taylor's work provokes needed conversations both here and across the country.

In the same Market Hall venue, New Stages director Randy Read brought a stunning production of "A New Brain," a complex musical which showcases 13 singers and 3 musicians, many with Stratford credentials, after which I marveled that, right here at home, in an affordable seat, I could hear such a score and ponder such a story line. The homeless woman in the cast asks passersby for some change. Change indeed.

This town is churning with learning. There was the talk by Gordon Laxer, author of the book *After the Sands*. There are blood donor clinics, toy drives, senior's singalongs, caroling in neighbourhoods, and "In from the Cold" concerts. No column is long enough to outline all the Peterborough works of charity and often, justice, which take place this month. All of them engender hope in the observer.

Poet Emily Dickinson wrote, "Hope is the thing with feathers/ that perches in the soul/ and sings the tune without the words/ and never stops at all."

From the Christian mystics comes some help. "The journey to the wellspring of hope is really a journey to the innermost ground of our being," wrote Cynthia Bourgeault. "Make your interests gradually wider and more impersonal," said British philosopher Bertrand Russell.

Maybe as wide as the globe. And as local as skating on the canal.

The Good Ol' Hockey Game Sure Has Changed
December 27, 2018

Toronto Maple Leafs Mitchell Marner and Auston Matthews laugh after Marner scored a goal against the Florida Panthers. NATHAN DENETTE/ CANADIAN PRESS

I wish I could write as well as Roch Carrier, whose short story "The Hockey Sweater" is a Canadian classic. But here anyway, is my Christmas hockey story.

I grew up in the hardscrabble mining town of Kirkland Lake, north of North Bay, where hockey was, shall we say, important. The local rink had been donated to the town by gold mining magnate Harry Oakes. It was both worn and wonderful, seating perhaps 1,200, but we generally used outdoor rinks anyway. My sister was a decent figure skater, but although I could trace a figure-eight, I was more of a rink rat. Pictures of me in that era show a grinning kid with a strange, cone-shaped, rabbit-fur hat. Always a style-setter.

We listened to the Leafs games on radio at 8 p.m. Saturday nights via the nasal voice of legendary Foster Hewitt. Our town produced for the NHL: Ted Lindsay, Dickie Duff, Ralph Backstrom, Larry Hillman, Bill Durnan and the dreaded Plager brothers, Billy, Bobby and Barclay.

There's a hoary old joke about Kirkland Lake I've heard many times. Seems a guy and girl, just acquaintances, were discussing Canadian small towns. And KL came up. "Ah," says the guy, "Kirkland Lake: hockey players and prostitutes." The girl is annoyed. "I'm from Kirkland Lake," she says. "Oh," he says smoothly, "which team did you play for?"

My three sons texted each other this past week around the issue, "What do we get Mother for Christmas?" They remembered my injunction to always "give experiences, not things," so they were thrilled when one of them came up with a ticket to the Leafs game December 20.

I last saw the Leafs at Maple Leaf Gardens on College Street. That's some time between games. Now I have to confess. Although it is capitalism gone crazy, a bread-and-circuses show writ large, a cheery, noisy, outrageously expensive happening, I enjoyed it.

I enjoyed the brisket sandwich, ($16) the sauce of which marked my jacket and the contents of which made mockery of my short-lived vegetarian pledge. Beer was $12.75. Parking at a public lot near the Novotel Hotel turned out to be only $6: some kind of mistake there, I think. Toronto is jammed with cars, of course.

Inside the rink, now called the Scotiabank Centre (that corporation having bought naming rights from Air Canada in the summer for $800 million), the party is on. I saw one baby happy because of heavy-duty ear muffs. I saw a teenager wearing a Marner shirt to which he had added "Magic Mitch" on the back with duct tape. I looked around at the crowd - a lot of young white men, making full use of the F-word in describing the play. Not nearly as diverse a crowd as at a Raptors game. Why is that?

One man wore a small plastic Christmas tree on his head. My seat, and it was on the third level, far from the platinum section, cost $120. Imagine.

I guess someone has to pay for Nylander's $39-million-for-seven-years contract. And the owners, ruled by the aggressive Gary Bettman, are very rich. It's far from its origins; even Bobby Orr now says so. Not affordable for the average family, it has become entertainment for plutocrats.

I am terribly compromised. And yet, to be here in person, one is mercifully spared TV ads, and commentators, especially Don Cherry, but is drawn in by non-stop diversion: T-shirts lobbed into the crowd, whole sections treated to Casino Rama tickets, a 50/50 draw worth $26,000. And of course the athletes, first and last. Skill, strength, precision, grace and balance.

The very day before my game, Marner and his buddy Auston Matthews had played cameo roles as cannon clowns in "The Nutcracker" ballet.

Who won? The Leafs did, 6-1.

Now for the Canadian Juniors playing in Vancouver and Victoria in a post-Christmas tournament. My love/hate relation with professional sports continues. But I can debate persuasively with my grandsons, and increasingly granddaughters, on hockey matters, when it matters.

Listen, Learn and Lead: Peterborough's Environmentalists Ready For 2019
January 3, 2019

Peterborough-Kawartha MP Maryam Monsef speaks to members of Peterborough Alliance for Climate Action at her constituency office. JASON BAIN/EXAMINER

In our small city, we have four national-quality environmental thinkers/writers teachers/activists. No, amend that: they are international-quality. They have acquired a vast education in ecology, biology, physics, and earth sciences. To say nothing of human psychology and behavior. They are always learning, paying attention to findings, reports and warnings, and at the same time noticing local manifestations of this great global change we are experiencing. Plus they can communicate with us at our grade-nine-level science capacity.

They both challenge us and hold our hands. We trust them because we know them, and they are civil. I am naming them "Peterborough's Heroes of 2018."

They are humble people, but assured at the same time. They feel a great responsibility to alert others to the need for urgent action, not by scaring us, but by patiently sharing what they know, putting it out for the public good, all the more persuasive because they do it voluntarily, without remuneration.

They are Prof. Alan Slavin, a retired physicist from Trent University and a founder of Sustainable Peterborough; Drew Monkman, a legendary teacher and now widely read columnist for the Examiner who co-authored *The Book of Nature Activities*; Kate Grierson, a retired high school literature teacher, grandmother of five and newly trained Climate Educator via the Al Gore Institute; and Prof. Bob Paelke, retired from Trent, who has greatly influenced hundreds of students, including my own son, since the '70s, and now makes powerful use of Facebook to continue teaching.

They are people whose inner strength does not let them give up. Nor does it let them throw up their hands at indifference, or at bad government policies, such as the recent Doug Ford proposal to let development into the Green Belt of Ontario.

So what's up that we need to know and act upon this new year?

I'd say personal resolutions for simpler living, but even more importantly, a resolution to join an environmentally active group here (the GreenUP Store can give you a list). Then to relentlessly pester, lobby, speak out and get political. It's a federal election year. We are behind on our promises from Paris in 2015 to reduce greenhouse gases.

Ask MP Maryam Monsef to bring Minister Catherine McKenna here to strengthen her arm in all negotiations and show her how really informed and resolved we are in Peterborough.

Civility is key. We won't rant, accuse or scorn. She is an MP from Ottawa, our Minister of Environment and Climate Change. Her email is bilingual and quite complicated: minister.ec-minister.ec@canada.ca. I used it last week to thank her for what she was able to do in Poland. I reminded her that I met her this year at the G7 meetings. Then I argued as vigorously as I could for Canada to move faster, further.

She needs the wisdom of Solomon on this crucial file. We are after all, a federation, and Alberta is heavily dependent on oil (and so are we!), whose revenues mightily help fund our budget and whose frustration at not getting pipelines to transport it to market is palpable, It must, in any fair solution, be taken in to account.

In Poland, ironically in a city in a coal-producing area, the UN convened COP 24 two weeks ago. COP stands for Conference of Parties, or countries. There were 186 countries there, galvanized by disturbing new reports of how quickly the world is moving to a tipping point.

There were desperate late-night negotiations. The U.S. as you know, is a complete outlier. They, Russia, Saudi Arabia and Kuwait, all four oil-producing nations, refused to endorse the scientific report calling for a cap on global warming at 1.4 degrees Celsius. President Donald Trump has threatened to pull out entirely from the 2015 COP agreement in Paris, although a new administration could return in 30 days.

In co-operation with our local and national leaders, let's make 2019 the year we personally got involved. Any one of the grassroots four will speak to your group. Kate Grierson offers her contact through this newspaper: kagrierson555@gmail.com.

Jane Bow is Peterborough's Quiet Fiction Writer
January 10, 2019

Jane Bow displays a copy of her latest novel *Cally's Way* in her living room in Peterborough. CLIFFORD SKARSTEDT/ EXAMINER

Living here for the last 40 years, undiminished in her creativity, Jane Bow is largely unknown to most Peterborough folks. An accomplished writer, with four novels and three plays over the past 20 years, Jane's modest presence and highly informed conversation are the outcome of a cosmopolitan childhood and youth lived in many countries.

Her parents, Malcolm Bow, originally from Edmonton, and Betty Roberts, a war bride, rose in the diplomatic service to become Canada's ambassadors to Czechoslovakia and then to Cuba during the Cold War.

As a child, Jane, who had been born in Edmonton, lived in these and other countries, went to boarding school as a teenager in England and spent holidays behind the Iron Curtain.

At York University's Glendon College, she met her spouse, Grant Collins, now a retired Peterborough lawyer; married, raised two children and taught at Fleming College and Trent University while writing. Always, she says, she used a fountain pen and unlined paper, "because when ink flows, there can be a convergence of thought and imagination."

Jane then commits her work to a computer, where corrections are easier to make. In the 1990's, she researched the life of Martha Holland Hutchison, the wife of Peterborough's first doctor, John Hutchison from Kirkcaldy, Scotland, who lived with eight children in the limestone house on Brock Street, which was built by volunteers in 1837 and is now lovingly kept by the Historical Society.

Impressed by the strength of Mrs. Hutchison, who was widowed at age 41 and lived on in the house with her family until financial straits drove her to Toronto, Bow wrote a play called "Through the Fire" that was successfully produced at Hutchison House. It portrayed Martha Hutchison both in the fullness of her life, and in her anonymity as the doctor's wife.

The play was presented to great success but some Hutchison House board members felt it negatively presented the doctor.

"It was a kind of early feminist interpretation of the silencing of a key figure in local history," Bow smiles.

Astonishingly enough, Sandford Fleming of railway fame, was a cousin of the Hutchisons and stayed in the house for some time at age 18.

Bow's first job was as a court reporter for a Thunder Bay newspaper, and she has long been interested in justice for marginal people.

Her newest novella, *Homeless*, explores the dilemma of a sophisticated forensic psychologist who is examining an accused woman by the order of the court. The accused won't give her name, and the narrative becomes a kind of mystery, as well as the journey of the 38-year-old professional psychiatrist to new self-knowledge.

In 2001, Jane Bow went to the Greek island of Crete with her daughter Sarah, a psychologist. She was taken by the place, and has returned many times. Her novel *Cally's Way*, published in 2014, is the story of a 25-year-old Canadian business graduate on a kind of pilgrimage to her mother's birthplace in an effort to understand her roots. Cally has an unexpected romance with an American draft dodger. The heroism of the people of Crete under Nazi occupation is dramatically portrayed in the story.

In 2005, Jane Bow was diagnosed with a form of multiple sclerosis. It has not deterred her from a full life and a rich writing life. She has studied her illness, and has been going to a movement class at Trent for a year. She walks with the assistance of walking sticks but also plays tennis, is unself-conscious, and drives and cooks.

"I meditate," she tells me, "and I read good fiction from all over the world." She recommends to me Pat Barker's *The Silence of the Girls*.

Jane Bow's calm and accepting demeanour conceals a rich and sophisticated inner life that bursts forth in unforgettable storytelling.

Car Crashes Down, Racist Incidents Up: This is Peterborough in 2019
January 17, 2019

Selwyn Township firefighters, paramedics and Peterborough County OPP work at the scene of a two-vehicle collision at the intersection of Chemong and Lindsay roads. CLIFFORD SKARSTEDT/EXAMINER

What is going on in Peterborough? Two recent year-end reports point to conflicting realities in our city.

The first, and we can thank everybody for this one, is that we are among the 10 top communities in Canada for low numbers of car accidents per capita. Put that up against our ongoing griping about "Peterborough drivers." Whether that is enlightened drivers, fewer kilometres driven, conscientious policing, or patched and bumpy roads that make one slow down, it shows a sense of responsibility toward others that is good news.

On the other hand, to our shame, Peterborough also ranks among the top 10 communities for racist incidents reported to police in 2018. We have work to do here. The New Canadians Centre thrives, and we have absorbed 300 Syrian refugees, mostly smoothly, but yahoos there remain in every age group and sector. That can be a new year's pledge, to spot and challenge and put a stop to racist remarks, jokes, taunts and actions. Do you know that recently the Kawartha Sexual Assault Centre held a sold-out training session entitled "Bystander Intervention Training?" I plan to take it next time.

There is another double-edged phenomenon. We have a lively, progressive set of people and groups in Peterborough, and yet we turned away a good, hard-working and effective MPP in June for an unknown politician who took four months to open his office, and now is a conforming junior member of Team Ford.

Wasn't one Ford enough for Ontario? The premier commits blunder after blunder, but his caucus remains loyal. The Conservatives in the province rejected a moderate leader in Christine Elliott for Mr. Ford.

I was chatting with writer Mary Breen over the holiday about this work of writing. She is a fine writer herself. She sent me this quote from Susan Sontag, a giant of an American philosopher, who said, "A writer, I think, is someone who pays attention to the world. That means trying to understand, take in, and connect with what wickedness human beings are capable of, and not be corrupted, made cynical, or superficial by this understanding."

Now that is a keeper, even for a casual scribbler. My recent interviews have been with those who put pen to paper, or finger to keyboard, Jane Bow and Ann Douglas. Inspiring stories.

Other realities that shape our daily life? I'd say what we read on Facebook is an increasingly important one. I love newspapers in hard copy, but I also find news snippets and good cartoons on Facebook.

That all depends on the source, of course. Fox News, no, never. Nor the Toronto SUN. Once I told an American hiking with me that I watched Al Jazeera TV for a refreshing view, not from Washington. She blanched in horror. I turned terrorist before her very eyes. She avoided me from then on. CBC Radio is a great source, all the time. One neighbour is attached to The New Yorker.

I hope high schools and colleges are teaching critical thinking. Online, I read The Daily Climate with its often bad, but sometimes good, news. I get a daily message of condolence put out by Little Lake Cemetery. Some of these are forgettable, but many are consoling. I get North 99, a progressive site for provincial politics, and Lead Now, and Dying with Dignity and, for huge satire, The Borowitz Report.

I read lay-edited Catholic sites such as Commonweal and the National Catholic Reporter. I will write more soon on the big February meeting Pope Francis has called regarding sex abuse of minors by clerics worldwide.

The big question is, do these links keep us connected and informed or make us more anxious and dispirited? In Commonweal, I recently read a memorable quote from Villanova professor Massimo Faggioli, "Trumpism is what you should expect in a country that has neglected the humanities: philosophy, logic, theology, history, literature and foreign languages."

To all you teachers and practitioners of these subjects, hail.

Speaker Visiting Peterborough Paints Portrait of Suffering, Crisis in Gaza
January 23, 2019

The United Nations has been warned that Gaza is expected to be "uninhabitable" by 2020. Electricity is on four hours a day. The barrier is a wire fence, backed up by armed Israeli soldiers.
LUCAS OLENIUK/TORONTO STAR

I'm going to plunge into a topic that is fraught with division and deep trauma on all sides. It is the situation in Israel, particularly the behavior of the government of Israel, and what it has done and is doing in Gaza (population 1.8 million) and the West Bank (2.5 million), which are "occupied territories" holding Palestinians.

I listened to the testimony of a highly educated and compassionate spokesperson for the Palestinians this week at Sadleir House, Jonathan Kuttab. He is a lawyer, who recently was guest professor at the York University law school. He is a Christian Arab, born in East Jerusalem, now based in Jerusalem.

Critics of the policies of the Israeli government, and there are plenty in Canada and around the world, including the Israeli newspaper Haaretz, face the possibility, nay probability, that they will be labelled "anti-Semitic." Or, if they are Jewish, they will be called "self-hating Jews." But name-calling cannot become a reason for reticence when one looks at the massive, long-standing and ultimately cruel occupation, and denial of basic rights in the two shrunken areas.

The United Nations has been warned that Gaza, (40-by-six-kilometres) is expected to be "uninhabitable" by 2020. Electricity is on four hours a day. The barrier is a wire fence, backed up by armed Israeli soldiers. Food is very expensive. Water is often contaminated. A Gazan hospital was bombed in 2014. Unemployment is 40 percent.

A Peterborough group headed by activist Margaret Slavin is in touch with a family in Gaza and knows the daily deprivation it suffers. Kuttab offered his listeners slides, maps and some history. After the Second World War, in which Europe tore itself apart and then faced a dreadful acknowledgement of the Holocaust, during which six million Jewish citizens of several countries were killed in death camps, there was a global feeling of revulsion, guilt and shame.

So in 1948, the British government, which had been in charge of Palestine, decided to make the territory a homeland for the Jews. Except that it was already home to four million Palestinians who had no say in the matter. This was the Balfour Declaration.

Then came simmering resentment and some armed resistance. For 70 years, attempts at finding a solution failed. Twenty-five years ago in Oslo, Norway, leaders came up with the "two-state solution." It might have worked, but separation was not so easy: Arabs were living among Jews everywhere. Progressive Israeli prime minister Yitzak Rabin was assassinated by a religious fanatic.

The pain in Kuttab's presentation regarding the suffering of Palestinians was breathtaking, but equally so was the utter absence of vengefulness or hatred. He is convinced, as are many Israeli writers and citizens, that the imprisonment they are administering has the effect of imprisoning them also, and corrodes the long-admired Jewish conscience.

Israel is a nuclear power. We have seen pictures of boys with sticks and rocks being fired on by heavily armed soldiers. Prime Minister Benjamin Netanyahu, a hawk, is further empowered now by Donald Trump. Illegal settlements in the West Bank now house 700,000 Israelis.

Many Israelis have a strong fear that Arabs will exact revenge. But Kuttab said, "We are all intermixed now. What is needed is a commitment to human rights for all: an end to the blockade and the provision of services to all. The international community must help."

Israeli's neighbours, Syria, Egypt and Jordan, must pledge to respect its right to exist in safety. Israel is a democracy with freedom of speech and of the press. Small steps in regional co-operation are needed. So is a conviction among Israeli leaders that justice for its Palestinian minority is crucial. Many lives depend on it.

NOTE: Reframe Film Festival will show a documentary entitled "Naila and the Uprising," set in Gaza, on Friday at 1 p.m. at Showplace. Visit www.reframefilmfestival.ca for details.

Peterborough Writer Ann Douglas Launches New Book
January 30, 2019

Author Ann Douglas, left, interviewed more than 75 parents and other experts for her book *Happy Parents Happy Kids*. CLIFFORD SKARSTEDT/EXAMINER

Ann Douglas, the nationally-acclaimed writer from Peterborough whose 32 books have sold more than half a million copies, wisely followed her intuition when, after the birth of her first child, it urged her to write, and to write on the closest experience in her life: parenting.

That decision has led to a full and productive life of experiencing, thinking, writing and publishing on the universal topic of being a parent. Today, Ann, in her 50s, having raised four kids, who are now 21 to 30 years old, is about to launch her latest book called *Happy Parents, Happy Kids*, in February, to be published by HarperCollins Canada.

Chapter titles include "Parenting in an Age of Anxiety," "Work-Life Imbalance," "The Why of Distracted Parenting," "How to Boost Your Enjoyment of Parenting," "The Guilt-Free Guide to Healthier Living" and "Finding Your Village." Her new book is based on in-depth interviews with more than 75 Canadian parents and other experts, and offers a series of parent-proven solutions, which can be tackled at the individual, family and community levels.

Meeting Ann - a very modest person who describes herself as an introvert but who, when asked by the publisher to travel the country and do book talks, devotes several months to travel and speaking - one is struck by her ferocious honesty.

She discloses her own emotional vulnerability, her Meniere's illness and the various mental health and neurodevelopmental challenges her kids struggled with during their growing-up years.

Her down-to-earth and humble disclosures have endeared her to readers, tired of experts with all the answers. In fact, Ann found in the parent interviews she conducted for this book (she also read 100 books on psychology, parenting and wellness to prepare to write), a disturbing trend: parents lacking confidence in themselves, who feel they are inadequate to the task of raising good kids and fear they are messing up.

"Parents are the recipients of harsh social criticism. What is new now is that it's all recorded and remembered. Why has parenting become so hard? How does one parent in an age of anxiety?"

Ann has some thoughts about this. For one thing, Canada does not have a national daycare program. The median cost for infant daycare in Toronto is a mind-blowing $1,758 per month, according to the Canadians Centre for Policy Alternatives. "This is my most political book, I think," she says. "Society is responsible for much parent angst. Economic pressure is huge."

With a childhood in Mississauga and a degree in history from the University of Toronto, Ann married her high school sweetheart, Neil, 32 years ago. Within two years, the couple had moved to Peterborough and welcomed their first child. That was a "eureka" moment for Ann. She always knew she wanted to write. Now she knew what she wanted to write about: parenting.

That was the inspiration for her well-known "Mother of All" series of books. Her style is welcoming and informal. She empathizes with parents who are feeling worried and uncertain about the family's economic future. "I have been precariously employed most of my life," she says. "Contrary to what many people believe, the writer in Canada is not a well-to-do person." She laughs. "I have probably earned 50 cents an hour on some of my book projects. But writing for me has never been about money. I believe that writers can change the world. We have the power to tell stories and shift conversations. It is an extraordinary privilege and a daunting responsibility."

I find myself awed by her prodigious energy, but she assures me she walks on country roads north of Peterborough every day and marshals her strength.

The day after our talk, Ann was on her way to the CBC studios in Toronto for her parenting program, which is aired across the country one weekend each month. I caught it on January 11.

Prolific, generous and insightful are the words that come to mind when in the company of Ann Douglas.

Peterborough Singers Offer a "Relaxed" New Musical Experience
February 6, 2019

The Peterborough Singers are performing at the Calvary Church on February 23 - the concert is inclusive and accessible to all.
SPECIAL TO THE EXAMINER

Would you agree that each one of us is disabled in some respect? Something physical, or a mental or emotional wound or weakness? Some immobility, discomfort or pain which we have to live with? How then can we participate fully in all the cultural offerings in our community? How shall we get there? What accommodations will have to be made so that we too can benefit from the arts? What subtle, if unintended, exclusionary practices have up to now rendered us somewhat undesirable as an audience member?

Look now at the Peterborough Singers. It is an acclaimed choir of 120 members, now 27 years old, directed by the gifted Syd Birrell, which stages four sold-out concerts a year, two classical, one seasonal oratorio at Christmas, and one in mid-winter from the popular genre.

Recently a creative idea, some stellar collaborations and a grant from the Community Foundation of Greater Peterborough have come together to do what we do best: work together to bring about something new, something valuable and something inclusive. All with a kind of modesty.

Meet the visionary Peg McCracken, the manager of the Peterborough Singers since 2011, and a member since 1990. First off, we swap personal music stories. When she took piano lessons, the cost was $2 for a half-hour. Years earlier when I did, it was only 75 cents.

Peg had heard of a movement started in the U.K. about five years ago called "relaxed performance" and attended a workshop presented in Peterborough by Public Energy and EC3.

Through the "relaxed" principle, modifications are made to several aspects of a concert - the communications to the public, the education of performers and musicians, the transportation and parking availability for attendees, the sound and light arrangements in the hall and the personal support offered by volunteers at a concert for the comfort and reassurance, should it be required, for everyone of any disability.

"We seek to share cultural experiences with all in our community," Peg says, "while maintaining the authenticity of the full concert-going experience. Our goal is that a friendly and positive welcome exist at every concert for everyone: the hard of hearing or the deaf, the sighted, the blind and the visually impaired, the wheelchair-assisted people, and people on the autistic spectrum." It is the very opposite of any notion that art is exclusive or elitist.

Undertaking an expansion of mindset such as this takes some planning. So Peg arranged a well-attended, two-hour training session at Calvary Church, led by Jason King, outreach co-ordinator for the Council of Persons with Disabilities, for singers, church staff and volunteers.

Calvary Church and its facilities director, Melle Jongsma, were well on their way to having achieved an inclusive setting. Built in 2002, the church has many well-thought-out features: ramps, washrooms, handicapped parking at a rate of two spaces for every 50, good sound equipment and a spaciousness in the 1,250-seat main auditorium that make it ideal. But even Calvary staff learned from King that the height of soap dispensers and paper towels is not quite right.

There will be ushers with large, lighted name tags, well-lit areas and even a "chill-out" room for anyone who finds the sensory stimulation overwhelming. Two large display screens will show pictures of people who wrote the songs or sang the songs when they were popular.

A detailed written guide explaining the new features of a "relaxed" concert, and the motivation behind them is now on the Singers website. It even contains information on bus service along Lansdowne.

The program is ideal for such an initial concert. Called "Roots and Rights," it will include 12 songs from the early African-American gospel repertoire, and then move into 12 rousing liberation songs of the 1960's, when civil rights were top of mind and music motivated change. "Roots and Rights" will be performed on Saturday, February 23 at 2 p.m. at Calvary Church.

I can only imagine that everyone will gain knowledge, understanding and delight at this initiative of the Peterborough Singers in February.

Catholic Crisis: Sex and Governance at the Vatican
February 13, 2019

The Pope announced that the Roman Catholic Church had faced a persistent problem of sexual abuse of nuns by priests and even bishops, the first time he has publicly acknowledged the issue. VATICAN MEDIA

"This is the most serious crisis in the Catholic Church since the Reformation in 1517," said historian Massimo Faggioli recently about Pope Francis's call for a big meeting of the world's RC bishops in Rome, February 21-24. "The crisis is global, but it has a North American strain, inseparable from issues of sexuality, homosexuality and gender."

I would say it is really a double crisis: one of sex and one of governance.

After a long delay, with increasingly damaging reports from all over the world about sexual abuse of minors, of seminarians by bishops, and just last week the rape of nuns in India by a bishop, the leader of the Church, Pope Francis, has summoned the leader of each country's conference of bishops (our Canadian man is Rev. Lionel Gendron) to Rome for a three-day meeting, ostensibly to discuss the "protection of children."

The Pope has cautioned that "expectations should be kept low." Mine are low. Consider who won't be there, speaking, voting or participating in any way: women, lay people and sex abuse survivors. Those optics are very bad, but the reality is worse. The meeting is meant to address the huge scandal of sex abuse of children by clergy, but it will showcase, too, other burning issues.

The faithful are leaving in droves. My perceptive friend Mary E. Hunt of Washington ruefully says there are three groups: nuns, nones and never agains. My circle is full of "never agains."

For me, that stubbornly held and backward view of women's second-class status, combined with an immature and punitive policy on all matters sexual, is at the very bottom of this crisis. And the monarchical, male-only, exclusive style of governing with its deep-seated fear of sexuality, and of ordinary people, is long outdated, ineffective and harmful.

Reform groups from Europe and the U.S. are calling for three reforms: the ordination of women, a new theology of homosexuality and the withdrawal of the condition of celibacy from the priesthood. All good, all helpful, but the continuation of absolute governance from above, the clericalism by which members give inordinate deference to the priest, which Pope Francis himself has decried, means that they won't go deep enough.

A Vatican Council Three, open to the insights of 40 years of prophetic feminist thinking about the divine, and structured as a democratic assembly, might stem this slide, stop the suffering and restructure a toppling institution.

Women's voices are already vibrant. Law professor Mary Leary at Catholic University of America calls for "an independent, outside, top-to-bottom review, not reporting to the hierarchy but to the public."

Anything less, writes Pat Perriello in the National Catholic Reporter, "will cement the church's inability to retain the respect and allegiance of its members, a remnant of whom will retain blind adherence, but others will continue to walk away from a church that doesn't even understand the full impact of its cataclysmic failure to be a light in the world."

Marie Collins, an Irish abuse survivor, and for three years a member of a Vatican-appointed commission for the protection of children, resigned in 2017, citing inaction and a lack of commitment from Rome. She calls for international standards, recognizing that some protocols are in place in the U.S., Canada and Ireland but lamenting that kids in Asia, Africa and South America are not protected.

Joan Chittister, the Benedictine nun from Pennsylvania, describes this church as a sinking ship. First the people begin to cast off, then to disappear, and then it is of little importance to them. "Authoritarianism, narcissism and pride mean the church sins as much as it saves."

When #MeToo comes to the Vatican, and becomes #UsToo, there is no going back.

Next week, part 2 of the Catholic crisis.

Church in Crisis: Can the Rome Meeting Bring About Change?
February 20, 2019

Members of ECA (Ending of Clergy Abuse) and survivors of clergy sex abuse pose outside St. Peter's Square at the Vatican February 18. Organizers of Pope Francis' summit on preventing clergy sex abuse met with a dozen survivor-activists who arrived in Rome to protest the Catholic Church's response to date and demand an end to decades of cover-up by church leaders. GREGORIO BORGIA/ASSOCIATED PRESS

The potential for this large faith community, Roman Catholicism, to be a force for good is immense. Its very numbers, its reach, its progressive theological work, its small communities that are bringing life and doing good. But that potential is mostly squandered today.

Pope Francis, an Argentine Jesuit with a strong sense of the poor, issued a powerful letter in 2016 on the environmental crisis. Such is the disunity in the church that traditionalists, who are a mighty factor, have dismissed it, and ordinary clerics have not read it or taught from it. Never mentioned in the parishes I know.

The Pope is just back from the Arabian Peninsula, where he led mass for 135,000 people and spoke about war, violence, freedom of religion and the exclusion of immigrants. He is undoubtedly a good, often brave, person. But he is a victim of history, and is blind about women and sexuality, which are rather major topics. All that impedes him from leading the radical changes that are called for.

He is no feminist, but he has a sense of discerning the times. For him, 2018 was like a bad dream. He had a disastrous visit to Chile and almost as bad a visit to Ireland. Abuse-related reports from Mexico, Australia, the U.S., India, Germany, France, Spain and Poland were issued, and a bombshell of an expose from the state of Pennsylvania on the same subject. It reported on 300 offenders.

It seems some thousands of clergy from around the world have been implicated over 40 years in the sexual abuse of minors. Just as bad has been the cover-up by dozens of bishops, not reporting to the police, moving offending clerics around and closing their eyes to the obvious.

Could there be a systemic flaw here? An addiction to power? A phobia about sexuality, a privileging of the celibate over the sexually active? Could we describe the fixation on sexual prohibitions a kind of "procreationism?" That was illustrated last week by the pronouncement from an elderly Vatican cleric that in some cases hysterectomies may be permitted, but only if the uterus has ceased to be capable of carrying a child. Such absurd policy-making could only come from a group that has not one woman's voice.

The summit will "take consciousness of the seriousness of abuse" and outline procedures for bishops to follow to protect children. There was a half-hearted attempt to set up a Vatican committee including victims of clergy abuse a few years ago, but it has floundered. Decades of a terrible affliction are now exposed.

Mary E. Hunt, a leading U.S. Catholic feminist who appeared on CBC News Network this week, speaks of her deep disenchantment with institutional Catholicism. "The apparatus of the Vatican is unable to carry the gospel," she says. "The institution flames out in paroxysms of clericalism, sexism and homo hatred. We women of faith seek not to clean up a mess that is not of our making, but to live a new democratic and egalitarian church open to all. Invite other leaders from other faith traditions, and secular professionals, to step forward to help our communities."

Many call a for a church that is locally based and circular: people being involved in selecting bishops, for example, a task that now in the hands of the Papal Nuncio who submits three names to the Vatican.

Meanwhile, in the Peterborough area, Rev. Rebecca Fuller of the Roman Catholic Women Priests movement, who lives in Bethany, has written to Bishop Gendron, and copied local Bishop Daniel Miehm, that the church has been the "primary carrier of the global toxic virus of misogyny, and the cure for that virus is equality." Fuller is one of some 275 Roman Catholic women priests worldwide, about 30 in Canada. They respond to invitations for the sacraments, have no parishes, and support themselves financially.

Pushing back against both structural and personal injustice may be the best we can do for now: being watchful and critical, and living out an alternative.

Climate and Conflict: Gwynne Dyer Speaks at Trent University in Peterborough
March 6, 2019

Gwynne Dyer spoke about global climate change at an event at Trent University in February. BARRY GRAY/HAMILTON SPECTATOR

When I take a week or so off from column-writing, I always counsel my editor to make space for the columns of one Gwynne Dyer.

Now that is a joke. This gentleman is a master of the craft, famous for writing a twice-a-week column in 175 newspapers in 45 countries around the world. He is encyclopedic in his international political and economic knowledge. Pick any region, any country, and query him about the current situation there. You'll receive a balanced and factual analysis that will both enlighten and enlarge your grasp. You'll be informed and entertained, and are never left without hope.

Dyer is 75 years of age, Newfoundland-born and London-based. I can't believe his age. I've followed him for, I suppose, 40 years, and have yellowed clippings of his writing on many topics. Most of those years, he has appeared in a leather bomber jacket. I'm only sorry it's been retired. He is a broadcaster, a filmmaker, a navy veteran, a graduate of Oxford and Sandhurst, and an Order of Canada recipient.

I know him also for his generosity. Gzowski College principal Melanie Buddle told the audience, which filled a lecture hall at Trent University on February 11, that he has been in Peterborough nine times in recent years. I know he speaks in high schools and colleges all over the country, and those gigs aren't known to be huge earners.

He was sponsored by Gzowski College and the Trent Student Association. The topic was a sobering one: Global climate change. Dyer spoke for almost two hours without a note, a graph, a power point or a handout. Real adult education, laced with fact and wry humour.

"Am I filled with hope?" He began.

"Not exactly. Our future on the planet is uncertain. Aware people now know a great deal from many reliable sources. One important source which I watch, but which is seldom consulted, is the military. Military people everywhere watch and figure and absorb information with one goal in mind: prevent chaos and war, including civil war, in their country."

Leap ahead to a disturbing scenario, 100 years in the future. Global temperatures have risen six degrees. Farmland is parched, starving people from the south are indeed pouring over the Mexico-U.S. border. But the United States is 30 percent Hispanic.

What citizens would endorse the shooting at the border of fellow Hispanics, and what desperation could trigger a second American Civil War?

We have always emitted carbon dioxide, he said, but for millennia its atmospheric concentration was at 180 parts per million. Now in the short period since 1950, we are up to 400 ppm. "It's not so much population increase as it is consumerism: we're flying all over," he said.

"The north is responsible for 80 percent of our woes. The waters are warming. The poles are getting closer to the equator in temperatures. The jet stream is meandering. The birds are confused. Arctic ice will be melted in 10 years. The permafrost, which is the land around the northern ocean, is melting, and its dead vegetation will release huge amounts of CO_2. The world's oceans, which are 23 percent of its surface, absorb CO_2 but it forms carbonic acid and harms creatures at the bottom."

At six degrees increase in warming, 90 percent of the planet would be desert, "good for flies and scorpions." Sea levels would be up 18 metres. Population would be 10 percent of what it is now.

"Yet we have the money and the alternative sources of fuel: wind, solar, geothermal, nuclear and hydro, to go off coal, oil and gas. 10 years ago, scientists showed an undertone of panic, now it is overt." Seven-and-a-half billion persons are now feeding from the same land that fed two billion a century ago. At risk would be corn rice and wheat.

Dyer touched on some possible technical fixes, such as injecting sulphur dioxide into the atmosphere to deflect incoming sunshine. But his masterful presentation was primarily a call for faster emission cuts and greater global co-operation.

SNC-Lavalin: The Women, the Choices and the Damage
March 13, 2019

Jody Wilson-Raybould ADRIAN WYLD/CANADIAN PRESS

It's deep breath time. I am going to reflect on the current contretemps seizing Ottawa; the SNC-Lavalin affair and the two cabinet ministers, both women, who have resigned over it. They have made public charges, expressed their loss of confidence in the prime minister and in my opinion, gravely wounded their party, their ministries and this government. Worse, their actions have carelessly put at risk the progress made for women, reconciliation with Indigenous people and Canadian families - progress they themselves greatly contributed to when in office.

I am going to call them out, even though I personally have admired them both, and I am a longtime feminist. But in a mature movement, critique of one another is permitted, needed and encouraged, if respectfully done.

I have waited three weeks to write. I have read widely, various opinions. Anyone who says Canadian media is dominated by the left has not consulted such strident recent voices as that of Rex Murphy, Andrew Coyne and Christie Blatchford, who have almost fulminated in rage, as if waiting for an issue they could latch on to and elevate to the status of a Trumpian outrage.

When one comes to understand the deferred prosecution mechanism and learns it is widely employed in other democracies (20-40 in the U.S. each year) to impose reforms on offending companies, fine them and subject them to monitoring, one quickly rejects accusations of corruption in government and ill-informed calls for the leader to resign.

One hears the testimonies of loyalty from 32 cabinet members, including the respected Chrystia Freeland, Catherine McKenna and Maryam Monsef, and one accepts the sensible assertion that the PMO was motivated by concern for Canadian jobs, and accepts that the lobbying of then justice minister Jody Wilson-Raybould was meant to increase her understanding of Canada as a whole. It was somewhat vigorous, I am sure.

Former deputy prime minister Sheila Copps said recently, "For heaven's sake, on one issue when in government, I was lobbied 150 times." I myself took a short course once on the "elevator pitch." You imagine yourself, full of your dearest cause, having 40 seconds riding in an elevator with an influential person. You need to deliver a persuasive, even urgent, message.

In Wilson-Raybould, I see a deep sense of grievance and annoyance, followed by short-term thinking marked by naivete about how politics works. As writer Rick Salutin said in the Star, this is about feminism and Indigenous identity, not about criminality. With Jane Philpott, I see a kind of sentimental sisterhood at work.

A longer view would, I believe, have shown both ministers the fact that the good they hoped to achieve when they entered politics would be undermined by their absenting themselves, with parting shots as they went. And just how to explain their early announcements that they both planned to run as Liberals next election, after putting caucus colleagues in danger of losing their own seats, should public opinion be formed against this government. Better they had retired, or run as independents. What Liberal will campaign for them?

A positive take-away is that the PM kept his cool and did not resort to hasty or critical language to describe the surprising events, which some describe as "mild sabotage." Another is that Canada may soon accept a rationale for dividing the two offices, Attorney General and Justice Minister. Yet another is the evidence that Canadians care a lot about integrity in government behaviour and have followed this story carefully. Another is the pledge that Trudeau has made to improve relations between MP's and his office. Yet another is the fact that his feminism has been tested and found strong. Add to that the statement of Indigenous leaders that the tempest "is not a threat to the promise and process of reconciliation."

This is a devilishly difficult country to govern, given regional differences, but we are better off from this challenge going forward. Still, I little credit the two agents of the disturbance, and I think they were off-base.

Peterborough Work is Part of Global Effort to Set Goals to Sustain Our Planet
March 20, 2019

Wind turbines generate power at the Sumac Ridge Wind Project east of Highway 35 southwest of Peterborough. JASON BAIN/EXAMINER

What are these SDG's and why do they matter? Peterborough is chock-full of globally minded citizens. Just this week, for example, I ran into Sharon Lajoie, who works for the Catholic school board in Indigenous Education. She and her spouse, Ollie Flyng, have a daughter in Ghana and a son who works for the UN in Turkey.

So it seems completely apt that our federal MP, Maryam Monsef, has a new appointment as minister for international co-operation. We in Peterborough can be her best advisers on this file.

Being global also means being entirely local, and believing that to be true, the visionary Julie Cosgrove of the Kawartha World Issues Centre, which is a bustling office located at Trent's Otonabee College, designed a two-day meeting to unpack the United Nations goals for 2030: "The Sustainable Development Goals."

There are 17 of these goals, and they were announced in 2015, but we in Canada were busy with an election, and they may have passed us by. Yet no great announcements get circulated by themselves, no matter how much they are present on the internet. It takes personal time and effort from local leaders, those among us who keep themselves constantly aware of large movements and important information.

Though the SDG's have not taken Canada by storm, they are guiding the work and thinking of people in poorer countries, Prof. Haroon Akram-Lodhi, who travels widely for the UN, told us. He was in an Ugandan village recently, where the SDGs dominated discussion and informed policy decisions.

I personally heard about the SDG's a year ago. Outside the United Nations buildings in New York on a huge plaza, there is a massive iron and bronze sculpture of our planet, deeply gashed and wounded. It makes one pause and meditate.

So I was excited to see that Peterborough was going to have an opportunity to study the SDG's and see how they are applicable to us. That was the hope obviously shared by 125 others who flocked to the Mount on Feb. 28 and March 1 to ponder the SDG's.

Coalitions get things done, and they overcome silo thinking. This meeting had 15 cosponsors, including: Fleming College, the Peterborough Regional Centre of Expertise (as in all things environmental), CanWACH, Ontario Council for International Co-operation, Green Up, Trent Oxfam, Camp Kawartha, Horizons of Cobourg, Trent University and that always empowering (with seed money) Community Foundation of Peterborough. There were funds from two trusts: that of Thomas Symons and that of Linda and Alan Slavin.

When one looked at the quality of presenters, it was easy to see that such an endeavour would cost some money. There was Charles Hopkins from York University who works with UNESCO, Steve Lee from the UN in New York, Julie Wright from Waterloo's Global Science Initiative, and Alison Sydney of Community Foundations Canada.

Wisely, the organizers highlighted the views and centring presence of five Indigenous leaders: Larry McDermott of PLENTY Canada, Dan Longboat of Trent, Anne Taylor of Curve Lake, Lorenzo Whetung, a councillor in Curve Lake, and Kristin Muskratt, who works with native youth. They framed the day, at the beginning and at the end, giving the lively discussion a spiritual resonance. We moved from mere tokenism, often present at meetings today, to receiving the wisdom of these Indigenous leaders. There were reps from academia, health organizations, NGO's, green groups, anti-poverty people, educators, politicians and youth.

The goals themselves may sound like motherhood: simple in words but far-reaching in result. Among them: No poverty, zero hunger, good health, quality education, gender equality, clean water, decent work, clean energy, reduced inequality, climate action, strong institutions, responsible consumption, sustainable cities and partnerships for the goals. Advocates and activists in all these fields gathered round for two hours of discussion on what we have in our area and what we need.

The event launched all our thought-leaders into new directions. Colourful posters are available at the website of the UN. We will soon be as informed and engaged as the Ugandan village.

Pop-up Peterborough Music:
It's 3 Alarm Choir to the Rescue
March 27, 2019

Peterborough's 3 Alarm Choir brings together singers of all ages for fun musical performances. RICK MADONIK/ TORONTO STAR

Inclusive, musical, creative, one-off, inexpensive, one well-loved pop song: What's not to love about pop-up singing choruses? And Peterborough has one, called the 3 Alarm Choir.

Anyone can turn up on the announced evening, get the lyric sheet, and sing low, middle or high. Everything is taught on the spot.

In my choir experience, I have always stood beside a person who can read music and follow that person along. My strengths are that I can keep a tune, and I accomplished Grade 8 piano with great effort in bygone years.

For 3AC, no experience is necessary. Everyone is welcome. It is family-friendly, though the event is usually held in licensed premises. The occasion is called a song blaze. One's commitment is just for the one evening, so it suits people who cannot schedule regular singing practices with any one group.

After two hours of practice under the direction of skilled and enthusiastic leaders, there is one final rendition which is videotaped. Done.

In Peterborough's case, the skilled and enthusiastic leaders for April 4 are Linda Clark (keyboard) and David Berger (guitar). Linda is a dual American-Canadian citizen who has lived here for 23 years and is known for sensitive work at the Unitarian Fellowship.

With a bachelor of music degree from the University of Texas, Austin, in piano and string bass, and a commitment to a happier community through singing, Linda formed the 3 Alarm Choir in 2015 with help from Janice Wuerch, a founding member of the Lakefield Singers.

Linda's musical partner David, is a fine guitarist and singer-songwriter originally from Newfoundland. He has worked for many years as an educator and union leader with the Elementary Teachers Federation of Ontario. He is keen on the community-building values of 3AC.

The 3 Alarm Choir has been inspired by the Toronto group Choir! Choir! Choir! which started in 2011. Toronto's lively group was founded by two young men to honour a friend's birthday by staging a singalong at the Clinton Tavern on Bloor Street. It touched a nerve and has had huge success and public profile, opening the Grey Cup in 2017 with the national anthem, and honouring Gord Downie at Yonge-Dundas Square in 2018, with "Grace Too."

I've seen some YouTube videos of both groups: the joy on the faces of the participants is something to behold. All together, they sound good.

As for the song choices, Linda makes most of them. I've fallen behind on pop music since my teenagers left home (whatever happened to AC/DC?), but even I know The Tragically Hip, Joni Mitchell and Leonard Cohen. Moreover, I watched, in some bewilderment, the Juno Awards recently (well, not the whole two hours). My Edmonton grandkids have tickets to Shawn Mendes this spring.

Songs are chosen for their widespread appeal. The 3 Alarm Choir has open, public song sessions three or four times a year. The last was December 6, and the song, in honour of her 75th birthday, was Joni Mitchell's "River," from her album of 1971.

3AC has had 11 sing events since 2016. The next one, April 4, will feature "Sweet Child o' Mine" by Guns N' Roses. I used to tell my sons to turn down Guns N' Roses, but I can be converted. It will be at the Lakefield Legion next to the Curling Club, starting at 6 p.m. with socializing. Rehearsing starts at 7, and the final performance is at 8.30. Admission is $5.

Janice Wuerch says, "Songs I didn't even think I liked turned out to be great fun to sing." Linda Clark hands out lyrics only. "Most people learn by ear," she says. The 3 Alarm Choir has been drawing about 70 people to each event, diverse in age, gender and musical experience. Children are welcome to come and sing, too, if accompanied by an adult.

Learn more at www.3alarmchoir.ca

New Canoe Museum in Peterborough will Inspire Canadians
April 3, 2019

Minister of Canadian Heritage and Multiculturalism Pablo Rodriguez announces $10 million for the new home of the Canadian Canoe Museum. April 1, 2019 in Peterborough, Ontario. JASON BAIN/EXAMINER

My experience with canoes began in the 1950's. In Kirkland Lake, I was in a family whose parents had never learned to swim. My father was determined his four kids would learn water skills, so he sent us to summer camps on Georgian Bay.

By age 15, I was a counsellor. Everyone learned canoe skills: the Big J, the Little J, the sweep and the draw. Fast forward to 2007. I joined a group of mature women, motivated by Joyce Mackenzie and Myra Collins of Lakefield, to sign on to a 10-day canoe trip along the Yukon River from Pelle Crossing to Dawson City, all under the knowledgeable direction of Lin Ward of Canoe North Adventures. The Yukon is a wide river with no portages and a nice helpful westward current for paddlers.

But at one crucial point, my canoe smarts deserted me. I was in the stern. We were attempting to land on a spit of terra firma, but had overshot it. I could hear Lin yelling, "Pry, Pry!" Do you think I could remember that stroke?

It has all made me grateful that we in Peterborough have what will be a magnificent canoe museum in a few short years. As Peter Mansbridge has said "All around the world, when you mention the word 'canoe,' people respond 'Canada, Canada!'"

Here is a beautiful national symbol we can all embrace: the Indigenous, the francophone and anglophone communities, and newcomers, too.

That boat is silent, graceful, beautiful and human-powered. The dictionary puts it, "The canoe is a small boat pointed at both ends and propelled facing forward."

In 2013, the Senate of Canada declared the canoe to be a cultural asset of national importance. Since 1997, right here in our hometown, there has been a collection of 600 watercraft lovingly gathered by the late Kirk Wipper of Camp Kandalore. There were early appreciators. One was Prof. John Jennings of Trent. He took a year off to cross the country lobbying for the canoes to be saved and properly displayed. Since then they have been housed in an Outboard Marine building and warehouse. Only 20 percent of the collection can be on display now.

This is a campaign to build an environmentally sensitive and beautiful centre for the 87,000 annual visitors expected. I notice a witty sign, "Just add water." It will be a LEED-designated facility, up to curatorial standards, an 83,000-square-foot structure with a grass roof, swirling alongside the canal facing the Lift Lock.

I looked at the guest book. A lad from Langley, B.C. had written "Fabulous." Volunteer Noriko Merrett pointed to a map covered with pins from all over the world, Europe and Asia heavily represented. Through the lens of the canoe, Canadian stories will be told. Indigenous culture and courage will be raised up. Moreover, the economic impact for our area is expected to be $111 million, from 2017-to 2021.

Heading up the campaign to raise $65 million is Bill Morris of Peterborough. Bill and his wife Betty are our most remarkable philanthropists. Modest and deeply committed, they have singly or together raised the money for Crossroads Shelter, for Hospice, and now for the Canoe Museum. In my view they should have the Order of Canada. Bill and his team have had success: $11.4 million pledged from the federal government, $4 million from the city, $9 million from the province and half a million from the county. The W. Garfield Weston Foundation is the largest private donor at $7.5 million. We small donors are crucial, too. I plan for $20 a month.

At present the museum has 180 volunteers and 1,500 members. Its remarkable design was done by Heneghan Peng of Ireland, with architects Kearns-Mancini of Toronto. One enthusiastic judge was Lisa Rochon, former architecture critic for the Globe and Mail.

Education is high in priority. Last year thousands of students came to the museum, and several thousand others learned by virtual classes. I sat down with executive director Carolyn Hyslop and communications director Alicia Doris. "Sometime in 2019," says Hyslop with determination, "the ground will be turned over."

New Community Garden Starts to Take Shape in Lindsay
April 17, 2019

Crayola Canada donates $42,620.80 to the United Way in Lindsay. L-R United Way community investment co-ordinator Shantal Ingram, 2018/19 campaign chair Kawartha Lakes Police Chief Mark Mitchell, United Way CKL board president Duncan Gallacher, Crayola HR manager Mike Soehner, general manager Paul Murphy and finance manager John DeBois. The United Way and Crayola are working together on a community garden project in Lindsay. MARY RILEY/METROLAND

Nothing can be as pleasurable for a teacher as running into a former student (from 25 years back), and being laughingly reminded of goings-on in class back then. Even more pleasurable is learning that this student is practicing service-to-community, which teacher had always hoped to encourage.

Such was the case recently with Shantal Ingram, who first took two courses with me in writer's craft at St Peter's in the early 1990's. She reminded me of the excitement in class when apartheid in South Africa ended in 1994. She said "You put the words of the South African national anthem on the board, Nkosi Sikelele Afrika and we learned to sing it." Did I? Don't remember. But it's a good idea.

The daughter of a farm family in Selwyn township, with parents Bill and Veronica Ingram, Shantal went on to earn a BA and a Master's degree, and for the past three years has been working with the United Way in Lindsay. It is her current project that is so interesting. It is a well-supported community initiative among three sectors, ones that often don't work together: the non-profit sector, the business community and the public sector (Trillium grant), all leaning in and developing a practical all-hands-on-deck project for food security and agricultural education. It will lead to the production of healthy local food.

All is being done with local arts people, educators and students of all levels and conscientious businesses, even a hotel!

It is to be the Edwin Binney Community Garden. (Mr. Binney was the founder of Binney and Smith, now the Crayola Company.) Crayola happens to be a neighbour of the United Way office in Lindsay. They came over one day with an idea: an offer that United Way use the vacant lot to the east of the Crayola building and develop 30,000 square feet into a large-scale garden, in a minimum five-year land use deal. It is to be an enclosed space, not open to the public except for volunteers and for educational workshops and special events.

The official opening will be a Garden Party on June 8 for all the partners. Tickets are on sale at the United Way office. City of Kawartha Lakes Mayor Andy Letham is fully in favour. Sponsors include Bee City Canada, Hill's Florist and Greenhouses, the Kawartha Art Gallery, Bob Mark New Holland Tractor, Fleming College's Sustainable Agriculture classes and the Lindsay Police Department.

The Kawartha Art Gallery came aboard with $1,750 in prize money for a competition in which artists design a mural depicting the impact of the project on food security and education. A business man, Daryl Buttar, saw the value in the idea and came forward with a tractor for the initial plowing. The Lindsay Collegiate Gold Star building program has committed to building sheds, a sun shelter and raised garden beds.

Fresh produce will be donated to the Good Food Box program, Meals on Wheels, food banks and school nutrition programs. People who visit food banks receive three days of food per month and rarely receive fresh produce, says Ingram. In Kawartha Lakes, 2,000 people use food banks regularly, and 40 percent are children. Hence the link to United Way. People on fixed incomes struggle to pay rent, get transportation or pay food costs.

There will be furrows for seeds and 24 raised beds, their sides painted in the Crayola colours. The whole thing is being watched with interest by Crayola's head office in Pennsylvania.

Fleming College agriculture students will earn credits for assisting in the garden. There will be encouragement to pursue agricultural careers.

Shantal Ingram is a runner and was "fresh" from a 30-kilometre "Around the Bay" run in Hamilton. This farm girl is blending her background, her studies and her zeal into an important and creative project that will help her community and inspire others.

Unity, Social Justice are Ties that Bind Different Faiths in Peterborough
April 24, 2019

Of those who declare a religion in Canada, 38% are Roman Catholic, 28% Protestant, 4% Islam and 1% Judaism. JASON BAIN/EXAMINER

When I was in teacher's college, we trainees were warned by several professors not to discuss sex, politics or religion in class. Bad advice, which I never followed. My chosen age-cohort, teenagers, needed and wanted open-ended, honest, and well-informed discussion on these topics as they moved through life facing a lot of complex challenges.

That bad advice led me to a lifelong interest in the place and force of the religions in our culture. For good and for ill. Yet the enduring power of the religions, their potential "renewable moral energy" is not usually recognized or commented on. Polite society rules out conversation about religious values and convictions for fear of offending.

Newspapers, which used to have well-educated religious reporters covering that beat, have no more. I was shocked when, last November, the Parliament of the World's Religions, bringing together 200 religions and 8,000 people in Toronto, got hardly a mention in mainstream media.   But look today at the global outpouring of grief over Notre Dame Cathedral in Paris. On the other side, look at the cynical ways political leaders use religious ignorance and fanaticism to advance their doubtful agendas and demonize others.   It sure bears scrutiny.

Looking at some figures for Canada, 24 percent of us profess no religion. The rates of adherence of the rest are steadily decreasing, if adherence is measured by weekly attendance at a church, synagogue, temple or mosque. It is predicted that 9,000 Canadian churches will close in the next decade.

Of those who declare a religion in Canada, 38 percent are Roman Catholic and 28 percent Protestant. Islam is at 4 percent and Judaism at 1 percent.

Canada has no official religion. Support for religious pluralism and tolerance is high. Our national anthem refers to God, but for the most part, and wisely so, we have no state religion. Practice is considered generally private. There are anomalies: Public funding for religious schools continues in three provinces (and should stop). The Quebec legislature debates whether to remove the Christian crucifix from its National Assembly.

I am teaching a course called "Women and God Talk" at Traill College. There is lively conversation among the 16 students, looking at four organized faiths; Christian, Jewish, Muslim and Buddhist. We agree that all are badly marred by patriarchy, rule by the oldest males. We examine the resistance to this situation by feminists in these faiths, their dissent from teachings, laws and governance.

One student came in and said firmly, "I am atheist. I know no religious language, so you will have to explain every term you use!" I was glad I could point her to my favourite atheist, Alain de Botton of Oxford. Another student said, "Why do we emphasize differences, when unity is so needed in this world?" Couldn't agree more: We will spend only so much time on the differences and then move to similarities. My conviction is that what is best for the world is broad-minded, spiritually infused, social justice work.

Peterborough offers up lots of examples. The Abraham Festival, a feel-good annual event among Jewish, Muslim and Christian believers, happens Sunday. I personally am completely inclusive. I bought a Muslim prayer rug for Lent, and Elizabeth Rahman instructed me on its proper use. I am thrilled to be invited to a Passover Seder supper this week at the home of Jewish leaders. I delight when Janet McCue drums and sings of humility in the face of the Creator as she did at the recent environmental "Die-in."

Last Sunday, a creative group headed by director Jane Werger presented the Retrial of Jesus of Nazareth for crimes of sedition. It was truly spellbinding for the 150 people present. Well-known Peterborians, lawyers David O'Neill and Shannon Smith, Judge Barry Macdougall, teacher Kevin O'Neill and actors Geoff Hewitson, Laura Kennedy and Jim Angel vigorously took on roles in what was a mostly ad-libbed, two-hour trial. As a refresher, as a tool of learning, and an ecumenical experience, this trial will long be remembered. In surprising ways, manifestations of a spiritual nature will continue to break in to our consciousness.

Conservatives Attacking CBC as "Left-Wing Conspiracy"
May 9, 2019

The future of the CBC and Canadian journalism is a major election issue. LUCAS OLENIUK/TORONTO STAR

I try to organize my philanthropic giving by annual commitments and monthly deductions. The list of groups I donate to, and which I follow closely, includes local, national and international causes. I know, from being a beggar for Jamaican Self-Help for many years, that good causes benefit hugely from knowing they can count on regular contributions. They can plan, budget, implement and then send out narrative and financial reports online (always look at the financial reports). Groups don't need to mail me paper.

Because my mind is so well-served and the democracy I live in so strengthened by it, my top Canadian cause these days is the preservation and support of national media, that is, journalism, the arts and truthful news. After the climate crisis, it will be my "ballot box" question on October 21.

Right now, the main defender of a healthy, well-informed Canadian media landscape is the non-partisan, nonprofit group Friends of Canadian Broadcasting. To my surprised delight, Friends has 364,000 supporters. It is focusing on the upcoming election and on educating the public about the conditions under which Canadian media entities are laboring. These involve completely unfair favoritism toward the global giants, that group of five soulless corporations, which some wag has called "FAANGS:" Facebook, Apple, Amazon, Netflix and Google.

Well, FAANGS need to be declawed. At present, they pay no tax on the revenue they gain from Canadian advertisers on their platforms. That means we are the eyeballs and earbuds served up to them free.

Who gets impoverished by this favouritism, which could be fixed by changes to the Income Tax Act, are Canadian writers, storytellers, musicians, reporters, filmmakers, newspapers. And therefore our sense of ourselves. All Canadian creators and media organizations are badly affected, but CBC most of all. How can we measure the delight and the learning that Paul Kennedy of "Ideas" provides, or Norah Young on "Spark" or Bob McDonald on "Quirks and Quarks?"

Right here in Peterborough there is a small, impressive group of "Friends" who can call on some 200 supporters. They meet in the back room of Dreams of Beans, and are planning a large sign campaign, "We Choose CBC: We Choose Canada," and a several public events in the coming weeks. They are headed by the indefatigable citizen-advocate and artist Kady Denton.

In 2015, Friends worked on the two issues: Secure funding for the CBC and a reform of the CBC board to include impartial and highly-regarded people with experience in journalism and the arts. Got 'em both, I'm glad to say, from the present government.

Now for 2019, the theme will be closing the gaping hole in the Income Tax Act. Netflix has said arrogantly it will be "unambiguously exempt" from Canadian tax law. Says Friends' articulate executive director, Daniel Bernhard, "We are fighting for an end to lavish subsidies for the likes of Facebook, which pollutes our democracy, and a for major reinvestment in CBC, which strengthens our democracy and bring us together."

Adds Denton, "We are alarmed that the Conservative party, which is leading in the polls, has consistently attacked the CBC. A leaked Conservative fundraising letter attacked the CBC as a massive left-wing conspiracy. That is reckless hostility to fact-based professional journalism."

Denton continued, "I am moved by the intensity of feeling for the CBC. It is seen as a trustworthy base in a confusing world."

This year it is a question of cultural sovereignty. Just to be clear, our public broadcaster is funded by government but independent of it. It costs a Canadian $34 a year, compared to the BBC at $100, and Norwegian Broadcasting at $160.

So the candidate who knocks on my door and isn't ready to talk knowledgeably about this issue, and on his or her climate plan, will be eliminated from my list of possibles. I am not into supporting Silicon Valley any more than I already do.

Female Roman Catholic Priests Lead a New Kind of Church
May 15, 2019

Rev. Roberta Fuller is part of a small group of women in Canada who have been ordained as Catholic priests. She holds mass at a United church near Bethany each week.
RON PIETRONIRO/METROLAND

At a recent course I was teaching, "Women and God Talk," at Traill College, a gracious, well-spoken woman came in and introduced herself as an ordained Roman Catholic priest, living in Bethany. That got everyone's interest.

Roberta Fuller belongs to a community of strong women who have, since 2002, defied Vatican rules and been ordained to ministry in a new form. There are 300 such women now, worldwide. Their work has caused the church to react swiftly, strongly and negatively. They usually receive a letter of excommunication within two weeks from the local bishop.

It began when a South African nun-professor Patricia Fresen of the Dominican order lost her patience with the slow pace of any church movement toward gender equality, and joined a group in Germany in 2000. Fresen had been teaching theology and homiletics (how to preach), in a South African seminary, showing young men what scriptures to choose and how to speak at services, but she herself was barred from preaching in public.

With great persistence, she went to Europe, and found a male bishop willing to ordain her, a man whose name was to be kept secret until his death. It was important for the rebelling women to be in the apostolic line of succession, even for the resistance movement, which was gaining steam. Seven ordinations of women were held on a boat on the Danube River.

In 2002, Roman Catholic Womenpriests came to North America and conducted ordinations on a boat in the St Lawrence River out from Gananoque. Full disclosure: I was on that boat with my spouse. There was much joy as one more barrier to women's full equality was broken through. Had women been involved in church governance and teaching, from the beginning, what a different trajectory it would have been. So much suffering avoided. So many children spared. So many harmful policies and pronouncements, especially on women and sexuality, never issued. So much more respect from the world earned.

Some Canadians were among the candidates for priesthood in 2002, and so it has continued. Fuller herself has a fascinating story. Toronto-born and raised, a convert to Catholicism, she worked for Trans-Canada Airlines, now Air Canada, for 25 years. She became bilingual and travelled widely, then leaving business for teaching. She was active in OSSTF union matters, travelling to Afghanistan and Nepal, all the while drawn to the study of theology at St. Michael's College in the University of Toronto. She earned her private pilot's license and trekked to the base camp of Mount Everest.

With a master's degree in theological studies, she was ordained in 2011 and moved to a farm property north of Bethany. Now, Roberta Fuller ministers to a small congregation and has mass twice a month at a welcoming United church in Pickering. Her community is known as St. Mary Magdalen Catholic Faith Community.

"I minister to divorced and remarried Catholics, to members of the LGBTQ community and all seeking to live in a model of church that is aligned with gospel values. I conduct weddings and baptisms, offer spiritual direction and anoint the sick," she says.

The mission of RCWP is to prepare, ordain and support women and men from all states of life who are theologically qualified and committed to an inclusive model of church. RCWP Canada now has a retired bishop, Marie Bouclin of Sudbury, and a Regina-based active bishop, Jane Kryzanowski. There is a lively newsletter called "The Review," full of stories of progressive happenings here and abroad in church reform.

A woman is to be ordained on May 31. Her name is kept secret for fear of retaliation in her place of employment. "This is called a catacomb ordination," Fuller tells me. Disappointed at Pope Francis's recent rejection of the idea of women deacons, Fuller nonetheless carries on. "There is a great need for a new and radical reformation," she says. "Our actions as women priests may hasten it." For more information, visit www.romancatholic womenpriests.org.

These Difficult Times are Right for "Women Deliver"
May 23, 2019

Dozens of protesters from the recently formed "905 Handmaidens Local" converge in front of the Grimsby Legion recently as Niagara West MPP Sam Oosterhoff held a community coffee event. MIKE ZETTEL/TORSTAR

There may be no better time for a large global gathering of gender-equality advocates and decision-makers than the upcoming Women Deliver conference in Vancouver in early June. Nine thousand delegates from 165 countries will honour Canada's work toward achieving gender parity, and assess the progress made for half of humanity since the UN Conference on Women in 1995 In China.

To put its importance in context, we are seeing the emergence of right-wing, patriarchal, anti-choice laws in the United States, empowered by a misogynistic president and carried out by breathtakingly dim legislators, such as Rep. Barry Hovis of Missouri, who said, "Most rapes are consensual."

In Canada, seven provincial governments are now Conservative, and although leader Andrew Scheer says he won't reopen the abortion debate, 12 of his caucus members (11 men, one woman) attended a March for Life recently. Longtime activist Judy Rebick says, "Don't trust his promise."

Ontarians, already bruised by the Doug Ford government on many fronts, have to endure 21-year-old MPP Sam Oosterhoff, assistant to the minister of education, as he pledges to make abortion "unthinkable."

Doesn't he understand it is a woman's sexual health issue?

Twenty-four years ago, almost a quarter of a century, I was retiring from high school teaching and heard about a United Nations Conference on Women to be held in China. "Who is going from Peterborough?" Linda Slavin asked.

Of course, Peterborough must be there. It did involve a bit of a leap of faith. China was the mysterious east, opaque, just opening up. It wanted to show the world it could pull off hosting a huge UN meeting. The UN required that the meeting must include a strong non-governmental component. Citizens, many outspoken, from all over the world must be allowed to come too. They came to witness, to keep an eye on their country's official delegation and to correct them when their self-reporting was too glowing about the situation back home.

In the case of this massive meeting, the situation under discussion was the well-being of women and girls. China agreed to this condition but clearly was suspicious of Western feminists. Would we disrobe at the airport? Sheets were tactfully hidden at entry points. Would the free flow of debate, of democratic ideas, enter the minds of the Chinese young?

We didn't disrobe and ideas did enter the minds of hundreds of formally dressed young Chinese women who worked at our site, Huiruau. While the government delegations from all the countries of the UN met in Beijing, 35,000 of us, in jeans, suits, saris and khangas, milled about a muddy site in the village some 20 miles away. There were huge tents, one for each of the 14 themes. Beijing produced a fine declaration called the "Platform for Action," which has guided women's advancement since.

To be positive, all indicators about women and girls and their well-being around the world are up. Life expectancy is longer, maternal mortality is down, there is reduced female genital cutting, there are higher levels of literacy, increased employment and, among developing countries especially, greater political participation of women. Swedish doctor Hans Rosling wrote *Factfulness* to remind us of the progress made in the 20th and 21st centuries. The world's poorest people (living on $2 a day) now number 700 million: a terrible figure, but better than the 1.2 billion in 1990.

Burning issues remain. No one can deny the deeply troubling reality. In Vancouver, child marriage, inequality in girls and women's access to health, the stubborn statistics on violence against women and male control over their lives will be front and centre.

Women Deliver's theme is "delivering for good," an inspirational rallying cry. I will be reporting on it.

Handmaids Gather As Peterborough's Rosemary Ganley Heads to Vancouver

Rosemary Ganley models her handmaid's robe at her home on Friday May 31 in Peterborough. Ganley is attending "Women Deliver" 2019 in Vancouver June 3-6, the world's largest conference on gender equality and the health, rights, and well-being of girls and women. CLIFFORD SKARSTEDT/ PETERBOROUGH EXAMINER

When activist, teacher and writer Rosemary Ganley learned she was heading to the Women Deliver conference in Vancouver next week, she decided to add a visual statement to her travelling wardrobe and had a handmaid's uniform made. Women have begun wearing the robes and bonnets, taken from the hit television series *The Handmaid's Tale*, based on Margaret Atwood's novel, to highlight the struggles women still face in a male-dominated society.

The conference, which runs June 3-6, will also include speakers like Prime Minister Justin Trudeau, Sophie Gregoire Trudeau, Sahle-Work Zewde, Tina Tchen, Julie Gichuru and Ziaudden Yousafzai.

Ganley writes a weekly column for the Examiner.

By Clifford Skarstedt
The Peterborough Examiner
May 31, 2019

Women Deliver

Activist, educator and journalist Rosemary Ganley in downtown
Vancouver dressed as a character from Margaret Atwood's *The
Handmaid's Tale*. Ganley was in Vancouver to attend the Women
Deliver global conference. Now in her 80's, Ganley has followed
the women's movement for decades, and has no plans to slow
down even if "it seems more like a young woman's game these
days." JESSE WINTER/THE CANADIAN

The Mount Community Centre is a Miracle on Monaghan Road
May 29, 2019

High school students from the Youth Leadership in Sustainability (YLS) program prepare a meal with local ingredients at the Mount Community Centre. CLIFFORD SKARSTEDT/THE EXAMINER

I went by the other day to visit the old convent of the Sisters of St. Joseph, which has dominated the landscape along Monaghan Road north for over 150 years. It was almost unrecognizable on the inside, confusing me about where I slept during retreats in the '80s, and where we visited when a Sister had died. But it's humming with new life, renovation, activity and smiling faces.

In a very few years, Peterborough's best qualities of daring, generosity and hard work have come together with remarkable results at The Mount Community Centre.

Three leaders met me for a walk and talk. It was edifying. Kate Ramsay, a local philanthropist, co-chairs the newest campaign for funds: a goal of $4 million by 2020, more than half of which has come in. Ann Farlow is with us, a Mount Community Centre board member from the earliest days, whom I remember in 2013 as making an appeal at a service at the new convent for people to make a social investment in a newly forming, non-profit group renovating the old building for housing.

It seemed somewhat like a pipe dream then, but Father Leo Coughlin stepped forward with a $5,000 loan, and within three months the group had raised $300,000. Two years later the Mount board was able to offer these investors their money back, if they wanted it, and 3 percent interest. What a story.

Guiding me also was co-ordinator of the whole project Andi Van Koeverden, a dynamic leader who knows everyone in the building, manages a hundred volunteers and leads me in my hard hat to areas where 17 skilled local workmen are installing plumbing, doing drywall and working with wires. I ask about the architect, and Andi tells me glowingly about Gregg Gordon, a Peterborough architect with an interest in ecological features. In earlier phases, it was Neil Campbell. I can't really imagine what they thought as they first saw the 1869 structure. Dreaming big.

Already, tenants live in 43 apartments, vulnerable people from the list of those many hundreds here in Peterborough who seek social housing. The Mount Community Centre is, wisely, many faceted. There are offices for small businesses and professionals. I enjoy meeting up with former Fleming president Tony Tilly, who has his consulting business here, with Peter Pula of Axiom News and with Chonee Dennis, of The Dennis Group, all of whom offer service to non-profits in management and fundraising. The VON Adult daycare is there.

In the Gathering Room, sometimes used for Theatre Guild productions, I find a warm and peaceful preschool called Rowantree, led by Jessica Lindiman. This summer, an outdoor educator, Mathieu Lavoie of St. Anne School, will run a two-week "Forest School," incorporating the philosophy that 60 percent of education time for children should be outdoors.

There is another highlight at the MCC: The Fulcrum Restaurant, where managers teach culinary skills to adults and provide catering to such places as the Silver Bean Cafe, the Kawartha Cardiac Clinic and Kyoto Coffee. I hereby invite my women friends, all those book clubs and cycling groups and bridge foursomes, to come to the Fulcrum someday between 8 a.m. and 2 p.m. for lunch, five days a week.

"We want people in the doors," says Andi, "but we know we are a well-kept secret right now." The Mount Community Centre has more than 132,000 square feet, and St Paul's Presbyterian Congregation of 185 persons has set up their worship space, and office for minister Jonathan Baird and administrator Elaine Kempt.

Interestingly, The Mount Community Centre is gradually losing its early identity as a Catholic convent. Religious icons of course are there no longer. The "chapel" is now the Austin Doran Hall, and pews are movable for art exhibits. It will take a while for that designation to take hold for generations of Peterburians. But weddings still take place in that space.

The Mount is now a secular community resource and housing and cultural centre. More next week on its transformation.

The Mount Thrives and Grows with Strong Peterborough Support

June 5, 2019

Police officers, paramedics, dignitaries and friends attend the 2018 Special Olympics Ontario School Championships kickoff at the Mount Community Centre, May 29, 2018. CLIFFORD SKARSTEDT/ EXAMINER

Nothing as big as the transformation of the century-old convent of the Sisters of St. Joseph into a diverse mix of housing, a food centre, offices for health and social services and community groups for the arts could have happened without massive amounts of vision, daring, commitment and mobilization of people. Then, there was the need for large amounts of money from many sources, and countless volunteer hours. All of these have been given in spades to the Mount Community Centre as it exists today, partly redeveloped but well on its way. And in record-breaking time.

For example: commitment, an essential element, is demonstrated by Su Muslow, a retired school principal with a cheery greeting, who works 40 hours a week at the Mount as a volunteer. Lawyer Stephen Kylie has been chair of the board since 2013. Early visionaries include John Martyn, housing advocate par excellence, Lois Tuffin, formerly of Peterborough This Week and now with Five Counties Children's Centre, Jim Russell, of the United Way and the late Theresa Daw, an accessibility champion.

I know from the early days of Jamaican Self-Help, when we borrowed $5,000 from the Peterborough Community Credit Union, that when one person commits, other people come forward. That's Peterborough. Though, maybe it's more broadly human. For the Mount, it was the Kawartha Credit Union that was its initial "angel."

And there is the phenomenon of professionals becoming volunteers as they come to believe in the project. Bill Pyle worked on the sale of the Mount as an agent and became active on the board. Many others give pro bono help. I don't know who has written all the successful proposals for money from the government, but the Mount's mission responds perfectly to the federal and provincial governments' emphasis on social housing at this time.

In 2014, a small amount from the Peterborough Community Futures Corporation, with support from the Federal Economic Development Agency, enabled the Mount to write a strategic plan. In 2015, there was $50,000 from the federal government's Enabling Accessibility Fund and $100,000 from Aviva to modernize an elevator in the south wing (the Mount has four floors).

In 2016 and 2017, a portion of the food centre manager's wages came from the Federal Economic Development Agency for Southern Ontario. Then, a breakthrough of sorts. Contributions in 2017 and 2018, $600,000 and $500,000, for affordable housing, through Canada Mortgage and Housing Corporation, matched by the provincial government. The Mount was seen as a reliable and accountable partner. I mention these figures because they show how crucial higher levels of government support are to social development. They please me as a taxpayer, though I am quick to point out, I am, first of all, a citizen, who pays taxes to create a better society.

Both the Peterborough Foundation (Nancy Martyn, Pat Hooper) and the Community Foundation of Greater Peterborough (John Good, Nicole Gagliardi and Jennifer Bues), who have the happy task of collecting money from the well-to-do here in our region and passing it out to creative projects, have generously supported the Mount from the beginning. One local donor, who chose to be anonymous, gave $300,000 for the skills-training kitchen.

Former police chief Murray Rodd turned his retirement party into a fundraiser, raising $25,000 for the cause. Along those lines, I suggested to Andi van Koeverden that one of the possible outcomes of a project such as the integrated Mount, is the "conscientization" of those with extra means. We discussed the word. I think it comes from the '70s and liberation theology!

In keeping with the Mount's mission, a partnership was formed with Shared Dreams for Independent Living, parents of five young men with varying abilities, to construct suitable combined housing at the Mount. What I come away with is the way in which the Sisters' original ministry - witness, education, sharing, and community-building - is being lived out in new ways. Maybe there really is nothing new under the sun, only new manifestations.

Canada is Leading the Way in Gender Equity
June 12, 2019

Activist, educator and journalist Rosemary Ganley dressed as
a character from Margaret Atwood's *The Handmaid's Tale.*

In the beautiful city of Vancouver, between the mountains and the sea,
I was in its white-sailed Conference Centre, bright with colour,
bubbling and alive, for four days in early June as women of all ages and
hues, in saris, African khangas, jeans, hijabs and business suits, from
130 nations, rallied around one theme: the global condition of girls and
women, 52 percent of the world's population.

There was urgency. In spite of, or perhaps because of, the massive
progress for many women in health, education, freedom and political
participation over the past 25 years, we are seeing the rise once again of
mean, misogynistic men to leadership, perhaps the worst being U.S
President Donald Trump, but also in Brazil, Russia, the Philippines and
China.

They have a lot in common, most menacingly the rollback of democracy,
but a central tenet among them all is the attempted control of women
and of women's sexuality. Women and girls are, by universal agreement
backed up by statistics, second-class everywhere: In institutions, in
faith communities, in science and politics and general culture.

"In no country in the world," says Phumzile Mlambo of the United
Nations, "has gender equity been achieved." I think of this reality often,
as a privileged, older, educated, healthy, white, Canadian settler.

Locating oneself is a start. Educating oneself is next. Finding good
sources, human, and via technology. Joining honest, action-and-then-
reflection movements. Taking the position of an advocate for change,
keeping in mind the most excluded, the most suffering. Have a global
outlook.

This is one indivisible small planet. My father, enlightened and humble, told us, "Always advocate for someone you are not."

So join the worldwide women's movement, I decided many years ago. Keep meeting and learning and reading and speaking up. And finding surprise and joy, too.

That all brought me to the Women Deliver conference last week. Eight thousand people, mostly women. Scores of workshops, films, plenaries, talks by world leaders. Just for one example, I met Tarana Burke, founder of the MeToo movement.

Before leaving home, I had the notion to have a handmaid's outfit made. Partly, it was a tribute to the prophetic Canadian writer Margaret Atwood, who, in 1985, discerned the real possibility that frightened societies might try to turn back progress for women. Partly I wanted to have something concrete with which to start a conversation (just as my button "Catholic Feminist for Choice" opens animated dialogue).

Enter new friend Cathy Ogrodnik, who said, "Sure, I'll do one up. You can just donate to Crossroads Shelter." Friend Sandi Burri said, "You just take it and go. I'll make the donation." That's called "sisterhood," well-known around the world.

We had meaningful fun in Vancouver with that outfit, many trying it on.

The message was quickly understood by North Americans, since "The Handmaid's Tale" on TV is entering its third season. Not so resonant with women from the global south.

Anyway, that gig led to the reporter and photographer in Vancouver asking me to pose on Burrard Street in front of a church, as passersby grinned in recognition. Some of them took pictures of me and the photographer. Hence my picture and quotes on the front page of the Toronto Star on June 7.

I gave the present government a B-plus when asked.

But on more reflection, the vast amount of money pledged for women's and children's health by our prime minister as he showed his profound grasp of the status of women, and the truly brilliant work of Minister of Gender Equality Maryam Monsef all make me rate this national leadership we have right now as A-plus-plus.

More next week on Women Deliver.

Progress for Women in Politics
Begins at the Municipal Level
June 20, 2019

Ta'Kaiya Blaney and members of BC's Indigenous community march in commemoration for the inquiry into MMIW in Vancouver earlier this month, during the Women Deliver conference. TESSA VIKANDER/TORSTAR

When I looked at the first day's offerings at the Women Deliver Conference in Vancouver two weeks ago, I froze. At any hour, on any day, there were about 20 good choices. Among the titles, "Advocacy Strategies," "Why Should I Care?," "Digital Campaigning," "Managing Stress and Anxiety," "Born into Crisis," "Nurses' Leadership," films on women artists and women athletes, "2SLGBTIQ Advocacy," "Male Engagement," "Sexual and Human Rights in Conflict Zones," "Comprehensive Sex Education in Schools," (Mr. Ford, take note), "Women and Spirituality," "Midwifery Today," "Child Marriage" and "FGM."

My first new learning happened early, "2SLGBTIQ" stands for "two-spirited, lesbian, gay, bisexual, transgender, intersex and questioning."

Someone described Women Deliver as "the Olympics for gender equity." Sold out for two months, with an estimated 100,000 more participating online, it is held every three years, the last one in Denmark. "It comes at a critical time for gender equity," said chair Katya Iversen. "It is not a women's issue, not a war between the sexes, but an integral part of national agendas." And of local agendas and of family agendas, I'd add.

So I regained my balance and decided on a rather modest workshop called "Women Transforming Cities," sponsored by the Federation of Canadian Municipalities, which has 2,000 member cities and towns.

That is 90 percent of our Canadian entities. Good for them to be prominent at Women Deliver. I believe that change happens locally. Moreover, my friend Jennifer Rowell Dailloux is on a five-woman municipal council in Haliburton. And Peterborough has Mayor Diane Therrien.   No dust on us. In terms of missing out on all the other offerings, I counted on getting together with colleagues in the evening over some Okanagan wine and sharing our gleanings.

"If you can see her, you can be her," urged the federal minister for small business, Mary Ng, as she opened the session. But at present in Canada, only 18 percent of communities have female mayors and only 28 percent of municipal councillors are women. "If a city is friendly to women, it is friendly to everyone," said federation executive member Celine Fung. Another term I heard and liked was "wise practice," replacing "best practice" in the scheme of things. Mention was made of the words of a great Lebanese philosopher, human rights leader Charles Malik, who said, "The fastest way to change society is to mobilize women."

Then to my delight, in came two women mayors, from two other countries; Bolivia and Ukraine. We can get so Western-focused, and miss the wisdom from other parts of the world. Anastasia Popsui is mayor of Irpin, a city of 60,000 near the Ukrainian capital of Kyiv. Think of life there, close to Russia, from whom Irpin has recently accepted 10,000 refugees fleeing Putin. In the ratings of the Global Gender Gap, Ukraine is 61st out of 144 countries. Women's salaries are 26 percent lower than men's. But Popsui keeps on working, particularly in housing. She is knowledgeable about, and can call on, the European Charter of Gender Equality.

From rural Bolivia, we met Patricia Guzman, who spoke through a translator. She is mayor of Vinto, and spoke of the tough chauvinism she faces. Of 339 municipalities in Bolivia, only eight percent have women mayors. Guzman concentrates on women's skill development, including basketry, as a means of economic empowerment.Bolivia has a progressive president, Evo Morales, who often trenchantly criticizes Donald Trump, but enlightened national-level policies have to be brought to the grassroots, said Guzman.

Outdoors, I followed an Indigenous procession in which several young men carried a large wooden canoe holding a young woman singing. It was to honour women. The procession made its way down many steps toward the sea, to a grassy area of longhouses. It was here I took part in "intergenerational dialogue" with the Young Feminists of Canada. An impressive lot, ready to lead.

Next week, some impressions of "Gender Transformative Education." That's for all my teacher friends, who already practice it.

It's Time For More Peterborough Men To Stand Up for Gender Equality
June 27, 2019

There was another theme I followed at the great 8000-person Congress called Women Deliver, in Vancouver recently. Fully 30 workshops explored the vital role of men and boys in the long journey to full gender equality. The word "allyship" was used, as in being an ally, meaning, in this case, the conscious habit of noticing discrimination against girls and women in any field and taking a stand against it, preferably publicly.

Any girl or woman will tell you how rare and beautiful that is.

In the Canadian context, it is off-colour and sexist jokes in schools, jibes in bars, male locker-room talk, anonymous "come-ons," unwanted touch everywhere, and of course much worse violence in some situations. A Catholic high school girl told me once that some boys in her class called the girls derogatory names, and then, as a final clincher, said, "And you dames can't be priests anyway." We have to make sure Pope Francis hears that.

Equality and respect. "All we are saying," as the song goes.

There is overwhelming evidence that the whole human race and likely the earth we inhabit, will benefit from equality. Babies will certainly gain from the firm grasp and gentle attention of secure fathers. Fathers will gain from growth in emotional intelligence and perceptiveness that comes with full family involvement. The burdensome old trope of the father sole-breadwinner as a source of identity will give way to shared financial responsibility between man and woman in a partnership. Women will gain full humanity, rights and responsibilities.

I keep a quote from the great African-American Maya Angelou on my desk. "The divine upon my right impels me to pull forever at the latch on freedom's gate."

Immense progress toward the reality of men being women's allies has been made. Truly strong male leaders will now say with pride, "I am a feminist," as Prime Minister Trudeau and United Nations Secretary-General Antonio Gutteres have both done.

My personal surroundings, family, spouse, sons, colleagues, and neighbours, I can only describe as enlightened. My oldest son, a high school English teacher, gives a one-month course in gender studies (11 teenage girls, five teenage boys) each year.

He says, "Nobody else would do it, and anyway, anything I'm not sure about, I can ask my mother!"

All over town, young men carry little ones on their chests or in strollers. They choose to coach girls teams. They challenge chauvinism by doing otherwise. They clean bathrooms and stay up with sick children and even do crafts and cookies for daycare when their turn comes.

A leading Canadian theorist, Michael Kaufman of Toronto, gave several sessions at Women Deliver on this theme. It is work he has done all over the world for 30 years, having co-founded the "White Ribbon Campaign: Men in Solidarity with Women."

Michael's new book is *The Time Has Come: Why Men Must Join the Gender Equality Revolution.*

He is an engaging speaker, 68 years of age. I hope some Peterborough men's group, service club, book group, church association, or business coalition, will bring Michael Kaufman here soon for a full-scale conversation. University and college students, special price.

After a stimulating Kaufman talk in Vancouver, I overheard a group of grad students, men (yes, in a bar), speaking of other titles they knew and valued. To my surprise, since the writer is a former Dominican monk, they spoke of Matthew Fox and his 2008 book *The Hidden Spirituality of Men.*

At the same time, wise woman Phumzile Mlambo, highly respected head of UN Women (the agency, I'm proud to say, that was brought in by Canadian Ambassador Stephen Lewis during his tenure), said wryly, "Men need to be protagonists in the journey to gender equality, but we need to ensure they are not treated as heroes. We don't praise fish for swimming!"

Downtown Peterborough and the Creek that Runs Under Our Feet
July 3, 2019

Jackson Creek runs right next to the Only Cafe (left side) on Hunter Street in downtown Peterborough.

There's nothing quite like a Sunday afternoon stroll with a knowledgeable guide through downtown Peterborough, following Jackson Creek. It was taken in June with an affable group of Peterburians at a leisurely pace, but the learning was rapid. Peering down storm drains, we walked northwest from the Chamber of Commerce building, across Sherbrooke Street and the parking lot of UNIFOR and CUPE, all the while either rejoicing at the open nature of the creek with its bubbling rush of cool-looking water, or lamenting the intrusion of so much concrete that covered it.

I didn't know that our city is on a drumlin (a hill formed by glaciers 10,000 years ago) sloping to the east into the Otonabee River and to the west to Jackson Creek, We are living in a watershed that has not been sufficiently respected. It now poses a challenge to environmental leadership, to our quality of life and to our access to natural features, which so enhances mental health.

I can quite imagine school trips along this route any June or September day. It's an ideal case-study for critical thinking. We have had a love affair with concrete over the past 50 years, and the private car has been given pride of place, so that now parking for vehicles is dominant in our (un)thinking.

But there are now enlightened projects all over Ontario to depave areas, to recover what is under our feet and can give us delight. The guide on this free walk was Trent graduate student, and president of the Peterborough Field Naturalists, Dylan Radcliffe. Like many gifted teachers, he wears his learning lightly and can soon make you a creek lover.

Before we built the downtown parking garage on King Street and the bus terminal on Simcoe, streams would flow freely across landscapes. They are still present, but now confined to underground pipes and largely concrete tunnels, subject to massive flooding.

I felt saddened to be staring down a three-foot-wide storm drain at the creek beside the most easterly bus bay. Maybe, Radcliffe muses, when the bus bay needs to be replaced, say 20 years from now, we'll have a chance to open this up.

The creek meanders westward and, sadly, picks up effluent and salty run-off from the streets. It continues, as did we, into Jackson Park, a natural asset that many Peterburians treasure and hope to keep pristine for public use and personal renewal.

Dylan wasn't here in 2004 during our great flood, but I was here, and later was a proud "Calendar Girl" in the subsequent fundraising effort for downtowners who has lost everything. He showed us the spot in Jackson Creek along King Street where the flooding from quickly accumulating rainfall caused water to explode "like a fire hose" into the downtown.

There was the famous photo of a beaver wandering on George Street. An equally famous shot was taken of Mayor Sylvia Sutherland reading The Examiner while treading water in Millbrook Pond.

The walk was one of several hundred across Canada each year called "Jane's Walks," to honour the memory of the great American-Canadian urban thinker, Jane Jacobs, whose influential book was *The Death and Life of Great American Cities.*

Jacobs left the U.S. for Toronto in 1981, choosing to live in a neighbourhood along Bloor Street. "Neighbourhoods," she wrote, "are the basis of social capital. Do we build for people or for cars?" I was glad I had biked down.

The dream is could we once again have a drinkable, fishable and swimmable Jackson Creek? Citizen groups called "Water Keepers" are educating and persuading decision-makers today. Indigenous people keep pointing to the sacredness of water.

Radcliffe showed us his favourite downtown rest stop along the creek, the patio of The Only Cafe. He studies at Trent with Dr. Thomas Whillans. We have among us knowledgeable people. I felt very much better informed.

Looking down, is as valuable as looking up.

Let the Stories Begin at the Lakefield Literary Festival
July 10, 2019

Authors Michael Redhill and Ian Brown attend the Lakefield Literary Festival 2018 at Lakefield College School. CLIFFORD SKARSTEDT/EXAMINER

Sometimes, in small places, remarkable things happen, kind of organically. Such is the story of the soon-to-open, for its 25th annual weekend, Lakefield Literary Festival, which began in 1995 in that richly endowed community and has flourished since then, thanks to wise decisions, smart people and deep volunteer commitment.

I once taught English literature at Lakefield College School and got to befriend the iconic Canadian novelist Margaret Laurence, who was Manitoba-born but a Lakefield resident by choice. I remember her house on Regent Street, lined wall-to-wall and floor-to-ceiling with books from Britain, America and the world. Literature from Canada covered another wall. She was inspiring, and Brenda Neill, a teacher, and Ron Ward, a Baptist minister, were inspired.

Thus began a modest summer gathering for Canadian readers and writers, to be celebrated around the time of Margaret Laurence's birthday. She had died in 1987.

Our area has been rich in writers - both famous, such as Catharine Parr Traill, Susannah Moodie and Drew Hayden Taylor, and the less famous - and also with readers. The high schools have always had strong English departments and eager readers, and the libraries are good. I'm sure there are 200 book clubs for adults here. Canadians are reading online for sure, but they also buy books and think that reading is important. We have, every March, on our national broadcaster, a week of book discussion called "Canada Reads."

Lakefield Literary Festival grew slowly but it is now of national importance. The committee decided some years ago to maintain its modest size, with no venue larger than the auditorium at Lakefield College School.

Canadian writers like to come: Summer in the Kawarthas is appealing. One of this year's highlights will be Booker and Giller prizewinning novelist Michael Ondaatje, in conversation with publisher Louise Dennys. It is stunning to realize that LLF has brought more than 60 important Canadian writers here, including Elizabeth Hay, Peter Gzowski, Jane Urquhart, Heather O'Neill, Lisa Moore and Rawi Hage.

The prices have been kept moderate. There has been a sensitivity, shown by such people as Stephanie Ford Forrester, to both the national and the local scene. Two other features of the festival are showcasing the work of Indigenous writers - this year, Lee Maracle, Columpa Bobb and Duncan McCue - and encouraging the work of young writers through a contest.

Lucille Strath remembers the late Alisdair Wallace in 1999 beginning this young writers project. This year there were 70 submissions of fiction, non-fiction and poetry from regional high schoolers.

Many Lakefield people remember with pleasure the wisdom of the late, great Richard Wagamese in 2014. Brenda Neill mentions how much help Shelley Ambrose, publisher of "Walrus Magazine," has been to the festival. Another memory includes writer Andrew Piper stepping in for the ill Wayne Johnston with an hour's notice. In the middle of the 2004 Peterborough floods, Mayor Sylvia Sutherland kept her commitment.

John Boyko is this year's chair. "We are small, but mighty," he says, "thanks to volunteers and sponsors." I plan on going on a literary walk with Mark Finnan, and to a session with Peterborough authors Jane Bow, Laura Rock Gaughan and Andrew Forbes. I'd like to meet Tima Kurdi, who wrote *The Boy on the Beach*, the story of the death of her Syrian nephew, drowning trying to cross the Mediterranean, whose picture so saddened the world. It will be part of a reading on leaving and coming home. It's relevant to me right now, as I just spent time in my hometown Kirkland Lake, on the occasion of its 100th anniversary.

There will be a children's book tent, in Cenotaph Park just over the bridge, and three opportunities for aspiring writers to discuss their hopes and plans with Wayne Grady, Drew Hayden Taylor and Kevin Silvester.

Lakefield Literary means enrichment in the summer, year after year; stimulation, consolation and imagination right here at home.

Going Home Again as Kirkland Lake Celebrates 100 Years
July 17, 2019

"Home is the place where/if you have to go there/they have to take you in." Robert Frost was a wise American poet, but in the case of my visit to my hometown Kirkland Lake two weeks ago to celebrate its 100th anniversary, this insight didn't hold true. Five days with my sister, surrounded by longtime friends and schoolmates, were rich in memory and gratitude.

Kirkland Lake was founded in 1919, a hard-scrabble gold mining camp full of prospectors, odd characters and muddy roads. It gradually acquired a police officer, a hospital, a school and, of course, a hockey rink. It was also the site of many deaths of miners in cave-ins and rock falls, a very heavy toll: almost 300 men in the years from 1914 to 2015. There is a striking black granite memorial sculpture to these men. There was no union in the early days. A famous strike in the bitter winter of 1941 didn't produce one (until 1944).

The "Mile of Gold" was seven gold mines strung in an east-west row. It is estimated today that 42 million ounces of gold came out of these mines between 1919 and 2012, worth $60 billion in today's dollars. Even with mining's downside, that's a lot of nation-building.

But gold ran out in the 1950's, and KL went into decline. What were being exported were hockey players: 44 young men have made it to the NHL, including Dick Duff, Ted Lindsay, Larry Hillman and Ralph Backstrom.

I remember the egalitarian nature of the high school. We all funneled into it from diverse school systems.

I remember the ambition of the sons and daughters of miners, many with unpronounceable names. Kirkland Lake was multicultural before that become common. Poles, Italians and Croats (and my two brothers) worked underground for $1.12 an hour.

When the earth shuddered, women ran to the mine gates to await word. Disaster was signalled by a whistle. There is a profound community solidarity that develops in such situations. The 1,000 former Kirland Lakers who came to the town last week told stories of the camaraderie, the material simplicity of their homes and the quality of resilience they developed here.

Kirkland Lakers who live now in Peterborough have these qualities. George Tough was deputy minister in more than one federal or provincial government. Dr. Harold McCartney has been a respected eye surgeon; Pat Casey has spent 37 years volunteering with the Petes.

We developed a much-needed sense of humour too, I think. When my sister and I went back to the church where I had been married in 1961, I saw that the crucifix was still a bit off-kilter. One old-timer came over to us and whispered, "Are you the Burns girls?"

Girls? "Yes."

"Well, your father and mother used to sit over there, so I think you should move over." You bet.

Most communities I know have a one-day reunion or, at the most, a weekend. Kirkland Lake's was two weeks. Daily wine and cheese gatherings at Northern College were highly social. I said hello to MP Charlie Angus, a great representative of the riding of Timmins-James Bay, who had come to unveil a prospector-with-dog sculpture at Toburn Mine site.

Musical stars Blue Rodeo and Serena Ryder entertained. There was Shakespeare-in-the-Park. An additional delight was the arrival of playwright Jennifer Wynne Webber from Nanaimo. We started a conversation with her on the street and heard about her play, "With Glowing Hearts," which she read from at the museum the following morning.

Fascinating story: Jennifer became interested while at the University of Saskatchewan in the heroism of the women of Kirkland Lake during the strike of 1941. So she wrote the play and read from it to an enthusiastic audience. It is a fine work and I hope it gets wide play.

My literary and feminist side was thus also nourished.

Girls are Being Trafficked Along Ontario's Busy 400-Series Highways
July 25, 2019

My columns, I hope and intend, have a consistent feminist perspective. This one will explore an issue too long hidden but which is essentially a foundational feminist issue: the trafficking for sex and labour of girls in Ontario.

Sexual exploitation and human trafficking of young women are long-standing and complex realities, but it now needs new attention and community awareness as the numbers are rising. The Durham Regional Police Service reports that it has helped 41 girls in the first six months of the year who were trying to leave the pimps who had lured them. The executive director of Victim Services for Peterborough-Northumberland, Emily Poulin, reports they have had 77 clients in 2018-19.

Most of the Ontario girls are transported and forced to work in motels along the 400 highways. Pimps isolate and shame the girls and make them fear for their safety if they leave. Online recruiting plays a part. A young person posting "I hate small towns" or "I got in a big fight with my parents" can signal to pimps that the poster is vulnerable.

The greatest positive effect in confronting this situation comes when several partners, from the grassroots to the professional, link hands, knowledge and strength to mount a coordinated response.

On Tuesday, at 9:20 a.m, all of the ONroute Travel Centres — 20 of them along the 400 highways in Ontario — will have a public awareness event. It is sponsored by Courage for Freedom, a registered charity in Aylmer (www.farmtowncanada.ca) that offers counselling and support to victims and sometimes uses horse training in psychological rehabilitation. The closest ONroute Centre to Peterborough is in Port Hope.

I plan to attend this Port Hope ONroute event along with Sheila Crook of the Business and Professional Women's Clubs of Ontario. The BPW is one of the sponsors. Good for them. I've long felt that educated and financially secure women must take up advocacy and support for their sisters in distress.

I'm not sure where the idea of using ONroute locations as a place for public education came from, but it's a gem. I plan to learn the signs of victimhood and what to do to be helpful. As an example, Durham Police Service (www.stopHT.com) has postcard-size handouts. They state that "Common recruitment locations are schools, malls, group homes and bus stops. The ages of those recruited are as low as 12 or 13."

Victims are from all income levels. The homeless and the marginalized are targeted. Indigenous youth are especially vulnerable to trafficking. Addictions and disability are added risk factors.

The police postcard goes on that the signs to look for are noticing that the young person is repaying a large debt through sex, shows signs of abuse such as bruising or cigarette burns, or seems fearful and depressed and cannot speak for themselves. Tattooing may be obvious, particularly branding symbols. The young person may not control their own passport and identity cards and may be submissive to an accompanying person.

Staff and volunteers in Peterborough go out at night to provide emotional and practical support. "Sometimes," says crisis worker Leslie Kirton, "we provide a 911 phone."

Last May, the province passed the Anti-Human Trafficking Act to increase protection and make it easier for victims to pursue compensation.

The July 30 event is intended to increase public awareness and show those being trafficked that there are people in Ontario who care about, and will help, them.

Human trafficking is a crime and a human rights abuse. It is not consensual sex, nor is it smuggling, since these victims are homegrown.

I can think of no worthier cause for feminists than this. The public is invited to an ONroute Centre on Tuesday. There will be a brave survivor speaking of her experience.

Organizers ask attendees (it is free) to RSVP at:
info@courageforfreedom.org.

More and More, U.S. Politics Are Being Fueled By Hate
July 31, 2019

TOM BRENNER/NEW YORK TIMES

Americans Must Live With a Demagogue in the White House

Does America have more lovers than haters? That's the crucial question for the citizens of the republic to our south, now and into the future.

Spewing venom, their president outdid himself last week. Like a kind of Frankenstein unloosed, he dominated the news cycle, other crucial matters left abandoned. We watched, shocked. Me, too. I watched three straight nights of CNN. Evil before our eyes becomes wickedly irresistible.

The scorn he heaped on four congresswomen, the insulting language used, the disregard for truth, and the lack of a smidgen of respect for American institutions, all gave us a fresh and frightening picture of a demagogue at the helm.

Then I read what the wise Indian writer Arundathi Roy said, "The danger of that kind of obsession with a single person is that you don't see the system that has produced him." That system for this president entails extreme wealth, a background in the shallowest of entertainment forms, a disdain for learning, and a profound contempt for women. All parts of the system are dominated by rampant, unregulated greed.

"The occupant of the White House," as Rep. Ayanna Pressley of Massachusetts likes to phrase it, tweets like a mad man. He has a vocabulary of insult like none other we've seen in public life, in my memory anyway, and he incites his followers toward anti-social attitudes and sometimes actions. Hate crimes are up 17 percent in the states since his election in 2016.

Could we have expected anything different? His first words in office were to cast doubt on the former president's citizenship, and then to call Mexican immigrants "rapists." It was then on to Muslims, and within all of it, the denigration of women and his power over them: the whole female gender.

One despairs at the state of American public education that has produced the middle-aged men who shout slogans at rallies, wearing MAGA hats, and the women who gleefully assert their undying support. Is this the Stockholm syndrome before our very eyes: having been so beaten down by your abuser you come in a perverse way to love your own humiliation?

Where has the education in civics been? Education in the history and the fragility of democracy? Lost, I think in fostering superiority and jingoism. Now I understand what "American exceptionalism" means: entitlement, and an absolute right to power. Around here, and across Canada, not "socialism" nor "liberal" nor "medicare" is a bad word. Get a grip, America.

The women's movement in America has also failed among white women. When 52 percent of white women support this leader, what other conclusion can one come to? Knowing a little history might clarify things now. Demagoguery is defined as a political leader appealing to the prejudice and ignorance of ordinary people rather than using rational arguments. The demagogue goes on to attack the news media, and make false claims. (Our Canadian, Daniel Dale, is the man to go to for a complete record of Mr. Trump's lies.)

Such leaders have appeared since the earliest days of democracy. There was the demagogue Cleon of the Greeks, in 500 BC. On YouTube, I watched "A Night at the Garden," footage of an American Nazi rally of 20,000 in Madison Square Garden in 1939 in support of Mussolini and Hitler. There were straight-armed salutes. There were chants and swastika emblems. Leader Fritz Kuhn railed against a "Jewish-controlled press." What a cautionary tale it is, should Americans study it. Seventy-eight years later, there was Charlottesville.

Several prominent people, Chris Cuomo on CNN, Stephen Colbert on CBS and Prof. Jason Stanley of Yale, author of *How Fascism Works*, have spoken with moral authority of the threat Trump poses to democracy and peace in his country. Even comic Dick Van Dyke complained, "Does he not know the difference between the Bible and the Constitution?"

In Canada, several provinces have recently flirted with right-wing, populist parties and unworthy leaders. We're getting a harsh wake-up call.

Lacrosse Brings Girls of the World Together in Peterborough
August 14, 2019

U19 Tournament Was a Celebration of the Sporting Spirit

Who among us knew that our proud, fast and skillful Indigenous sport, lacrosse, is now being played at all levels and among both genders around the world? Wales, lacrosse? Korea, lacrosse? Ireland, lacrosse? You bet.

The 10-day tournament here in Peterborough has come as a delightful surprise, along with the midsummer arrival of 440 teenage girls from 22 countries. Lois Tuffin, who has worked for two years on a planning committee for the event, tells me I should use the term "nations," not "countries," because an Indigenous team, the Haudenosaunee, is here. I'll try to use the term.

Lois herself "runs tings," it seems to me, up and down from the VIP tent to the media booth to the front gate. On the day it rained heavily, she was ushering all players and fans into the Athletic Centre. The whole field is fenced off, tickets are $10 for the whole day, maybe five games, and there are scores of friendly volunteers and fans, greeting each other with warmth.

I sit on the unforgiving metal bleachers and watch the Haudenosaunee team. I ask a nearby parent, "Is that Number 18 your daughter?" "Yes," he says proudly. "I'm from Tyendinaga, and she's played since she was three."

As a well-known fashion expert, I can say the outfits are pleasing to any feminist eye. Skirts and sensible tops, and goggles too, since those sticks can hurt. No beach volleyball attire here.

Perhaps 3,000 people attend major games, Parking is, of course, at a premium. I talk to one Peterborough couple who had parked up near the Hamburg Cabin on Armour Road. Others walked across the bridge from Gzowski College. These were the locals. Everywhere, I hear contented stories from visitors of being in Peterborough. Some were at motels, some at Airbnbs, some camping.

I want to salute the committee that pulled this off, the producers of the colourful program with headshots of every player, the media, especially the fine writing of Mike Davies of the Examiner, and the pictures of photographer Clifford Skarstedt, who got some beautiful shots, and the sponsors, including the city and the province.

It has a professional touch: The national anthems, the pledges of fair play by athletes and referees, the flags of each nation flying, the weather in full co-operation, the mood, happy.

A midsummer lifter-upper.

I think that internationalism for the ordinary person comes from small groups meeting small groups, not so much from immersion in a 10-million-person capital city.

I of course was following the fortunes of Jamaica. It has been a replica of "Cool Runnings," when Jamaica sent a bobsled team to the Calgary Olympics, the basis of a hilarious John Candy movie. For nine of these 22 teams, it was the first time participating at this level. The Jamaicans showed, ahem, a certain lack of experience. Catching that darn ball or scooping it from the grass is a challenge. But never mind, the players sang and danced reggae as they lost five in a row. Came close with Taipei.

Down at FreshCo, the checkout women tell me everybody who comes in is talking about the tournament. At the Silver Bean Cafe on the water, the Belgian team, hot and sticky, decides to take a swim. On campus, three food trucks serve up poutine or Mexican food, and a nearby Indigenous man instructed others on the art of stickmaking.

A father from New York City points out his daughter to me. She is playing for Israel, since her mother is Israeli (formerly of Argentina). The girl has an Israeli passport. Special cheers go up for Peterborough player Skylar McArthur and coach Alison Daley, both with the Canadian team.

Maybe the best of our world right there, on those Trent and Fleming fields.

Angela Stultz's Life is Full of Signs and Wonders Indeed
September 4, 2019

Dedicated Jamaican Care Worker Launches New Book

Back in 1998, in the gritty, often forbidding inner city of Kingston, Jamaica, our friend Father Jim Webb, who lived a heroic life there, summoned me and my late spouse, John, to chat.

"I've met a remarkable Jamaican social worker/leader down the street," he said. "Her name is Angela Stultz. Take a look at what she is working on: an after-school tutoring and homework program for kids who are falling behind, a daycare centre, a health clinic with a lot of AIDS education, a chicken-raising project, a callaloo garden and serious peace-building among rival gangs. She is fearless."

"Nooooooo," we said reluctantly, "we are in over our heads financially and human resource-wise now."

"Well, just meet her," he finished. "She gets a bit of foreign aid from Christian Aid in the U.K." Our fate was sealed then and there. We met Angela, a tall, beautiful Rastafarian queen with a brilliant smile, mile-high heels, bright swirling clothes and hairdos with extensions to die for. No nonsense though. No challenges from anybody, the roughest "rude boy" among them.

When she arrived each morning, the whole neighbourhood lit up. It was as if they were important enough to get the attention of this great lady. "Gang members, the 'dons,' also want their kids to be safe and to read and write," she told us. "I know them. I am not a police informer, but I know them. They trust me enough to agree to meet at secret locations here in West Kingston."

Years of productive joint work went on. Angela and her centre, the S Corner Community Development Project, became a trusted partner for our organization, Jamaican Self-Help (JSH). She did the reporting we required. She came to Canada in 1998 to charm people here and to give the annual JSH lecture, "It Takes a Village, Plus the Neighbours."

She absorbed our teenage volunteers year after year, giving them meaningful tasks, explaining Jamaican culture and keeping them safe. They could walk about the ghetto with her, utterly unmolested.

Some time in there, she found space and time to go to the U.S. to earn her master's degree in social work. I remember she did not have a first degree. John spoke on the phone to the college registrar. "Your community would be privileged to have this woman among you," he said.

Then she unofficially adopted a foundling from the street, taking her into her single-mother family with three kids, and raising her to adulthood.

Prince Charles, whose foundation, the Prince's Charities, sponsors development projects among the very poor around the world, visited Angela in Kingston and asked her to Buckingham Palace to meet people and be honoured. The woman can dine with royalty and not be intimidated, and she can walk with humble folk. In fact, she will leave royalty with thoughts to ponder.

In passing one day, she mentioned to me she had had a call from the U.S. Embassy telling her she had been named a "Woman of Courage," and was one of only seven women from around the world selected by the State Department to be honoured on International Women's Day in 2008 in Washington.

So it didn't completely amaze me when she announced in 2019 that she had written and published her memoir, entitled *Signs and Wonders: Sojourn in the Inner-city*.

Jamaican Self-Help of Peterborough is still very much alive. It has survived the originals such as myself, and now is entirely volunteer-based with no office. But so much goodwill toward JSH remains in our area, it raised over $60,000 last year for Jamaica.

It has eagerly organized a book launch with Angela Stultz, to be held Saturday from 5 to 8 p.m. at By the Bridge cafe and bookstore on Water Street.

A little reggae music too, of course.

It's Time to Take Stock as We Head into a Federal Election
September 11, 2019

Progress Has Been Made in Socio-cultural Affairs in the Past Four Years

We'll soon have another chance to define the country we are and hope to be. There is a national election October 21. Time to seriously consider both large ideas and the practical laws which try to deliver on those large ideas.

It's not easy work, this business of deciding one's vote. But when neglected or corrupted by special interests, including foreign ones, we put our citizenship, for which many have died to preserve, on the back burner, and place the grand project of building a country worth living in, at risk. I am dismayed when I learn that only 2 percent of Canadians belong to any of five political parties, (that's where you have the most influence), and that just 60 percent of us vote. That describes a lazy democracy.

A couple of observations: Cynicism should be rejected, and realism should be adopted. Human beings run this project and are forever susceptible to flaws, fatigue, pressure, naivete and self-interest. So, perfectionism as an expectation has to be jettisoned in nation-building. I salute the wry remark of the 19th century German chancellor, Otto Von Bismarck, who said, "Politics is the art of the possible, the art of next best."

This country is big, spread out, and diverse, with strong regional identities. Coast to coast to coast, from a temperate climate to the Arctic, and a long border separating us from an empire in decline. This Liberal government has managed the tempestuous Mr. Trump pretty well.

I depend on the ideas of the thinker and activist, Mary Jo Leddy in her new book, *Why Are We Here*, which many of my contemporaries in Peterborough are discussing. Leddy, once a Sister of Sion, born in Saskatchewan, for many years taught Canadian theology at Regis College in Toronto. I once took a course with her, and we were invited to a spaghetti supper at her place on Jane Street. She founded Romero House for refugees in 1991. I'll never forget what she said as we looked out on an old garage in a nearby back lane. "One of my refugees looked at that and marvelled, a house for a car!"

Leddy, a loving but critical patriot, writes that Canada has been both a victim of colonialism (British, then American) and a perpetrator of it (Indigenous people). We now could become slaves to mad consumerism. She urges us to make our ambition to create a good, not a great, country.

So I hail the progress made in socio-cultural affairs in the past four years, and I reject the right wing's desire to go backwards.

I am also a fan of John Pavlovitz, a progressive Christian blogger from Syracuse, who has a way with words. He said recently, "There are far more people working for justice, equality and diversity than opposing them. Don't let hopelessness trend in your mind."

With these big ideas brimming, I look at what the federal government has achieved in four years.

- A carbon tax. That's an important way to go in reducing carbon emissions. Ignore the gas pump stickers asserting otherwise.
- A huge effort, with increasing success, to reconcile with Indigenous people.
- The beginning of a national pharmacare program.
- The lifting of 850,000 children out of poverty.
- The establishment of a cabinet-level ministry, "Women and Gender Equality," with the appointment of our own MP to head it up.
- The creation of more jobs than at any time in 40 years.
- A national housing strategy with money for Peterborough, including Habitat for Humanity.
- The resettlement of thousands of refugees across the country, ordinary Canadians doing the welcome.

A very likable prime minister, a genuine family man, with inclusionary and progressive views, who has made some mistakes, but is rated by 40 scholars at having achieved 50 percent of his promises and partially achieved another 40 percent. Any school teacher will tell you that's an excellent grade.

The 360 Clinic Offers an Equal Opportunity to be Healthy in Peterborough
September 18, 2019

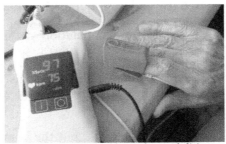

The 360 Clinic offers health care for people living on
the margins. RICHARD LAUTENS/TORONTO STAR

I am walking in downtown Peterborough, this late summer day, actually on my way to a doctor's appointment in the Turnbull Building to get test results. On Simcoe Street, just at the north end of Peterborough Square, I pass by the doorway to the city's nurse-practitioner-led 360 Clinic. I've always been curious about what goes on there. I go in.

Spacious and welcoming, with two smiling receptionists and a lot of positive posters, it is the practical face of a visionary concept: that every Canadian, no matter what status, should have "equity in health care."

The elderly, the poor, homeless people, the undernourished, people who use substances, the confused, the doubtful. Everyone. People who have just taken down their tents in Victory Park.

I am keenly conscious of my privilege: White, older, with a secure if small place to go home to. I am free of well-known addictions, with a basic income in retirement, socially connected, without visible disabilities, and registered at a family practice of physicians.

The 360 is a progressive, community place, a "low-barrier" centre, where people can come off the street, usually see a nurse the same or the next day; receive help from a social worker in navigating the systems requiring the forms that enable them to get the benefits to which they are entitled; and find "few-questions-asked" acceptance.

A team of two nurses, four nurse practitioners, two social workers and a dietitian collaborate in a non-judgmental atmosphere, with the purpose of creating what widely-respected Clinical Director, Kathy Hardill calls, "health equity."

We as a society aspire still to achieve it.

The Clinic, which sees about 250 people a week, some on repeated visits, keeps some statistics: 77 percent of the patients do not reach the "Low Income Cutoff" (LICO) for income. This standard varies a little from province to province and community to community, but it is roughly $41,500 annually for a family of four, and $27,000 for a single person. We have 13 percent of our population at this level. That is 5 million Canadians. Eight percent of 360's patients identify as Indigenous, 12 percent as LGBT2. Many clinic patients have greatly increased levels of anxiety, depression, heart disease and serious mental illness. 13 percent are homeless and 45 percent are food insecure.

The poor are sicker, says Kathy Hardill, but the homeless poor are in double jeopardy. What we are seeing is scarcity: the result of cutbacks in social income support programs going back to the Mike Harris era.

The 360 Clinic offers showers and laundry facilities. When I ask what the public could donate, I am told, "Toiletries, especially for men: soap, toothbrushes, shaving supplies."

The chair of the nine-member, community-based board which runs the clinic is Beth Day. Sitting on the board is Dr. Rosana Pellizzari, Peterborough's medical officer of health, who knows keenly the effects of the "social determinants of health." The 360 Clinic opened in 2011, after the city of Sudbury showed the way in bringing together trained and available nurse-practitioners in the community and the large number of people not registered at any family practice. On opening day in Sudbury, there were lines around the block.

Hardill grew up in Bridgenorth and earned her BScN at the University of Toronto. She earned a Masters in Public Health at York University. She has extensive experience with vulnerable populations, and a cheery manner. At the same time, she advocates politically for better support systems.

It is challenging work. "Our patients are vulnerable, often stigmatized," says Hardill. "They have multiple needs: food security, mental health services, harm reduction support for drug and alcohol use, and affordable housing." Funded entirely by the provincial Ministry of Health, Hardill tells me MPP Dave Smith has visited The 360 twice. But it has experienced a cutback in funding recently.

Canadians take a lot of pride in our health system: this clinic attempts to make it complete.

Women in Politics Share Their Stories in New Book by Peterborough Author
September 25, 2019

Over the past three years, I've often caught sight of Betsy Mcgregor of Lakefield, who was federal Liberal candidate in 2008 and 2011 in Peterborough, hard at work in one corner of the Planet Bakery in the Trent Athletic Centre.

She started at 7 a.m. and, during the day, toiled amid books, papers, her phone and computer, taking breaks for food and for fitness upstairs. It was a huge labour of love to interview and record the insights of 95 Canadian women who had ever run for office, at all levels of government, successful or not. There was the job of finding pictures, getting permission and enlisting a publisher.

She did it all.

The result is a handsome 243-page volume, attractive to look at and to pick up, called *Women on the Ballot: Pathways to Political Power* (Plum Leaf Press). In brilliant colour, and in their own voices, 95 women tell remarkably frank stories. They are from all provinces and territories, and all political parties They describe their motivations, their experiences, their hard work, their disappointments and defeats, and their resilience.

Their stories span a 50-year period in Canada, from 1968 (Hazel McCallion) to 2018. It should be in every high school across the country, in every public library, university and college; in women's studies courses, political science, civics and history. It is a lively and relevant reference book to be promoted among girls and women considering politics, and the general reader, too.

Recent public research shows that women have not reached a critical mass in public positions and remain disadvantaged in Canada. In the House of Commons, women are at 26 percent. The present government makes heroic efforts to right the balance with its gender-equal cabinet, but other levels have not stepped up, nor have public attitudes changed fast enough. In many cases today, women candidates are sacrificial lambs, given unwinnable ridings and less money for campaigns than male candidates.

The book has collected page after page of appealing and diverse faces: Canadian women who have run in elections. It is a rich sampling of powerful, personal stories. The process of entering politics is demystified. The women speak frankly about the toll on family life, the financial and career sacrifices, and the fatigue. In these times, online harassment and even threats need to be heeded and dealt with.

I hail Betsy McGregor's work, her assiduous research and numerous cold calls to politician's homes and offices, her vast knowledge of personalities in Canada, and her vigour in bringing the book to completion.

Full disclosure here: In 2010, I ran for a city council seat in Northcrest and was defeated by two men. So I appear in a minor way in this volume. But it is not just tactics and tools. There is practical advice for girls and women contemplating the next step. Many women look at a certain policy - for example, cutbacks to health, education or social services - and say, "That's it, I'm running."

McGregor gives advice on getting training and attending non-partisan training schools, either in person or online, such as the ones offered by "Equal Voice."

Twelve local women are featured in *Women on the Ballot*, including Maryam Monsef, Linda Slavin, Diane Therrien, Sylvia Sutherland, Barb Jinkerson, Kemi Akapo, Mary Smith and Kim Zippel. There are 37 MPs, four Indigenous leaders and six mayors.

"Women run for purpose, not power," McGregor says. "They need to slay the dragon of doubt. There is no job description for politics."

McGregor maintains that in a campaign, 90 percent is actually out of the local candidate's control. It has to do with the brand, the leader and the policies being promoted. "Only 10 percent is you."

I waited too long, in my 70's, to run for office. This book will assure that hundreds of other women start early. And finish strong.

Maryam Monsef has been Good for Peterborough and Good For Canada
October 2, 2019

Peterborough-Kawartha Liberal incumbent Maryam Monsef speaks during a Trudeau campaign stop at the Evinrude Centre September 26. CLIFFORD SKARSTEDT/EXAMINER

The Maryam Monsef story to date is a spectacular one, one of great opportunity offered in Canada, of formidable ability and of a person's deep morality and prodigious work ethic. Altogether, her achievements, done in a short time on a national and indeed international stage, all while accompanied by sharp scrutiny and criticism at all points, place Peterborough and women squarely at the centre of political life and influence in our country.

Globally, Monsef and Canada are hailed for brave leadership, backed up by real money. I have seen it with my own eyes, at the United Nations in New York, and at the Women Deliver Conference last June in Vancouver.

About 15 years ago, my spouse, John, said, "I want to learn more about Islam. I'm going to the Eid dinner at Trent."

"I'm too tired," I answered. "You go."

He came home glowing. "I met a fantastic young woman, a Trent student," he told me, "selling red scarves for women in Afghanistan. So I bought 10."

Into our lives came the remarkably talented and genuinely good young Maryam. She was highly intelligent, a very quick study, and ambitious. She arranged to meet mentors, often older women, in downtown cafés as she weighed her political options, choosing to run for mayor and then to seek the Liberal nomination in 2015, though other parties courted her.

For me, a longtime advocate for women's advancement, this was a dream come true. It seems it was for Liberal Leader Justin Trudeau too, because after she won this riding, he put her, a young woman without five minutes experience in the House of Commons, in charge of the new cabinet post of Democratic Institutions.

Around a cabinet table of 30 people was a young woman from Peterborough, a strong voice. At that time, I went to town hall meetings of the issue of proportional representation. I could see that Canadian voters were about evenly divided on the wisdom of tinkering with the electoral system. As I expected, the new prime minister took the issue off the table for the moment. It wasn't a winning one. Many Canadians still need to be persuaded on this one.

Monsef's stature grew as she became minister for women and gender equality and minister for international development. She is a reasonable, civil and gracious politician, showing leadership. I went to community gatherings she organized, one for ministers of religions, one for young women leaders, another for rural women, and yet another for people involved in international development; always consulting, just as she had started out. She brought high-level public servants and decision-makers to the city, keeping both a local and a global view.

There has been money to invest locally, nationally and internationally. That must be the joy of it. This empowers such pro-woman projects as "Homeward Bound," the YWCA, Trent University, Habitat for Humanity, anti-violence campaigns, and now, anti-trafficking programs.

So we come to Election 2019. I am stupefied that any Peterborough woman or her partner, who looks the world over, would fail to vote for this MP. But then, some women voted for Donald Trump over Hillary Clinton in 2016.

I am suspicious of the Conservative party, on sexual and social issues. I am appalled at its lack of a climate plan. I am uneasy about the patriarchal attitudes left in many of their candidates. I'm unhappy that Premiers Doug Ford and Jason Kenney and Leader Andrew Scheer are in a kind of right-wing alliance.

Most of all, I admire Monsef's strength of character, deep local attachments, and vision of a better world where all are equal. If power and influence are to be placed in anyone's hands, it is good they are here. She has been heard to say, "Canada needs more Peterborough."

Let's rise to that. It's an easy vote for me.

Discovering the Wit and Warmth
of the People of Scotland
October 16, 2019

Edinburgh Castle is one of Scotland's most familiar landmarks.
TORONTO STAR

On my very first day, ever, in Scotland, I happened upon a noisy football rally (a "footie"), in George Square in Glasgow. The rivalry between the Rangers and the Celtics puts any Habs-Leafs competition in the shade. In fact, some bars warn you not to wear team colours inside.

I was there for a religious retreat on the mystic island of Iona in the western Hebrides. More on that next week. Also to honour my mother, who was a Hogg, and to learn something of the tumultuous history of the 5 million people living in Scotland now. The Scots are survivors of a harsh climate, years of clan rivalry, a mighty struggle with the English over 700 years, and much out-migration (from which Canada as benefited). And now North Sea oil.

When I travel, I jot down wry and interesting public signs. Here is one, "Disabled Toilet." Another, "Weak Bridge Ahead." Would you chance it? Finally, in a warm and friendly pub, I saw, "When I read about the perils of drinking, I gave up reading." Scots I found funny, friendly, resolute and hearty.

"Ladies, you can stand all day at that bus stop and not catch anything. Number 14 stop is two blocks up," said one lad. On the bus, one can actually tap the fare (one pound, 70). Tap, with your credit card, on a bus!

I walked long distances uphill in Glasgow, past Strathclyde University, to the famous Glasgow Cathedral, (dedicated 1136), blackened and majestic against the sky. Readers know that certain scenes from the vastly popular TV series "The Outlander" are filmed here. The fictional Claire lay in state in the underground chapel of Glasgow Cathedral.

Why are the Scots so well educated? One story has it that the fiery anti-Catholic reformer John Knox in 1560 thundered that all Scotsmen should learn to read so that they could themselves interpret Scripture and not depend on Roman Catholic clerics.

Whatever the reason, Scottish literacy and public education was 200 years ahead of their English counterpart. Scotland produced such thinkers in the enlightenment age as philosopher David Hume, economist Adam Smith, engineer John Watt, poet Robert Burns, writers Robert Lewis Stevenson and Sir Walter Scott.

Nowadays it is J.K. Rowling, from a hotel in Edinburgh.

My philosophy of travel is this: prepare eagerly and conscientiously, endure the trip itself with all its joys and uncertainties, fatigue and confusion, and then enjoy at leisure, the reflections afterwards. For me, on the confusion side, there was the humiliating experience of stalling a stick-shift car on a busy roundabout while seeking exit 4.

I interviewed longtime friends Gill and Sandy Sandeman (Sandy is a grad of St. Andrews University). I borrowed books and maps. *Scottish History for Dummies* from the public library was a help, though I've forgotten the names and dates of many battles.

I was analyzed by Ancestry.ca, ignoring the skepticism of my sons. I was told I was 78 percent Celtic. No breakdown of Irish/Scots was offered. I am also 10 percent Norwegian.

"That'll never get you a Nordic passport," one wag told me.

Since I knew my Irish side pretty well, I needed to discover my Scottish roots. I must confess I have become pretty proud of both. I know what "toasties" are, and "cullen skink" and "neeps." I find that Glenfarglas whisky is one I can't afford on either side of the Atlantic. I took an hour's cruise on Loch Lomond, a lovely lake more than 30 kilometres long, and hiked part of the West Highland Way.

Edinburgh, the capital, has a hop-on, hop-off bus with 14 sites of interest. Or just keep going around and round. I was keen to see the 1999 Parliament with its 131 members, in a thoroughly modern building designed by a Spaniard, a building much like a concert hall. Cheeky newspapers call Prime Minister Nicola Sturgeon "Nic," and they call Queen Elizabeth "Maj."

People of this wit and this warmth will never be erased, Brexit or no Brexit.

A Week at St. Columba's Abbey on Iona
October 23, 2019

St. Columba's Abbey on Iona

Tiny Island off the Coast of Scotland is
the Perfect Pilgrimage Destination

My life of travel, in these later years and even before that, seems to show a strong pattern of quest. Of pilgrimages: a search for meaning, for new knowledge and insight, and for religious reflection.

I know I am not unique in this often-restless search for greater meaning. It's in the human condition.

In high school, I had opportunities for occasional weekends of silence and meditation, through a church-based group called Youth Corps. Then at the University of Toronto at the Catholic college, there were routinely scheduled, though not mandatory, days of talks and prayer.

This was in the 1950s, and the sessions consisted of the presentation of ideas and inspiration; talks largely given by a priest, not even by a nun; lit candles in the chapel, and readings from Christian scripture.

Then as newlyweds, with the struggles of new relationships, and with a grievous, early bereavement, my husband and I were strengthened by Marriage Encounter weekends, offered by the churches.

I am still always alert to centres of contemplation.

I have spent time at Oka in Quebec, on the Camino in Spain, at Loyola House in Guelph, the Desert House of Prayer near Tucson, Arizona, and at Villa St. Joseph in Cobourg.

Even great art galleries can be sites of meditation, such as the Hermitage in St. Petersburg. As can walks, paddles and sleeping out in creation.

Then a year ago I heard that a much-admired friend, Rev. Bob Root of Peterborough's Mark Street United Church, had led pilgrimages to the remote island of Iona, off Scotland's west coast. Considered for many centuries a sacred isle, a "thin place" between the human and the sacred, Iona had been settled in 563 by St. Columba, a monk who came by small boat from Ireland with 12 followers. He farmed and built an abbey, wrote and missionized.

For a thousand years, the Abbey at Iona sheltered a community of monks, and in 1200, a community of nuns. It is considered the founding place of Christianity in the United Kingdom, and it is Celtic in nature, not Roman. An American group called "Pilgrim Quests" made all the arrangements. As the newsletter expresses it, "Iona is the ideal setting for exploring a new religious paradigm: one that is inclusive, intellectually and scientifically honest, and soul-satisfying."

"If the call is heeded," wrote famous thinker Joseph Campbell, "it is a dangerous adventure, moving out of the familiar, crossing the threshold to places where dualistic rules don't apply." (*Hero with a Thousand Faces*)

Geographically, it was an adventure to get to Iona. Fly to Glasgow, drive three hours north and west through the lightly-populated, and hauntingly beautiful Scottish countryside to the oceanside town of Oban.

Then take a ferry to the large island of Mull, and a two-hour bus trip on a one-lane road across Mull, through the most astonishing landscape of crags, glens and sheep, to the village of Fionnasport, from whence another 10-minute ferry ride lands you on Iona. Only three miles in length, with a population of 150, the island lives on farming and fishing and visitors, many just for the day, to the abbey.

The abbey is now re-roofed, and managed by a vowed, ecumenical, Christian community of 300, only a few of whom actually live there. Led by the Abbey people, Iona has a small school with seven students. On Climate Action Day in September, the children held a rally, and made the front page of the Guardian newspaper.

For a week in a small hotel, I heard the bells tolling for services at 9 a.m., 2 p.m. and 9 p.m. I felt like a monk. I hiked up steep hillsides to holy wells and to beaches with labyrinths.

The Celts had a monastic tradition of "peregrinatio," the spiritual practice of holy wandering. Their ways may just be the key to a renewal of the religion of Christianity for our day.

Peterborough Artist Kathryn Durst Brings Paul McCartney's "Hey Grandude" to Life
October 30, 2019

Kathryn Durst illustrated the new children's book by Paul McCartney. "Hey Grandude!" is a hit.

Nine months after submitting four sketches to her agent in the U.K. in regard to a new children's book being prepared, artist Kathryn Durst of Peterborough and Toronto received exciting news.

Paul McCartney, the Sir Paul McCartney, one of the creative geniuses of the Beatles, now in his 77th year, had composed a story for kids, and after looking at her work, had invited Kathryn to illustrate it.

He has eight grandchildren whom he refers to as "chillers," and they call him "Grandude."

His book was to be called "Hey Grandude!"

It's a fantasy about four children, bored at home on a rainy day, who are saved by their grandfather, who presents postcards illustrating faraway adventures. The cards, along with a compass, have the magical power to whisk the kids away to these places and immerse them in dangerous happenings.

In the South Seas, fun on the beach is interrupted by swarms of attacking crabs. In the Wild West, cowboys and cacti provide delight until a herd of rampaging buffalo disturbs the peace. After escaping the stampede, the chillers and their grandude make it to the Swiss Alps, where singing and strumming amid the wildflowers charm them until a roaring avalanche comes surging down the mountain.

Safe and sleepy, the foursome and their guardian welcome home again. To dream.

McCartney's book has made it to the top of the bestseller list for children's books in the New York Times. And Kathryn Durst hopes its success and her part in it will allow her to continue her work illustrating children's books and to make her home in Peterborough. She has four nieces and nephews nearby to whom she dedicates her work.

Durst grew up here and went to St Peter's, where she says she was encouraged by teachers Mary Claire Nepotiuk and Greg Burke. Then she went on to Sheridan College in Oakville for its animation course.

Her dream has always been to illustrate children's books. The Dursts were always an artistic family. Grandmother Durst, Kathryn's paternal grandmother, entered the Ontario College of Art and Design at age 50.

Daughter of Dan Durst, a well-loved teacher at St. Peter's and Holy Cross, who himself taught photography and technical subjects, and of Loretta Durst, who works at Trent in student aid, Kathryn tells me over coffee at Dreams of Beans that her decision to engage a British agent was a good one. The largest children's book conference in the world is actually in Bologna, Italy, she says. "That is a fantastic gathering."

I have known Dan and Loretta Durst from their longtime volunteer work with the local charity Friends of Honduran Children. Kathryn spent time with them in Honduras.

She was amused when Paul McCartney asked her to make the Grandude somewhat slimmer in her designs, and to make him "a little eccentric." Hence, grandude has a receding hairline and a white ponytail.

A large and colourful book, "Hey, Grandude!" shines with energy and a sense of fun. Kathryn, who plays accordion, manages to slip one into a scene. The kids' clothes are typically and often mismatched. Wildflowers bloom profusely in Switzerland. Kathryn consulted friends who had travelled there and researched pictures to get it right.

She can't estimate how many hours of work are represented here, but McCartney invited her to London recently to take part with him in the book launch and to sign autographs along with him. She is doing some talks and encouraging Sheridan students particularly.

Another Peterborough young person succeeds.

A Post-Mortem on the Election Results in Peterborough and Across Canada
November 6, 2019

Conservative candidate Michael Skinner poses with NDP candidate Candace Shaw at The Venue in Peterborough, October 21, 2019, after he had a close race with incumbent Maryam Monsef who won the election. JESSICA NYZNIK/EXAMINER

Priority Now is to Heal the Divisions Between Regions

With relief, I saw right-wing ideology turned back in my country on October 21. I saw almost 65 percent of my compatriots turn down all aspects of Trumpism, and vote for faster climate action and for an inclusive, fairer country. I saw that, apart from a few nasty comments, such as Andrew Scheer calling Justin Trudeau names during the national TV debate, it was generally civil in tone. It was still not substantial enough in discussion of issues.

The campaign certainly was civil in Peterborough, though some letters to the newspaper displayed deep animosity. I saw people, feminists, bringing flowers to the offices of both Candace Shaw and Maryam Monsef. I saw citizens of opposing parties reinserting campaign signs that had fallen over for their neighbours.

My two brothers made a joke of taking their opposing front lawn signs and moving them to the backyard on each other, overnight.

Peterborough thinker Ben Wolfe posted a graceful post-election message. He thanked those who voted strategically for winner Monsef in order that Conservatives not be elected, and then he thanked those who voted with their hearts, for the NDP and the Greens.

We may have dodged a bullet.

Voters should know now that Scheer's team of advisers included Hamish Marshall, who co-founded the right-wing media site The Rebel. Georganne Burke, from Scheer's team, worked on American elections and continued to support Donald Trump online. There are other small benefits from post-election time: hearing less from the Eeyore in our midst Andrew Coyne, who sees disaster behind every rainbow, and less from self-described anarchist who refuses to vote at all Rosie Di Manno, in the Toronto Star.

I rejoice that these people were re-elected: Joyce Murray, Elizabeth May, Hedy Fry, Bardish Chagger, Karina Gould, Patti Hajdu, Catherine McKenna (a heroine against hate), Chrystia Freeland, Carolyn Bennett, Marc Garneau, Ahmad Hussen, Adam Vaughan and delightful surprise (since his father and stepmother live in Peterborough) Adam van Koeverden, in Milton. I will miss the ever-reasonable Ralph Goodale, and Randy Boissonnault, the Rhodes scholar from Edmonton who became the prime minister's point man on LGBTQ issues. Randy has encyclopedic knowledge of the status of LGBTQ people around the world. I am sorry that Pierre Poilievre, the attack man on the front benches of the Conservatives in the House, is back.

On women's rights, I learned that fully half of the Conservative candidates were endorsed by the hardline, anti-choice group "Campaign Life." The House now has 98 women members, up from 88 in 2015. That's 29 percent. Not exactly glowing. Six hundred women ran in the election, says Eleanor Fast, of Equal Voice. Let's watch 25-year-old Mumilaaq Qaqqaq, who was elected in Nunavut. Here is an interesting note: if we had had proportional representation, Mr. Bernier's People's Party of Canada would have six members in the House today. For the future, Canadians will have to learn and practise both new and old ways of co-operating and compromising. Put the women in charge, perhaps.

My friends in Alberta feel completely misunderstood. They believe they subsidize Quebec especially, with their contribution to the national budget through equalization payments, and yet Quebec, for environmental reasons among others, won't develop its own natural resources. They ask how soon the ROC (Rest of Canada) and the ROW (Rest of the World) will get off oil. They tire of eastern "holier-than-thou" pronouncements about the tarsands when the people making them depend on oil. With all this reconciliation work to be done among ourselves and our regions, Canada must also stand tall as a liberal democracy in the world.

No more talk please, of cuts to foreign aid or shutting down our borders. Or of separation as a threat made by self-serving politicians. The potential for progress in the future with a Liberal minority dependent on support from the smaller parties is enticing.

The More We Read, the Stronger We Are
November 13, 2019

Peterborough is a community of book lovers and avid readers. HANNAH YOON/TORSTAR

Canadians read. They read, buy, borrow and talk books. Maybe on Kindle or Kobo, but just as likely in hardcover.

Every person not strap-hanging on the TTC is reading. In Peterborough, Knotanew and Mark Jokinen's, Hunter Street Books and that funky By the Books on Water, which specializes in used social-justice works, plus Happenstance and Lakefield Station Bookshop, all make us a bookish region. That's not even including Chapters, or online shopping.

Although I miss the card catalogues at Trent's Bata Library, all that opened space serves more readers. At Peterborough Public Library, the one with the fine new art installation outside depicting a book cover blowing in the wind, I had an hour's free tutorial with a librarian, Laura, striving to make me more computer literate (starting with the deletion of multiple Facebook accounts).

As a nation, we avidly follow five new titles on radio every March, on "Canada Reads." Then we read all five to make up our own minds.

We've just concluded a national election. Sixty-five percent of us voted for political parties with progressive values. I put that prevailing view, which to my delight is a deeply anti-Trumpism one, down to the influence of reading. People who read, learn, revise their opinions, consider, ponder and are made more sympathetic.

Count the number of book clubs around here. Mine, originated by me, is a solo effort. I am doing the choices and my apartment is doing the hosting. It has 10 participants and is just two sessions in length. No use wearing ourselves out, though I once knew a woman who read a book a night.

Recently we discussed with enthusiasm Melinda Gates' personal memoir, *The Moment of Lift*. Next month, it will be the cheery, reassuring *Factfulness* by the well-known TED Talks man, Hans Rosling of Sweden.

Gates took her title from her father's work on the space program in Texas, but she broadens it to include her own journey to feminism and her profound social conscience, which has led her to make huge, repeated donations to partner groups in the global south, those working in women's and children's health.

Two weeks ago, looking at the perils in her own country, she announced one billion dollars over 10 years for American women in leadership. I had the pleasure of meeting her a couple of times on a committee in 2018, when I served on the Gender Equality Advisory Council to the G7. She is a warm, intelligent and listening person with great insight. I found myself saying in a friendly manner over wine one night, "Melinda, I don't agree with any system that makes one so rich so fast, but if anyone has $400 million to give to the world's neediest women, I would trust you to do it."

She readily agreed. She said that when she began this philanthropic work 20 years ago, Hans Rosling himself said to her, "The last thing we need is billionaires in here messing up." Gradually, the two became comrades with a common vision.

Melinda Gates is also conscious that private philanthropy, which actually makes up only about two percent of world development aid, will never make all the changes needed. Still, private money can be a catalyst for state responsibility.

She has obviously sat listening to women on a grass mat in India and Burkina Faso and other places for many hours. The Gates Foundation in Seattle employs 1,500 people, many Canadians, and both she and her husband Bill write their own newsletters.

Our book club includes a physician who works in global health and spent 12 years in Thailand, and a woman who basically does not believe in foreign aid as it is delivered today. We hold those tensions, and then enjoy spanakopita, brought by a former librarian and peacebuilder.

Gates is an honest writer, who reveals a great deal about her family, the challenges of her marriage, her relationship with her church and her idealism.

(Don't miss the new Netflix documentary, "Inside Bill's Brain.")

Your World is Getting Better, Even if it's Hard to Tell
November 20, 2019

Dr. Hans Rosling, known for his animated lectures, uses rolls of toilet paper to illustrate world population growth for a standing-room-only audience. CATHIE COWARD/TORSTAR

These are dreary times. Not just because it's November and we tighten our shoulders against cold winds, but because the global news is worrisome. Almost everywhere, climate disasters and suffering, human greed and stupidity. People generally are unhappy.

I chuckled when I saw the T-shirt of my hairdresser last week, "I am Happy, and it Drives Everyone Crazy!"

I remind myself that people in other historic times endured great grief and loss. The study of human history is always instructive. So is an investigation into antidotes to glumness, such as political activism and spirituality. Mindfulness, gratitude, a sense of the sacred, can be increased and deepened. It is crucial today.

Twenty-five years ago, a great German Jesuit priest named Karl Rahner wrote, "In the world to come, we will be mystics, or we will not be." Also of help is a bracing dose of Dr. Hans Rosling, of Sweden, who served 20 years as a physician in rural Mozambique and then committed his energetic self to enlightening the world with facts.

His thesis is that the world is getting better but no one will admit it. Rosling draws his facts from United Nations statistics. That body is assiduous about collecting facts, and a good thing, too.

His son, Ola and his daughter-in law, Anna, help him get the message out. They are technically hip, and have designed a "Bubble" technique to go with his TED Talks, preserved now on YouTube and well worth a look. Rosling is dedicated to "helping people carry only opinions for which there are strong supporting facts." He says, "I fight against devastating ignorance."

Misconceptions abound, he finds. Playfully, he asks every reader to take a 13-question quiz about the state of the world. For example, what percentage of the world's girls finish elementary school: 20 percent, 40 percent or 60 percent? The answer is 60 percent, but fewer than three in 10 people get it right.

Rosling is a fan of the ability to keep two facts in one's head at a time. Things can be bad, but still getting better. He takes as his reference point the year 1800, and he uses as a framework "Four Levels" at which the world's population lives.

At Level 1, people live on less than $2 a day (extreme poverty) and total one billion people. At Level 2, three billion people live on $8 a day. At Level 3, two billion live on $32 a day, and at Level 4, one billion live at $64 and up.

"People such as you and me must struggle hard to grasp the reality of the six billion people with much less than us," Rosling says. In 1800, 85 percent of people lived at Level 1. Now it is 12 percent.

"We can now drop the term 'developed' and 'developing' and use the Four Levels with more accuracy." We skew our views toward negativity because "there is more surveillance of suffering," than ever before, and there is "selective reporting."

Also, we have 10 habits of mind that need to be challenged. These, Rosling calls "instincts." The gap, negativity, straight-line thinking, fear, a misunderstanding of size, generalizations, blame, urgency, a single perspective and destiny. To illustrate generalizing, he reminds us there are 54 countries in Africa, one billion people, and great differences.

Rosling's 2018 book, completed just before his death from the cancer he had lived with for 40 years, entitled *Factfulness*, is our book group's second study. One of our members brought a refutation of Rosling's "optimism" (though he calls himself a "possibilist") with an essay from www resilience.org. It argues that he does not pay sufficient heed to climate change. It is going to be a case of holding two different ideas in one's head, I think.

KWIC is Connecting for Change in Peterborough and Around the World
November 27, 2019

Students participate in a workshop entitled *Stories of Water in Nogojiwanong* during the "Local Global Youth Day" conference presented by Kawartha World Issues Centre (KWIC) on March 23, 2018 at The Mount Community Centre in Peterborough, Ontario. CLIFFORD SKARSTEDT/EXAMINER

Dynamic Youth-led Resources Make a Difference in our Community

The Kawartha World Issues Centre is the amazing little group that has fostered many progressive projects over 30 years in our city: GreenUP, Teaching Outside the Box, Kawartha Food Share, ReFrame Film Festival and TRACKS for Indigenous youth. These are organizations that shape our values.

I have lived in Peterborough for 50 years, and for 30 of those years I have had a small hand in, and watched with admiration of, the development of a group started by the community and then enlarged to include the university. It is today a highly influential, dynamic, youth-led resource which shapes what we stand for as a city and whom we elect to office.

And with one and a half staff.

The Kawartha World Issues Centre grew, as healthy movements do, organically. In the early 1980's, a few people interested in international affairs and in Canada's role around the world, who were operating as volunteers in such groups as Oxfam and the International Development Education Program at Fleming, merged their small budgets and their person-power. Some names are still active 30 years on: Alan and Linda Slavin, Don Quarrie and Stephanie Benn, for example. "It was a caring, connected, joyful social-justice community," says Debra Morales, who wrote a 44-page history of KWIC in 2004.

The name for the organization was suggested by Alan Slavin, and it had a nice ring, "KWIC." The group moved from Fleming College to 106 Murray St. in 1998, making it more accessible to downtown. The late Jim Anderson and teacher Don Quarrie guaranteed the mortgage for the space. In that period, the Canadian government was supporting global education centres across the country. In spite of their achievements helping Canadians learn accurately about the world and take action to better it, the federal government withdrew support. Peterborough's is the last Ontario one operating.

From its current home on the Trent campus in the Science Complex building, KWIC operates as a nonprofit, run by an active board of directors. It benefits from the passion and knowledge of its longtime executive director, Julie Cosgrove, and commitment from many sectors. Offering resources of all kinds, hosted by enthusiastic students, KWIC is a hub for students and community members. It organizes city-wide events, such as the International Women's Day gathering, and brings in impressive guest speakers, such as those who came to the workshop last March on the United Nations Sustainable Development Goals for 2030. It networks with high schools, community groups, service clubs and graduate students. On its newsletter list are 500 Peterborough people.

If our city has a provincewide reputation for progressive politics, has a globally educated population and is known as a welcoming place for newcomers, KWIC can take a lot of the credit. Newcomers who want to get involved in leading-edge local activities might want to consult KWIC's newsletter. Its budget is currently around $200,000. Three-quarters of this amount comes from grants and donations. The other quarter comes, to their eternal credit, from the 8,000 Trent students who give at the time of tuition payment about $3 per semester.

To everyone's consternation, the provincial government's "Student Choice" initiative (a Doug Ford plan) enabled students to opt out of these fees. In a time of cuts to student loans and grants, there is increased pressure on students to find savings anywhere they can. (Stop the press: this policy was just denied by an Ontario court.)

KWIC's creative energy was demonstrated again in October with a two-day session led by popular educator and unconventional academic Bayo Akolomafe, a Nigerian living in India who is globally renowned for his fresh take on the global crisis, civic action and change. Bayo was suggested to KWIC by volunteer Faith Mwesigye. His workshop at the Mount drew 90 students, teachers, members of Indigenous communities and NGO leaders in a remarkable encounter across generations, locations and ways of life. It was another KWIC success: courage and ingenuity in service of community and change.

Stephen Lewis Inspires During Peterborough Talk at Trent University
December 4, 2019

I wish I had had a chance to go to the Stephen Lewis School of Oratory. At age 82, the Toronto-based diplomat, humanitarian and political leader kept a large audience at Trent spellbound on November 18 as he launched the week of international education.

The recipient of the Order of Canada and 33 honorary degrees from universities in Canada and the U.S, he tells with great good humour of the fact that though he attended four institutions of higher education in the '60s, he completed none. Lewis gives the status of "college dropout" a new distinction.

He rued his lack of success in electoral politics as leader of the Ontario NDP, and then paid tribute to two Peterburians: Founding Trent president T.H.B. Symons, and the late former MPP and Kenner teacher Walter Pitman.

I can never think of Stephen Lewis without thinking of the influence which his wife of 48 years, journalist Michele Landsberg, a giant of the early women's movement in Canada, had on the social history of the country. She wrote a not-to-be-missed column for the Toronto Star for many years. I think too of his prolific daughter-in law, Naomi Klein, whose writing on climate and inequality is honoured around the world.

But not to diminish the power of the man himself. He is possibly the best public speaker Canada has ever enjoyed, and one with encyclopedic global knowledge. Combine this with a finely honed sense of morality and a deep compassion for human suffering, and one has a truly great world citizen.

Lewis has many deep interests. The AIDS epidemic, mostly in Africa, has consumed him for a long time. The virus still spreads, especially among young women. He repeatedly calls for education and services in reproductive health. He has a fiercely feminist vision and has for a long time. I remember many years ago at a discussion at McGill University in Montreal, he refused to sit on a panel because it was all male.

Lewis briefly discussed the impeachment focus, nay obsession, in the U.S. (calling President Donald Trump a "nitwit completely without knowledge") and trade with China, "distractions." Rising resentful populism in Europe and threats to democratic institutions are more critical. Chile, Lebanon and Yemen "seethe with ceaseless hostility," which is followed by street demonstrations, police repression and then the rise to power of autocrats. "It takes education to understand it all," Lewis asserted.

I could see Cam Douglas, the visionary secondary school teacher with Kawartha Pine Ridge School Board, itching to recall his class at five o'clock.

Lewis called the extent and degree of continuing sexual violence "an annihilation of the soul." He spoke of the Rohingya in Myanmar, of the situation in Zambia, of kidnapping in northern Nigeria, and widespread rape in India. He could have also mentioned the stubbornly unmoving statistics in Canada on rape and assault. The MeToo movement has drawn thousands of signatories. I am one of them. It was of a minor nature when I was 12, but I remember my confusion and I wanted to add my name to the lists. "What you can do," he said is, "simply teach little boys to respect little girls." Lewis himself has two daughters and four grandsons.

Global sex education, so greatly needed, is compromised by the "crazed concentration on abortion." The U.S. has instituted the "global gag rule," no funds for maternal and child health centres which even refer for abortion. Fundamentalists from all the religions lobby for this damaging policy. It is one reason I am active in the NGO Catholics for Choice.

Finally, he spoke of 70 countries around the world which still criminalize LGBTQ relations. That led to cringing for me: Jamaica, my second home, is one. Classrooms in an educated society should be "fearlessly discussing all these issues."

I cannot even include Lewis's remarks on climate, the 11 years we have left for massive changes. That he enlightens, amuses and moves people at the same time is a remarkable feat which Peterborough witnessed last month.

Nuclear Threat Against Humanity
Never Went Away
December 12, 2019

An allied correspondent stands in a sea of rubble
before the shell of a building that once was a movie
theater in Hiroshima September. 8, 1945. On
August 6, 1945, an atomic bomb instantly destroyed
almost all of the houses and buildings in Hiroshima.
The bombing of Hiroshima and Nagasaki brought
about Japan's unconditional surrender. STANLEY
TROUTMAN/ASSOCIATED PRESS

This week's column is on a topic I've never touched on before, and one
our culture hardly mentions, with all the other global concerns. But it is
big. And ominous, too, with reckless strongmen running things. It is
nuclear weapons. The world bristles with them. In the 1980s, we were
scared to death about an incoming Soviet bomb or missile. Then to
everyone's relief, we got an international treaty, limiting their creation,
acquisition and use. The Soviet empire collapsed. Now, U.S President
Donald Trump withdraws from treaties. Who is noticing? We are not
safer, for sure. The nuclear "club" includes China, the U.S., the U.K.,
France and Russia. The accumulation is 4,000 warheads, enough to
demolish the planet many times.

But small groups of conscientious objectors have always existed. In
recent weeks I've seen word of an American resistance group, seven
ordinary people, in this case, all Roman Catholics, acting out of their
faith, who take inspiration from war resisters of the 1960s, who
committed acts of "faithful civil disobedience" at the time of the
Vietnam War. Today, In St. Mary's, Georgia, in Kings Bay, there is a
berth for six Trident submarines. The "Kings Bay Plowshares Seven," as
they are called - in April 2018, while singing and praying, cut a hole in
the security fence there, pounded a Tomahawk missile with a hammer,
poured human blood on the seal of the base and left a copy of Daniel
Ellsberg's 2019 book, *The Doomsday Machine.*

Then they awaited arrest. Last October 21, the seven were tried and convicted in Brunswick, Georgia of conspiracy, destruction of government property and trespassing. The judge allowed no defence or witnesses based on faith; no theologian or nuclear war planner, although one defendant, Steve Kelly is a R.C. priest and another, Martha Hennessy, is the daughter of well-known New York peace activist, the late Dorothy Day. A third is Elizabeth McAllister, age 80, who took part in the non-violent actions against weapons in the '60s.

The Kings Bay Plowshares Seven await sentencing in January. Kelly chooses to stay in jail; the others are at home under curfew. The defendants assert that they want to awaken the conscience of the nation and avert "omnicide." Considering the destruction such weapons could unleash, this seems not too strong a word.

Whatever the sentencing next month, it is clear that such dissidents are having an impact on the church as a whole. Pope Francis now calls nuclear weapons "immoral." Up to recent times, the Catholic Church allowed for the creation and keeping of such weapons permissible for deterrence. Now, the Church is moving to outright condemnation.

The Pope was just in the Japanese cities of Hiroshima and Nagasaki, where 150,000 people and 75,000 people respectively were killed by the atomic blasts of 1945. He turned his attention from environmental degradation and inequality to nuclear peril.

For me, it has a dark sense of deja vu. In the '60s, John and I and other Montreal-area people played host to Fr. Daniel Berrigan, the American poet-scholar who was protesting the Vietnam War. At Cornell University, he was counselling students not to report to the draft, and he decided he must also take some risk. With a few other peace activists, he and his brother, Philip entered a draft office in King of Prussia, Pennsylvania, gave flowers to the shocked staff, and poured human blood over draft files.

"Better the burning of paper than the burning of children," he said. Then he went on the lam and we had the strange, almost comic sight of FBI agents, almost all Irish Catholic, hunting up a priest.

Dan Berrigan served three years in prison, and died at age 94 in New York in 2016.

There are signs, says Paul Elie in The New Yorker magazine, that the Church is coming around to the position that such activists have resolutely maintained for decades.

That is grounds for hope.

From Trent to Degrassi and Back Again for New Chancellor
December 18, 2019

Stephen Stohn and Linda Schuyler on the Degrassi set in Toronto in 2013. Stohn is the new chancellor of Trent University. KEITH BEATY/TORSTAR

I belong to the Trent Athletic Centre, it being the closest fitness place to my home. I get to see posters of upcoming events and free lectures at the university. This place of learning has many renewed links to the community, I find. And now, there is a brilliant appointment to deepen the community-university relationship. I recently met the new chancellor, appointed in June for a three-year term.

I chatted with Stephen Stohn of Toronto, a Trent grad of 1969, and his spouse, the decorated television producer, Linda Schuyler, over coffee at Gzowski College. I came to see their profound interest in our region, in Trent, in students and in liberal values.

Each is very accomplished. Stohn, an entertainment lawyer, and former producer of the Juno Awards, is a Canadian cultural powerhouse. He was inducted into the Canadian Music Hall of Fame in 2011. Over more than 20 years, the company he ran with Linda produced many hundreds of episodes of critically-acclaimed television for teens including the iconic Degrassi series. About growing up in Toronto, the Degrassi series tackled teen drama unflinchingly: Drugs, sexuality, gender identity, cyberbullying; all the joys and the angst of teenagehood.

The chancellorship all fits. While at Trent studying philosophy and economics, (now there's a good combination for life), Stohn was influenced by founding president T.H.B. Symons, and he helped start the Arthur newspaper and Trent Radio. A lifelong interest in music marks his career and philanthropic work.

With zest, modesty and charm, Stohn plans to enter into university life with at least a weekly visit, turn up at gatherings large and small, share his story, befriend students and professors and enhance life in Peterborough generally.

"Trent has always emphasized interactive learning," he says. "It rates very highly in every survey of student satisfaction, and takes a critical approach to thinking in all disciplines. These habits of mind are the very ones needed in our time. The unique guiding principles of Trent have been foundational in my life."

Schuyler wears her Order of Canada pin, earned for her creative work with Degrassi. She taught for eight years in a Toronto junior high school, observing the diversity there and the teenage lives. "I am a storyteller" she says, "and first of all, an educator." I recall many 50-year-old friends telling me they had most of their sex education from watching Degrassi.

"There was no human issue we would not explore," Schuyler says. "We were determined to tell the truth about young lives, and to keep our actors at the same age as the characters. No 24-year-olds playing 16. All our stories had three components: a dilemma for a young person, a choice to be made, and then some presentation of the consequences of every choice. We were sending the message 'You are not alone.'"

The series has been seen all over the world, in 140 countries. It is the longest running Canadian half-hour drama series ever. Rapper, actor and now ultimate Raptors fan, Drake (Aubrey Graham), got his start on Degrassi.

In 2007, Stohn and Schuyler worked with the international development organization Free the Children to take the Degrassi cast to Kenya, where they lived and worked among the Masai and helped to build a school. "That was an occasion for team-building," says Stohn. "They came back better actors, too."

The couple has been fuelled by a sense of social injustice. An episode about two transgender youth won a Peabody award in 2010. Other stories have included the character Marco "coming out" as gay in 2003.

"What a fantastically long way social attitudes have come," they say.

Recently Schuyler joined a panel to speak to Trent teacher candidates. Collaborative, modest and witty, she will no doubt make a large contribution to the arts and to education there. They will be more than one-plus-one in impact, but together model what determination, idealism and talent can achieve for society.

Peterborough Charity Helps Promote Change in Jamaica
December 26, 2019

For 45 years Rosemary Ganley has been involved in development programs in Jamaica. Progress has been slow, but it has occurred and been a worthy journey. MATHEW MCCARTHY/FILE PHOTO

Almost 45 years to the day of my first fateful arrival, I came to Jamaica again last month. It was "fateful," in that life and relationships there shaped my next five decades. What a ride it has been for me, my family, Peterborough and points beyond. In 1975, I was a raw recruit in the world of international development, and in fact that term itself had only been in our lexicon since 1966, when Canadian labour leader Romeo Maione suggested we Canadians might want to help overseas causes and people.

That is still true. On a recent morning I was at Kenner Collegiate, a very special, warm and outward-looking high school, where students Eliana Schartner and Emma Poley led a two-hour Amnesty letter-writing session where 200 students and teachers wrote appeals for nine prisoners of conscience around the world, who are under 25 years of age, and for one Canadian cause, that of Grassy Narrows Reserve in northern Ontario where people wait for clean water.

Back in 1975, I was being led by my adventurous husband to take three little kids to the teeming and turbulent city of Kingston, Jamaica where he would teach accounting to young adults at the community college. I had never even had a black friend.

But, "say yes" has been a kind of guiding motif in my life (though not, of course, in compromising situations my mother would not approve of.) In this case, my puzzled parents held their tongues as we took their grandchildren far away.

Jamaica was and is a kind of geographical paradise; sun and light, mountain and the sea, fruits and fish, talent and energy, and an open spirituality one sees in Africa and other islands of the Caribbean. It had a free press, a university, two daily newspapers and no leader as vulgar and repulsive as the current occupant of the White House. But also, it had widespread poverty, large urban slums and a troubling level of violence, mostly gang violence, but other crime too. There was a vigorous socialist government under Prime Minister Michael Manley, a man trying to tackle the deep social ills caused by classism and a long history of colonialism.

We didn't know much, but we needed to learn, fast. Back in Canada our sponsor, the Canadian International Development Organization, provided a first-class orientation course at Carleton University. We were advised that, for all our good intentions, we were in fact making an "intervention" in another culture and that could have mixed results.

The aid organization Jamaican Self-Help started here in Peterborough in 1980. (A shameless pitch here: the story is told in my 2016 book *Jamaica Journal: the Story of a Grassroots Canadian Aid Organization*.)

That's almost 40 years. Today JSH thrives because it is real, small and relevant. Its budget is, astonishingly, $60,000 a year. No expenses. No staff. Three Kingston projects, in education and skill training. Those harsh streets are now protected by armed ZOSOP members, "Zones of Special Operation." I spoke with one mother who feels at ease sending her daughter to school now.

With me were four members of JSH's planning committee under the leadership of Joyce Mackenzie, highly skilled people who deal compassionately with Jamaican leaders, guiding them in simple budgets and reporting. Also along is Annie Ross, Joyce's 18 year-old granddaughter on a kind of awareness trip.

I devour the newspaper, The Gleaner (75 cents a copy, seven days a week). The International Monetary Fund itself is praising Jamaica for dramatically reducing its debt. The Chinese, it must be admitted, are getting involved in the Caribbean. They make gifts of money for infrastructure and roads, and loans at four percent.

The Minister for Gender Affairs, Olivia "Babsy" Grange, announces the opening of Jamaica's first-ever shelter for abused women. Thirty women take part in a workshop on sexual and reproductive rights. And 50 young men participate at the university in the first-ever "Walk a Mile in Her Shoes." All encouraging.

Twenty-five Years After Beijing, Women's Struggles Continue
February 13, 2020

Benedita Da Silva (Brazil), Vuyiswa Bongile Keyi (Canada) and Silvia Salley (USA) cheer at the conclusion of the "Women of Color" press briefing during the Fourth UN World Conference on Women in Beijing 09/13/1995. Racism issues have not been addressed strongly enough in the Platform for Action. GREG BAKER/ASSOCIATED PRESS

I'm back. Thanks, Examiner editor, for the leave of absence. I went to Jamaica on what I planned as a farewell visit, these being the years of farewells before the final one, and I came in to contact with a dengue-bearing mosquito. One in 20 mosquitoes is carrying the virus these days, says Kingston, Jamaica Public Health. My luck to run in to this minority population, or he to me.

Jamaicans, among my favourite people, are nonetheless obstreperous and fiercely skeptical, so when health authorities came in to spray neighbourhoods, ("fogging" to use the correct term), they were chased out with brooms, since they might be introducing even more poisonous materials.

However it happened, dengue, which I had had when living there 40 years ago, is called locally and accurately, "break bone" fever. The joke going around is that the doctor says, "The good news is that you have dengue fever and you aren't going to die, the bad news is that you have dengue fever and you aren't going to die."

This setback means that we are already two months into 2020 by the time I reflect on this important year for women.

It is the 25th anniversary year of the great United Nations conference on women held in Beijing, China and in a nearby village of Huairou.

That conference drew 1,000 official delegates from 183 countries who met over 10 days and drafted and approved a final statement, which has never been bettered. It described women's status under 12 headings and called for action, state by state. It was called the Platform for Action, 153 pages in length, available from UN Publications online for a fee. But I have a treasured hard copy. Call me a Luddite, but I prefer hard copy to any other means of reading. For absorption, that is.

The 12 areas of focus are women and poverty, education and training, women and health, violence against women, women in armed conflict, women and the economy, women in power and decision-making, institutional mechanisms for the advancement of women, women's human rights, women and the media, women and the environment, and the girl child.

Just think for a minute of any one of these headings and the realities of our culture. You could spend a lifetime working to improve women's well-being under any one topic. Violence - figures stay the same, stubbornly, (MeToo has shown it); poverty - wage gaps remain, the vast majority of the poor are women and their dependent children; inequality in income - grows and leads to social instability, resentment politics and gated communities; the media - Fox News contaminates the airwaves with misogyny; and the girl child – the trafficking of girls continues.

So 2020 is a year to remember, reassess and see what must be done, only faster. I looked up the report on Canada done by a think tank I respect, the Canadian Centre for Policy Alternatives. It is called "Unfinished Business" and is a careful, well-documented analysis of the progress made in our country since Beijing. And there has been lots, especially at the federal level, with the leadership we have. Then, the serious gaps. Indigenous women, Inuit women, the sexual exploitation of athletes, the marginalization of newcomers, Islamophobia, the policy platforms of neo-conservatives seeking to roll back reproductive rights.

No shortage of work to do. Here in Peterborough, on International Women's Day, March 8, there will be various events. I choose the one organized by KWIC and KSAC, which includes a downtown Women's Walk, and art projects that afternoon at Seeds of Change.

I, the old white feminist, will co-host with Faith Msegiye, the young black feminist student. Intergenerational.

I am putting together a booklet of 20 of my columns, mostly published in the Examiner, from Beijing in 1995, and a few from the review of Beijing the UN sponsored in 2000. Sister, carry on. Male allies, welcome.

Revolutionary Hip-Hop Musical "Hamilton" is Particularly Relevant in 2020

February 27, 2020

Lin-Manuel Miranda and the cast of "Hamilton" perform at the Tony Awards in New York in 2016. The acclaimed musical is now playing in Toronto. EVAN AGOSTINI/ASSOCIATED PRESS

In December last, two of my three sons, who were heavily involved in professional and personal responsibilities in Alberta and B.C., forgot me and Christmas. I mean "forgot" in the sense that there was nothing in the mailbox delivered by an actual postal person.

So, I expressed myself. In families, it's generally best to be honest. They lamented and made amends, big time. Knowing my Christmas principle, "Give experiences, not things," they arranged for a big envelope to come to my address. It contained a prize ticket to the hit musical "Hamilton," now playing in Toronto.

I was thrilled. But I needed to prepare.

In my past studies, the American Revolution, that conflict after 1776, in which the 13 colonies in America rose up against the British who ruled them,(the Redcoats), declared they were independent and fought battles and skirmishes over a period of eight years in order to "win" the war, to send the British packing and begin to create a country.

Many names from that dramatic time come to me in a jumble: Washington, Jefferson, Adams, Madison, Burr. Well now, I get to sort them out via that most pleasant of learning techniques, the song.

It's an astonishing story, really.

In 2015, off-Broadway audiences in New York were stunned by a highly literate hip-hop musical, every word sung. It seems a composer and lyricist named Lin Manuel Miranda, a newcomer to New York from Puerto Rico, inspired by a long biography of one of the framers of the new nation, Alexander Hamilton, wrote, produced and starred in "Hamilton."

What a way to learn your history. It turned out to be a two-hour rap event, delivered by talented and diverse actor-singers, tracing the life of Alexander Hamilton, a fourteen-year-old orphan who arrived in New York having been born illegitimately on the Caribbean island of St. Croix to a white mother and a Scotsman. Brilliant in mind, with an assertive personality and a power with words, he rose quickly to become an officer in the revolutionary army, a war hero, and then a favourite aide to new American president George Washington. Along the way he made many enemies. Political debate raged, largely through the use of newspaper articles. Hamilton's output was prodigious. He often wrote under pen names chosen from Roman times.

He would be assailed by men such as Thomas Jefferson and James Madison, earning lifelong adversaries. The thinkers were passionate about the shape of the new country. The division of powers: should it be more to the national state or to the individual states? It was the beginning of the two-party political situation we have today. He wrote most of the 76 essays on American government called the "Federalist Papers." He created the banking system, the tax and customs policies. What his enemies charged was that he wanted to restore a monarchy in America like Britain's, whereas he argued for strong executive powers in order to prevent chaos.

Maybe that's why "Hamilton," the musical, is so popular and so relevant these days, nine months from a U.S. election. Alexander Hamilton married, had children and also dallied. I won't divulge his sad ending at age 47 in 1804. Something to do with duels, a matter of honour at the time.

I listen to the CD of "Hamilton" in order to catch some of the rapid-fire delivery beforehand. I watch the YouTube of Lin Manuel Miranda sing at one of those White House culture nights the Obamas sponsored. Michelle Obama said later it was the best offering they had presented there. At one New York performance at which VP Mike Pence was present, the cast stopped and called out Pence for his Trumpian administration. Hip hop, or rap, is a form of popular music developed by inner city African-Americans. It is rhymed speech that is chanted. I know something of block parties and reggae from Jamaica, so I should be OK. Sons are now forgiven.

Hard Lessons from the Jean Vanier Revelations
March 5, 2020

Jean Vanier speaks in London March 11, 2015. An internal report reveals that L'Arche founder Jean Vanier, a respected Canadian religious figure, sexually abused at least six women. LEFTERIS PITARAKIS/ASSOCIATED PRESS

The depressing news about L'Arche founder Jean Vanier's abuse of six women who were associated with L'Arche over a 25-year period, and who came to him for spiritual counsel, has some salutary lessons for us.

The first that strikes me is that no one should be put on a pedestal of holiness by others. Such an attitude reveals an unhealthy attachment, which is encouraged by all kinds of modern celebrity, but is essentially a dependence, an immaturity on the part of the devout, the penitent, and the vulnerable.

Religious figures, especially, may appropriate to themselves a kind of virtuousness that impresses some but which we should find suspect, because it tempts the counsellor to exploit.

Therefore, no hero worship in any community of believers, no matter the community.

Vanier, the fourth of five children of former Gov-Gen Georges Vanier and his wife, Pauline Archer Vanier, of Quebec, founded the L'Arche movement outside Paris 50 years ago.

L'Arche, now in 38 countries, brings together the intellectually disabled with the able-bodied in mutual friendship and living arrangements. Vanier died last May at age 90.

Over the years, he wrote spiritual books, gave retreats, delivered the Massey Lectures, was honoured with the Order of Canada and had many schools named after him. He seemed above reproach.

Only after his death did L'Arche initiate an investigation carried out by a reputable English firm, GCPS Consulting, which works with organizations globally to ensure the safety of children and vulnerable people. It issued a 48-page report in early February.

It revealed that Mr Vanier had been influenced by a disgraced Dominican priest named Fr. Thomas Philippe for many years, and had taken advantage of women in sexually abusive relations. In the words of the report, "coercive and non-consensual." Jean Vanier claimed to be an instrument of God, and said that the women should submit in order to be healed. He referred to scripture, at times to the Song of Songs.

Then he lied about having anything to do with Fr. Philippe, yet defended him publicly in 2009. It is the abuse, the lies and the hypocrisy that has shaken Canadians.

As life has had it, I knew Pauline Vanier while living in the Montreal area in the 1960's. She was in retirement, a Catholic widow of genuine piety and goodness, with a chapel in her house. She let it be known that she would welcome small groups of faith and justice activists for occasional prayer and discussions at her home. We eagerly accepted, along with a few of our friends from Dorval. Pauline Vanier was tall, gracious and humble. I remember I have the same shoe size, very long, and I often wore her slippers for the evening.

In her last years, she decided to move to the French village where Jean was, in order to counsel and encourage, not so much L'Arche members, but the young searchers who came from all over the world looking for meaning in their lives.

It is the L'Arche organization that has come now to be admired. They have ordered the report, made it public, and are carefully informing the members of the community. Tina Bovermann of L'Arche-USA says, "We stand on the side of the women who have been harmed."

In an insightful piece in the newspaper National Catholic Reporter, columnist Jamie Manson says, "The radically patriarchal leadership structure and theology of the church are at the root of sexual abuse cases in the church. There is a special class of spiritual men entitled to use women and children."

Writer Robert Mickens of La Croix International says flatly, "Sex abuse is not about sex."

Forty years after the first stirring among Catholics and others in regard to the widespread and pernicious nature of this behaviour, this might be a turning point.

Choosing a Dream Cabinet for the U.S. Government

March 12, 2020

The West Wing of the White House on the evening of January 7, 2020, in Washington. ALEX BRANDON/ASSOCIATED PRESS

Not every Canadian is as political a nerd as I am, but I'd guess that almost every Canadian has been following with fascination and trepidation the long, drawn-out American political drama leading up to the presidential election in November. Everyone has opinions about who can beat Trump. There are even a few among us, one of my relatives for example, who favour Trump's return to office, though this is scarcely comprehensible to me. My friends and contacts are in deep worry, even despair, at the overall mess south of us. It's not easy to be ruled by a despotic, unintelligent, manipulative man who hurts others and tears at the fabric of society daily.

So it's not too strong a word to say I rejoiced while reading the February 26 column of one Thomas Friedman, an award-winning columnist with The New York Times. He must be on holiday in Florida, because he published these thoughts in the Palm Beach Post. I'd say the Post editors got a scoop that day.

I'm going to quote widely from his thinking because it is so forward-looking, fresh and hopeful. The last thing we need is defeatism. Friedman advises the Democratic Party to put together a slate, a national-unity group of people, and offer it to the American voters before the vote. That way, everybody can claim some representation.

He is no slouch as a thinker: age 66, born in Minnesota, educated at Oxford, able to speak Hebrew and Arabic, writer of seven books, and a serious man with a sense of humour. For example, one of his books is called *The World is Flat* and another, *Thank You for Being Late*.

Ideologically, he describes himself as a "radical centrist." He is plain-spoken - "Mr. Trump is an undiagnosed sociopath."

We all know America couldn't have achieved all it has: More than 200 years of democracy, a superior post-secondary education system, though often private; innovation and entrepreneurship, a military force which engaged in two world wars, and a rich artistic and literary tradition, without talent, intellectual capacity and, often good leadership.

But in recent years America has fallen back. Since the election of 2016, there is deep national malaise, and the politics of insult, stupidity, shame. So Thomas Friedman calls for a national unity platform, and he names for positions. If Mr Sanders wins the presidency, these are the recommendations for cabinet posts.

At last, some creative thinking for readers to chew on. For vice-president he recommends, for her decency and moderation, Amy Klobuchar. For commerce, Mitt Romney, a Republican; for health and human services, Elizabeth Warren; for housing, Cory Booker; for treasury, Mike Bloomberg, because "he wants to address income inequality;" for attorney general, Kamala Harris, "to restore integrity" to the battered Justice Department); for energy, Andrew Yang, and for foreign affairs, Joe Biden, because he knows everybody and has the personality to build bridges so recklessly burned by Mr. Trump. Finally, Pete Buttigieg for Homeland Security, and Adm. William McRaven for defence. And, delicious thought, Alexandria Ocasio-Cortez, called (AOC), as U.S. ambassador to the U.N.

Now there's a new image of America for the world.

I remember being impressed when our prime minister issued a mandate letter to each of his chosen cabinet members, and made these letters public so we could refer to them and hold these leaders accountable.

But I've never heard of a proposal such as Friedman's, to tell the electorate in advance that you plan to invite the following people to assume these posts if you are elected. It will make for far better-informed voters for one thing.

Since I have been watching these folks debate and persuade for weeks now, I get to imagine them being in the posts which Friedman recommends. His last piece of advice to Democrats is to bring together moderate and progressive wings in their party. There will be no victory without that.

Bystander Intervention:
Looking Away is no Longer an Option
March 21, 2020

Two-time elected member of Parliament for Oakville North-Burlington, Pam Damoff. NIKKI WESLEY/ TORSTAR

We can't go very long or very far today without witnessing, though we may be reluctant to see it, an incident of bullying, harassment or just plain nastiness against a stranger.

These situations tend to defeat me: I am a slow reactor. The Enneagram (a personality test) tells me I am a number 3, acting from the heart, whereas courageous, quick-acting people are ones and eights, acting from the gut! Whatever the analysis, I have been seeking to extend my competencies, and just needed a push.

That came when I read about the assertive and helpful action of a woman in Ottawa recently. At midnight, at an LRT stop, with few people around, she intervened. So I called her.

It was December in snowy, downtown Ottawa, after a Christmas party on the Hill. The two-time elected member of Parliament for Oakville North-Burlington, Pam Damoff, was taking public transport home, when she saw "a man coming on to a young woman, asking inappropriate questions, and I just felt something wasn't right."

"I am tall and I am older and I would probably have said something like, 'Get lost, mister.' But this was a twenty-year-old and she looked uneasy. I walked up, put myself between them and gave my attention to the young woman, chatting about her backpack. The man moved off. Then the girl, Abby, asked me to ride with her on the LRT to her stop, which I happily did. I thought nothing more of it, until Abby posted the story and even came to my office on the Hill to say thanks again."

I call that intergenerational solidarity. The feminist kind.

It was the reaction of a strong, fit woman, a champion for cycling in her riding, who, after a career of 25 years working on Bay Street, ran for office and former co-chair of the House of Commons Committee on the Status of Women, along with being parliamentary secretary to Hon. Marc Miller, Minister of Indigenous Services.

I see it as extraordinarily brave and pro-social.

I was inspired to learn more, so I registered for a free, two-hour workshop in mid-March on "sexual harassment in the workplace, and bystander intervention" offered by the Kawartha Sexual Assault Centre and the Community Legal Clinic. It's a kind of stand-with-the-victim course, providing skills for the bystander to use to protect the person who is under threat without escalating the situation for many reasons one of which is that the perpetrator may be unstable, on drugs or drunk. But looking away becomes no longer an option.

You see compassionate kids doing this for their beleaguered peers all the time. My granddaughter, 10, is a champion at it. She recently won her school's monthly citation for "justice."

With hundreds of refugees and newcomers in Peterborough and with street people of all kinds, we all need to be ready to practise the virtue of solidarity at the drop of a hat.

In 2018, a national report showed that one in three Canadian women and one in eight men were subjected to unwanted sexual behaviour in a public place or the workplace.

Responding to these dreary numbers about Canadian society, the federal government has been providing funds for education at the local level to counter them. Here in Peterborough, the Kawartha Sexual Assault Centre and the Peterborough Community Legal Clinic have been offering powerful workshops: free, two-hour sessions to any group that asks. Dreams of Beans cafe stayed open late on March 11 so that a small group of us citizens could take the training.

I learned a lot. About the prevalence. About the forms of harassment. About techniques that can be used by the observer to confront it.

Each agency brought a helpful perspective. Over one-third of Canadians have been sexually or physically assaulted since age 15. So much awareness is needed.

And the instincts of Pam Damoff are to be hailed.

This Federal Government is Competent
March 26, 2020

Blockaded rail lines in sympathy with the We'tsuwet'en reserve in northern B.C. were just one of the big challenges Canadians have already faced this year. LARS HAGBERG /CANADIAN PRESS

This article might well be called a "counter-column."

Much heavy criticism has been directed at federal leadership in recent days, some of it from legitimate sources, but then again, much more in nasty, hateful, anonymous posts on social media (is that what are called "trolls?"). Avoid them.

Here, then, is one voice in approval of the federal management of our crises. It may be drowned out. But it represents the feelings of many in the silent majority.

We Canadians have been rocked by three unrelated shocks since the new year. There was the dreadful shooting down of Ukrainian Airlines Flight 752 on January 8 by the Iranian military, with the deaths of 176 people, 57 Canadians.

Our government reacted swiftly and compassionately. Prime Minister Justin Trudeau visited the bereaved, and sympathetic arrangements were made for families, including the immediate grant of $25,000 for urgent expenses. Foreign Minister Francois-Philippe Champagne, who is experienced and energetic, invited the countries with citizens involved to a meeting in Europe at which they demanded an honest Iranian investigation and restitution for victims' families. Iran responded partly, taking responsibility for "human error."

Canada absorbed the tragedy, angered, yet whole.

Crisis 2 followed quickly upon it. From February 5 through to March, 2020, Indigenous groups blockaded rail lines in sympathy with the Wet'suwet'en reserve in northern British Columbia, who were objecting to the natural gas pipeline proposed by CoastalGasLink to run through their lands on its way to the sea, from the Dawson Creek area to Kitimat, some 650 kilometres. Across the country, other Indigenous groups and their allies rose up in solidarity with the Wet'suwet'en. The method used was the blockades of rail lines. National travel of people and goods was for a time stopped. Some strident voices called for vigorous police intervention. The courts had granted injunctions against the blockades. The RCMP stood at the ready. But the prime minister and his advisers, especially Chrystia Freeland, Bill Blair, Marc Miller and Carolyn Bennett, all of whom are profoundly committed to the long and arduous process of reconciliation, made it clear there was to be no force, no bloodshed, no removals. It was the practice of heroic patience, and patience is a virtue much admired and practiced by Indigenous people. "It is never appropriate to send in the army against Canadian citizens," said the Prime Minister.

"Protect our future; no more pipelines," said Native leader, Roxanne Whitebear. Quebec Premier Francois Legault weighed in, "Solutions must be found so it never happens again." Canadians were learning a lot about Indigenous reality. Late perhaps, but vividly. There are hereditary chiefs and there are elected chiefs in these communities. Who has the legitimate authority? Along the route, elected band councils had signed a benefit agreement with the development company. Hereditary chiefs insisted they also be at the table. Meetings, statements, tentative agreements poured forth. Via Rail reported that 1071 trains had been cancelled, affecting 165,000 passengers. The financial losses are yet to be completely calculated. But on March 12, Parliamentary Budget Officer Yves Giroux said the disruptions had shaved two-tenths of a percent off economic growth in the first quarter. Patience and good faith continued. The Mohawks near Montreal moved their encampment to a green space near the Mercier Bridge. The Tyendinaga protesters near Belleville dispersed. The New Brunswick blockade was ended.

Settler Canadians had learned a lot. Thirty-seven percent of us showed some support for Indigenous grievances. Then has come COVID-19. Led by the prime minister, who has been personally affected, and by Heath Minister Patty Hajdu, the Canadian response has been calm, intelligent, science-informed and effective. Tests cost $1,100 in the U.S. Here they are incorporated into medicare. I was struck by a lyric by American jazz musician and poet Mose Allison, a white artist from Mississippi, who wrote in the '80s: "And will there be heroes and saints, or just a dark new age of complaint?" Salute our government and its talented cabinet.

Let's Try to Avoid a Nervous Breakdown in Peterborough
April 2, 2020

A reporter applies hand sanitizer as Medical Officer of Health Dr. Rosana Salvaterra speaks to reporters on March 27, 2020 in Peterborough, Ontario. CLIFFORD SKARSTEDT/ EXAMINER

We sure are being challenged these days, even in little old Peterborough. The relentless, sad news, rising illness and economic distress, self-isolation, and the radical change of daily habits are, all together, causing us profound dislocation and anxiety. We can get depressed. These three realities are intensified many times over by the ghastly denial behaviour of the leader of the great country along our border.

Let's start with No. 1: Data about the sick. One of the mixed blessings of our age is quick data, and at this writing there are 900,000 cases of COVID-19 worldwide, 171 countries are affected, with more than 4,000 deaths. In Canada, we have 5,000 cases and 63 deaths. There are over 100,000 cases in the States, which is now the epicenter of the disease, and chastened by dire predictions.

No 2: Job loss, closings, and layoffs have become a huge worry among individuals and families, causing widespread anxiety about paying bills.

No. 3: Being alone with too much negative thinking, too much access to media voices, too little comfort from friends and family, too much restriction on physical movement. But, look to the other side, always.

There are thousands of antidotes for these stressors, right at hand. Listen to CBC for your information, but only twice a day. Give up CNN for Lent, and Fox News forever. Listen to classical CMFX out of Cobourg for blissful escape.

Walk outside at an appropriate distance. See the greetings which our new Maritime-style friendliness is bringing out, and the compliance with regulations practised almost everywhere. Bikes, kids, teens, old couples all are respecting the necessary spacing. There is some spring sunshine. The PM, our newfound elder, is chastising and encouraging us from his front lawn every morning. His finest hour.

Somehow, supportive legislation, such as the Canadian Emergency Response Bill (CERB), gets passed in Ottawa. We are all socialists now, with new regard for big government. Our powerful, unprepared neighbour, the U.S., reels and fights, suffers and competes for life-saving equipment. The projected number of deaths is apocalyptic. An idea comes forward from the president: Station U.S. troops at the border. I'll tell you which way the traffic will be. Not south.

The lieutenant-governor of Texas calls on seniors to sacrifice our lives for the economy. Not so fast, mister. I don't know how Daniel Dale, who went from the Toronto Star to CNN with his uncanny knack of spotting lies, can stand another day doing what he does.

We are Canadian, more than ever. Psychological resistance, combined with great sympathy, will lead us. Actor Ryan Reynolds posts a wry statement asking us to socially distance and challenges other celebrities They step up: Shania Twain, Justin Bieber, Shawn Mendes, Jann Arden Connor McDavid, Michael Buble and so on.

Kids in my neighbour chalk-draw flowers on my walk. Sam, of downtown Peterborough's favourite sandwich shop, posts a tearful message thanking her customers. My birthday becomes a ZOOM dinner. I am sated by watching nightly operas from the Met in New York, offered free at 7.30 p.m., with buxom sopranos and tenors on stage to glorious music. A blessed new regard for all the arts is surfacing.

In Nova Scotia, Premier Stephen McNeill, touched by photos of family members visiting their loved ones in long-term homes by shouting through windows, orders that 800 tablets be issued to seniors' homes.

Megan Murphy, great communicator, inspires Peterburians to leave groceries on their front steps, and volunteers pick up two tons of food for Kawartha Food Share.

Wise words come from American author Dave Hollis. "In the rush to return to normal, maybe use the time to consider which parts of normal are worth returning to."

That's our communal task now.

Women Shine as Medical Officers During COVID-19 Crisis
April 9, 2020

Medical Officer of Health Dr. Rosana Salvaterra of Peterborough Public Health has been providing daily COVID-19 updates in Peterborough. CLIFFORD SKARSTEDT/ EXAMINER

There's another tale yet to be told in this pandemic that we are suffering through. Of 14 provincial and federal medical officers of health across Canada, seven are women.

They are now becoming well-recognized, widely consulted and trusted. Their calm presence and clear presentation of information are having a big impact, especially on young women and little girls, who are noticing.

The medical officers are talking at daily media briefings with poise, sound data, and, in some cases undisguised feelings of compassion. The political leaders are wisely giving pride of place to the officers.

In the case of the prime minister, already showing strong leadership, he is happy to give the lead to Dr. Theresa Tam, the Hong Kong-born, British-trained chief medical officer for Canada who is, according to one Canadian writer, "steely and authentic."

Another woman making a strong impression is Minister of Health Patty Hajdu, who was once a shelter worker in Thunder Bay.

Contrasts are impossible to ignore, and we see with distress the bombast and weird musings of the president of the U.S., whose team doesn't even attempt to show the social distance he advocates, and whose spokespersons, except for Dr. Fauci, do not inspire confidence.

In Toronto, medical officer of health Dr. Eileen de Villa is one of these leading women. Though ordinarily dead serious about our situation, De Villa also is having a bit of online fun with Raptor basketball player Serge Ibaka, about their stylish scarves. A bit of levity is welcome these days too. In Newfoundland and Labrador, it is Dr. Janice Fitzgerald, and in B.C., Dr. Bonnie Henry, who wept with compassion as she announced deaths in long-term care homes. My daughter-in-law on Vancouver Island tells me there are wrist bands going around with "WWBHD" on them. That stands for "What Would Bonnie Henry Do?"

In Alberta, Dr. Deena Hinshaw adopts a "Dr. Spock-like tone" says one journalist, and she has worn a dress patterned with chemistry's periodic table. Many of us considered Dr. Benjamin Spock our child care guru in the 1960's. In New Brunswick, Dr. Jennifer Russell leads the fight. Everyone trusts veteran epidemiologist Dr. Alison McGeer, who took us through SARS 18 years ago and speaks authoritatively on radio. In Peterborough Dr. Rosana Salvaterra conducts fact-filled daily briefings. She is in the eye of the local storm day after day. Last week, my neighbours sent her an African violet.

A clothing company in Calgary, Madame Premier Clothing, designs and produces T-shirts honouring the women, the first with the faces of Hinshaw, Henry, De Villa and Tam. They sell 1,200 a day.

Dr. Heather Morrison, medical officer for P.E.I., has a cow named after her. She is flattered, she says, and happy with the attention to her work.

Fifty-five percent of new students into medicine are women, but their proportion is not reflected in leadership roles. There is a gender gap in medicine, with almost no women deans of medical schools or CEO's of hospitals. A welcome exception soon to come is the appointment of Dr. Jane Philpott, former federal health minister as Dean of Health Sciences at Queen's University in September.

Altogether, and accidentally rather than intentionally, this pandemic will be seen to have contributed greatly to the rise of women in Canada All the women provide a unifying and rallying centre

Another benefit coming from the rise of medical officers of health as trusted guides, whatever their gender, for an anxious population is the growing conviction among citizens that public health departments are critical to our well-being. Statistics show that such departments have been reduced, some will say "starved," in recent budgets including Ontario's. So, in these unfortunate circumstances, their strength is being valued in a non-partisan way. It may well rise to the top of issues which will dominate future elections.

COVID-19 Threatens Gains Women Have Made in Peterborough and Around the World
April 16, 2020

Members of two former G7 Gender Councils have made a series of recommendations to address gender inequality during the COVID-19 pandemic. GRAEME FRISQUE/ TORSTAR

G7 Gender Councils Draft Recommendations for Coronavirus Response

In late January 2018, at supper hour, I received an astonishing phone call. Prime Minister Justin Trudeau is a man of great charm. "Rosemary," he said, "I've been reading your CV. We teachers have to stick together!"

Canada was to host the annual meeting of the G7 leaders in June that year in Charlevoix, Quebec. That would be Angela Merkel, Theresa May, Shinzu Abe, Guiseppe Conte, Emmanuel Macron and Donald Trump. The Prime Minister wanted to lift up women's inferior global status to great prominence at the meeting. He was setting up an Advisory Committee of 17 internationally-known women and one man to write a report for the leaders.

How on Earth I came to be on this committee is a mystery, but it turned out to be a memorable experience. When I asked Trudeau why me, he said, "For your voice, your experience and your grassroots connections." Well, I have those, and they serve me well in Peterborough.

Macron was impressed by this gender analysis work, while Trump nearly scuttled it, gender not being his strong suit. I think he despises women, actually, and at our breakfast on June 9, he was late, rude and difficult. However, France continued the format when next it hosted the G7 in 2019.

I hesitate to mention that the 2020 G7 meeting is scheduled for Camp David in June. I'm sure there will be no Gender Council for that one.

Now the world faces the terrifying COVID-19 pandemic, and the two Gender Councils have drafted a strong, short statement directed at the G7 leaders. It is called "Step it Up, G7." Though not yet universal, applying a gender-based analysis (GBA) to every policy, every decision, and every remark, is becoming more common. Canada is leading.

"Desperate times call for determined leadership," wrote the two councils. "The COVID-19 virus is a common challenge to the whole world and reminds us as never before of our interdependence."

"Girls and women experience the health crisis differently," the councils say, and "deep-rooted gender inequality" still exists in all parts of the world. The G7 countries must take "emergency joint action to prevent the deterioration of gender equality and women's rights worldwide."

Women have, as a study of their status since the great conference in Beijing in 1995 shows, made strong steps forward toward equality. There have been hard-won gains, in health, education and longevity. But it is always precarious. Hard-line fundamentalist forces and right-wing politicians are ever ready to stop the progress and drive women backwards. "Women make up 70 percent of health care and social service workers," say the councils. They must be given proper equipment and supplies to do their life-saving work. "They also hold the majority of lower-paid retail and service jobs, which puts them at the forefront of the economic crisis."

It is usually in the area of sexual rights that reversals in rights take place. As the Canadian government has recognized, women and their children, under COVID-19 policies, are asked to "shelter in place." Often that shelter is not a safe one. Fifty million dollars in new funding for sexual assault centers and shelters has been pledged. Calls to the Kawartha Sexual Assault Centre are up by 30 percent. France has just booked 20,000 hotel rooms for just this demographic. School closures make inequalities in education worse for girls. In the contested area of reproductive services, they are at risk of being reduced. Finally, the councils call for equal sharing of household tasks among men and women, and for data to be collected that is differentiated along male/female lines. "The times call for humanistic leadership, free from sexism, racism and economic mercantilism. We must light up these dark times."

It is a helpful word from some of the world's best leaders. Me, I was proud to be among 37 women and two men to sign, as were six other Canadians.

After the Deluge, Peterborough and the Rest of the World will be Very Different
April 23, 2020

Painted stones thank health-care workers for their support outside Peterborough Regional Health Centre during the COVID-19 virus April 2020, Peterborough, Ontario. CLIFFORD SKARSTEDT/EXAMINER

Canadians, for many reasons, have an outward-looking attitude toward the world. Immigration, wide travel, education and a certain humility as citizens of a medium-sized power, prepare us for significant understanding of the world.

Recent research shows that we support the United Nations, especially the World Health Organization, (take that, Donald Trump), and we seek unapologetically to co-operate with other countries. This Canadian view has become even more popular in the COVID-19 crisis. We accept that it is a pandemic jumping borders, and will finally be defeated with a vaccine. Most of us don't demonize China. (I just learned a new word, "Sinophobia," or irrational hatred of China).

Paradoxically, that reasonable, rational and open attitude renders us even more effective at working locally. The global mind and the local application of it is our strength.

Healthwise in Peterborough region, our case number is low. There is grief for the family of our one victim and there will be extra attention to seniors' homes. In the new age: complete redesign of those buildings, some built in the 1950s, and for a long time underfunded, will be paramount.

The extent of volunteering is astounding. I myself have to field at least three calls a day from acquaintances who have listened to the advice to "check in on their seniors."

Meals on Wheels continues, businesses have made a quick pivot and now manufacture personal protection gear; the United Way announces a new fund for COVID-19 relief, the PRHC is prepared for a surge in cases should it come, the media give us hard numbers and also heart-wrenching stories of bravery; Facebook is full of encouraging poems, pictures, bird calls, and recipes.

Worship services, including the Abraham Festival April 18 go online; seniors learn programs to link them with loved ones; and every time I hear the bouncing of a basketball, on either side of my place, my heart soars. Prime Minister Justin Trudeau and I have a date on CBC TV each morning at 11:15 on his lawn.

As for at-home teaching and learning, I have yet to hear one person, young or old say that it is easy for either side. That's for me, "existential courage," shown by teachers and learners. Now as the greatest health crisis in this century passes over us, some voices, are undertaking to imagine a possible new world. Some are worth listening to, though not "the wrath of God, repent of your sins" ones.

It will be about the global survival of planet earth.

Looking back, it would be understandable should such thinkers as Naomi Klein, Katherine Hayhoe, David Suzuki, Andrew Weaver and Elizabeth May (there's five Canadians), plus international visionaries such as Vandana Shiva (India), Wangaari Mathai (Kenya), George Monbiot (U.K.), Greta Thunberg (Sweden) and Bill McKibben or Thomas Berry (USA), not to mention local heroes such as Al Slavin, Carlotta James, Kate Grierson, Cam Douglas, Shirley Williams and Drew Monkman, stand up and say, "We told you so."

But they won't do that. April 22 is the 50th anniversary of Earth Day. It was in 1970 that the world began to listen to voices of concern about pollution, deforestation, overpopulation, earth-warming emissions and plastic in oceans, floods, fires and hurricanes. The earth has been crying out for some years, but humans haven't been listening. Now we are inundated with news of the fates and the suffering of people all over the world.

This re-envisioning, in which we can all play a part, is an exercise in a kind of prophesy, a sharp, fact-based critique of the present and the presentation of an alternative future. The guides are out there. The minds of people are in movement. Damage from this illness are seen and felt everywhere. It is a virus, starting in Asia, jumping to Europe and North America and now, fearfully, to the Southern hemisphere. It doesn't respect wealth or class, education or location. That makes serious motivation to change.

Wise Words From Women ~ Build Back Better
April 30, 2020

A sign posted at Empress Gardens Retirement Residence shows support for health-care workers on April 28, 2020 in Peterborough, Ontario. A new COVID-19 virus outbreak has been declared at the facility. CLIFFORD SKARSTEDT/EXAMINER

As we negotiate this week's emotions and its additional grief and shock over Nova Scotia, our fatigue is deepening, it seems to me.

What I do is relish the words of three women of wisdom: one, a Jewish woman in America, Rebecca Solnit, who habitually counsels hope in the dark; another, a Christian in India whose father was Hindu, and who won the Booker prize for fiction in 1997 with *The God of Small Things*, Arundhati Roy; and the third, an African-American poet named Sonya Renee Taylor.

Finding them has been salve for my soul. The comfort found in reading is called bibliotherapy. I rejoice when I see my grandchildren finding it out.

Rebecca Solnit wrote recently in The Guardian, an English newspaper.

"As we struggle to learn the science and statistics of this terrible scourge, our psyches are doing something equivalent, adjusting to profound social and economic changes, studying the lessons which disasters teach, and equipping ourselves for an unanticipated world."

Ah, this might explain my fatigue. Overload. Unfamiliar territory. Maybe it's worse for those of us accustomed to extensive planning!

As the current witticism says, "Introverts, look in on your extrovert friends. Unlike you, they don't know how to handle this!"

Arundhati Roy, now deeply involved in Indian politics, writes, "Historically, pandemics have forced humans to break with the past and imagine their world anew. This one is no different. It is a portal, a gateway between one world and the next. We can choose to walk through it dragging the carcasses of our prejudice and hatred, our avarice and data banks, our dead ideas and dead rivers and smoky skies. Or we can walk through lightly with little luggage, ready to imagine another world. And ready to fight for it."

In a domestic parallel, a lot of people I know are using the days to clean out drawers and attics and sheds, giving away or discarding things. It's a beneficial practice for minds too, and attachments. And ambitions. Ambitions for larger, faster, more modern, more impressive things.

These thinkers point to a break with the past, and breaks are always disorienting. But the same-old, same-old isn't going to save us either.

I've been involved in international development for 50 years. The world, ever shrinking, is not a fair one. There is massive wealth and massive poverty: over-accumulation and scarcity.

I once asked an expert what standard of living would be required for everyone to live decently. "Pre-war England," he replied. "Apartment living, public transport, daily small shopping." Does that mean no Walmart, Costco, monster homes, three-car garages, annual plane flights to warm places? Maybe so.

My third reference these days is Sonya Renee Taylor. She is blunt. "We will not go back to normal: our pre-corona existence normalized greed, inequity, exhaustion, depletion, extraction, confusion, rage, hoarding and hate. We have been given the opportunity to stitch a new garment that fits all of humanity and nature."

There is really no debate now that, after this health crisis, the earth herself must be regarded and tended with a whole new attitude. The $100 billion which the Canadian government has pledged for relief of citizens who have lost their jobs includes some inklings of a green new deal: money for the decommissioning of thousands of "orphan" oil wells marring the Alberta landscape. Let's hope that our minister for the environment, British Columbian Jonathan Wilkinson, has a pre-eminent place at the Cabinet table.

Just as we women have fought for and largely achieved at the federal level anyway, the application of a gender lens to all legislation, there must be an environmental lens for all expenditures from now on. Breakdown gives us a chance for breakthrough.

It's Time for Sexual Education to Take a Big Step Forward in Peterborough and Across Canada
May 7, 2020

Toronto students walk out of class to protest sex-ed curriculum changes in Toronto September 21, 2018. NATHAN DENETTE/CANADIAN PRESS

Now for a complete change of pace.

It has to do with the health and safety of the young. Who among us doesn't care about that? To be specific, the education we are providing for their sexual health and well-being. Under Canada's division of powers, health and education are provincial matters. But the federal government wields much power and influence.

My sex-ed was almost non-existent in school. It largely consisted of don'ts and warnings. And some biology. But that was a long time ago. Now a new report finds that sexuality education across Canada, though widely accepted as necessary in schools, is inconsistent, partial, dated, and in the case of religious schools, ideologically driven.

The quality depends on the teacher, the principal, the school board and the parents. When I asked teacher friends about their assessment of sex education in their schools, the answer was, "It depends."

It depends also on the availability of local resources such as sexuality educators who can be invited in and who understand youth's evolving modern context, a dominant social media culture for one. Here comes a frank, lively and well-researched study, 82 pages in length, called "The State of Sex-Ed in Canada," and an additional resource for teachers and parents, called "Beyond the Basics," both produced by an Ottawa-based, nonprofit organization called Action Canada for Sexual Health and Rights.

The group is a progressive, pro-choice, charitable organization committed to advancing sexual and reproductive health and rights in Canada and globally. Information for the report was somewhat hard to come by. It was drafted by eight people from French, English and Indigenous resources, guided by a national youth advisory board and endorsed by many experts, including Dr. Danielle Martin of Women's College Hospital in Toronto.

The team consulted curricula from across the county and interviewed scores of young people academics and educators. The term is "Comprehensive Sexuality Education" (CSE). It is usually placed within the framework of health. It calls for cross-Canada delivery of knowledge, skills, attitudes and values to enable the young to develop respect for themselves, their bodies and others. It covers the cognitive, emotional, physical and social aspect of sexuality. Research shows that good sex education has many benefits; healthier, more confident people, with stronger ability to make decisions about their lives; less violence and coercion, and more inclusion of diversity. Strong majorities of parents support good sex education that is positive and age-appropriate, using correct vocabulary, at all levels of schooling.

A branch of the United Nations, UNESCO, headquartered in Geneva, developed a definition in 2018, "Guidance on Sexuality Education." It keeps an eye on us too, and UN Special Procedures criticized Ontario in 2016 for drawing back from a new sex-ed curriculum. A minority of parents were objecting to it. The language of human rights is now used: The young have a human right to accurate sex education. But sexuality education is often politicized. Conservative forces, often from the right-wing in the religions, ignore or think dangerous newer concepts, which arise from an emerging understanding of gender equality. One of these is consent. Another is gender diversity. One parent from New Brunswick told me, "We teach our teenage age sons to respect girls, above all. And wise condom when the time comes. We want them to look on sexuality positively, as joyful." Comprehensive sexuality education addresses sexually-transmitted diseases, which are common in Canada, and male violence against women. It teaches boundaries, self-assertion and self -respect.

Margaret Laurence, the great Canadian writer, said, "Sexual encounters should be tender, mutual and communicative."

Action Canada is an amalgamation of three groups: Action Canada for Population and Development, Canadians for Choice and Planned Parenthood. Its work is to prevent gender-based violence and to see everybody thrive. In 2019, Health Canada endorsed a fine report called "The Canadian Guidelines for Sexual Health Education." Now to get them implemented. This snapshot from Action Canada is a good place to start.

On Comforting a Senior,
and On Reading a Good Book
May 14, 2020

Outgoing Chief Justice of the Supreme Court of Canada Beverley McLachlin smiles at the conclusion of a news conference on her retirement, in Ottawa on Friday, December 15, 2017. JUSTIN TANG/CANADIAN PRESS

I was scrolling Facebook recently and stopped to look at a touching post showing an elderly man in a seniors home who had been sleeping beside a picture of his deceased wife. A caregiver, with great insight, came in to surprise him with a pillow, imprinted with a picture of his late wife. He broke down with joy. It got me thinking about such a small, real consolation that readers might want to consider for their seniors.

So I called Ricart's Trophies in Peterborough. A nice man said, "We don't do things like that, but I can give you the contact information of a woman in Lakefield, Aileen, who does. Her business is 'Pillowstuff.'"

I called Aileen and she said yes, she could do it if I sent a photo of my loved one as an attachment on email, and she'd send me a picture of three fabrics and I could choose. She'd do it up and I could pay by e-transfer and she'd deliver, at a proper distance.

Done and done in a few days. It's 16 inches square and has a zippered removable cover. That's my homey item for this week.

On the reading side, I favour heroic Canadian women of late. Here is one: the memoir of Beverley McLachlin, Chief Justice of the Supreme Court of Canada, 2000 to 2017. Called *Truth be Told: My Journey through Life and the Law*, her book is an appealing piece of plain writing, as benefits a judge who had to write hundreds of important decisions for the court, while keeping in mind ordinary Canadians.

It is also a frank and warm account of growing up in rural Alberta, becoming a serious student, getting a BA and a law degree, and teaching for seven years at UBC. Her personal story is inspirational: Happily married for 21 years and with a teenage son, she suddenly became a widow in 1988. Hers is a modest summary of considerable achievements moving to judgeship. It has a positive patriotism mixed with a sense of international solidarity.

Beverley McLachlin is 76 years old. I remember once about 10 years ago being at the Stratford Festival. One of the attractions was a session, a mock trial, considering the guilt or innocence of Shylock, the wronged Jewish merchant in the play "The Merchant of Venice," who insists on a pound of flesh promised by his adversary, Antonio.

Chief Justice McLachlin, a lover of the arts, had agreed to hear the evidence in a highly entertaining "mock trial," led by gifted actors, and to render a judgment. The large audience delighted in her performance.

Her decision was balanced: a moot judgment on Shylock.

In humble beginnings, McLachlin was born in Pincher Creek, Alberta, a town of just 2000 people, to German immigrant parents, rancher-farmers, whom she describes as "fundamentalist Christians." The eldest of four, she was no promising student but checked out two books a week from the Pincher Creek Library. For two years in elementary school, she took correspondence courses, since the family lived too far from the school in town.

Not until the University of Alberta did she begin to shine. Appointed Chief Justice of the nine-member court in 2000, she participated in dramatic cases, often charter-related: Same-sex marriage, dying with dignity, various Indigenous rights cases, some reproductive rights cases, and the return of Omar Khadr from exile in Guantanamo.

On her retirement, McLaghlin began to write fiction, a novel called *Full Disclosure*.

Justice Richard Wagner succeeded her as chief. The court has five women and four men, one of whom is Michael Moldaver of Peterborough. McLaghlin continues to help other countries in the development of their legal systems. Her energy, intelligence and sense of social justice shine in this book.

"I love the law," she says, "but the law I love is there for everyone, high and low, imposing obligations to be sure, but also offering protections and benefits."

Let's Put the Word "Misogyny" into Everyday Understanding
May 21, 2020

What a relief it was to hear Public Safety Minister Bill Blair use the word "misogyny" at the all-important news conference on Parliament Hill on May 1.

It was part of what one observer called "the best news conference" he had ever seen, with completeness, moral passion and good sense: the announcement of an immediate Order in Council by the federal government to ban the sale, importation and use of 1,500 types of assault weapons in Canada.

"Today," Prime Minister Justin Trudeau, "the market closes."

The three leaders who laid out the case, and implemented the actions so long hoped-for, actually since the Montreal massacre of 1989, were the prime minister, Blair, former chief of police of Toronto, and Deputy Prime Minister Chrystia Freeland.

Freeland gave the 10-minute speech of her political career, laying out the history of mass killings in Canada carried out by these weapons and their particularly deadly effects on women and girls.

"The weapons aren't for hunting" she said, "they are designed to kill people and to look like they can kill people. Gender continues to be a determining factor in whether you feel safe in your home or on your street. From 2010 to 2015, there were 476 victims of domestic homicide, and 79 percent were women: on average one every three days. Let that sink in."

I looked up the meaning of the word "misogyny." It is hatred of women, contempt for women, or ingrained prejudice. We aren't, as a society, coming to terms with it.

Often, says the magazine "Psychology Today," men don't even know they have a misogynistic personality until some crisis. The attitude is probably related to some trauma in childhood, and is fostered by a "macho" culture.

This COVID-19 pandemic, not surprisingly, is worsening the situation. In the past 36 days in Canada, there have been nine cases of men killing women: In Brockville, Winnipeg, Portapique, Calgary, Osoyoos B.C., Hammonds Place, N.S., rural Alberta and Hillsboro, N.B.

Feminist analysts have written perceptively about it. We cannot ignore any longer the link between mass killings and hatred of women, says Elizabeth Renzetti in The Globe and Mail. Why are officials "scratching their heads again wondering how such horrible event could occur?" Behind many acts which we deem "senseless" is misogyny.

They are not "senseless and isolated acts," continues Renzetti. "That releases us from responsibility for the hard fixes needed to ensure the chain of violence is broken."

On April 24, Robyn Bourgeois, a professor at Brock University, wrote that the most prominent link connecting Canadians and killings has been that all the accused perpetrators were men and mostly white. Male violence begins in domestic abuse, she writes, and many males are socialized into violent masculinity. Finally, Johannah Black wrote in a Halifax paper, *The Coast*, "Call it what it is: misogynist violence." Black also points out that it is mistaken to paint rural communities as "quaint" and free of violence against women.

Blair, with his craggy, all-man persona, was just the person to draw it all home. He is an older white man, a police chief at one time. I often expect such people to spout vaguely anti-woman perspectives, such as one hears in bars and hockey dressing rooms. But no, Blair showed his deep understanding of the gendered dimension of violence, using the word "misogyny."

For many years, we feminists have been trying to get decision-makers of all kinds, mostly men, to grasp the deep-rooted, often unrecognized aspects of crimes that show a deep hatred and fear of women.

The prime minister, with his credentials as a feminist who made the cabinet gender equal, only has to be there to underline the importance of this move. Of course, the new law is partial, and just a start. It tackles the weapons, not the attitudes, the socialization, the business of weapons and so on.

But it is a long-delayed start, and will make Canada safer.

A Single, Sad Issue Unites Church and State in the USA
May 28, 2020

I'm one of the vast majority of Canadians hoping our southern neighbour replaces its national leader next November. With horror I saw that Catholic leaders in that country had chosen to "single issue" the election, a blind and dangerous choice, and then to endorse the sitting president on the basis of this one issue.

That single issue, rating ahead of health care, poverty, racism, climate and immigration, is, predictably, abortion. Last November, the bishops met in Baltimore and endorsed a program called "Forming Consciences for Faithful Citizenship." They voted 143 to 69 to make abortion the "pre-eminent issue" in the 2020 election.

Intellectually bankrupt and stubborn, the American bishops, led by Cardinal Timothy Dolan of New York, (that's the rector of St. Patrick's Cathedral) are counselling the faithful to vote for Donald Trump in 2020. Cardinal Dolan was fawning in praise of Trump on Fox News.

This might be considered just internal church stuff, but the Catholic vote may well help foist this damaging president on all of us this fall. So, it is of public interest.

There are a couple of burning questions. How has it happened that members of the church follow such direction? Over what period of time and through what means have church leaders appropriated to themselves a superior spiritual and ethical consciousness?

The second question is to what extent will the Catholic voter, the Catholic woman, follow these bishops, and relegate their own reasoning to a back seat?

It is "Father knows best," taken to extremes.

For modern Catholics there are four disastrously mistaken teachings: No birth control, no abortion, no same-sex marriage, no stem-cell research. Not one of them is theologically sound. Attitudes toward women and sex comprise the official Church's Achilles heel.

I read Fr. Hans Kung's *Infallibility: An Inquiry* in the early 1980's, and abandoned any notion that church authority could do no wrong. Kung is a Swiss theologian who investigated the claim by church authorities to be above reproach in certain teachings.

I am also impressed with feminist analysis. The writers (Ruether, Johnson, Schussler-Fiorenza, Maguire, hundreds of others,) all Catholics, all critical.

Except for this serious blind spot, Pope Francis is great on most of the important issues: Poverty, peace and the environment. This week marks five years since his groundbreaking statement "Laudato Si."

The generosity and goodness of many Catholic believers and groups is uncontested. What is at issue is the misogyny and blindness of the institution. It has harmed so many women and children. Different countries have vastly differing leadership. Today, it is the U.S. Catholic bishops who are out of step with the Pope. They have gone rogue. They have given in to the temptation to render all to Caesar, in hopes of gaining some influence, some questionable moral victory and some money.

In 2016, many Catholics voted for Donald Trump. Even the women did. Witnessing his complete failure as a leader, it is hard to grasp that many Catholics still support him and are encouraged by most of their bishops. Who stands up to them? The nuns, that's who. Two communities, the Sisters of St, Joseph of Carondelet and the Sisters of Providence issued strong statements.

"We are very concerned about your unqualified praise of President Trump," they wrote to Dolan. "We were very discomfited by your praise on Fox News, April 26. He is notorious for consistently lying to the public and for poor judgment. He sows animosity and polarization instead of offering moral leadership. He is a philanderer whose business activities have taken advantage of the poor and vulnerable. His support of one or two religious causes (abortion and financial support for Catholic schools) is designed to create the impression that he supports Catholic values. The scandals of the past few decades call us to a much higher standard."

As American democracy declines before our very eyes, I grieve that the present Catholic Church leadership there aids and abets the decline.

The Family Zoom Call: a Modern Tale
June 4, 2020

Some people I know are Zoomed out. Tired of sitting still, looking groomed, making small talk, or big talk, as businesses do, waving and smiling or frowning, enduring awkward pauses, unmuting oneself.

Seems like a lifetime ago, I learned the technology.

We Ganleys gave the task of setting it up to No. 2 son Michael in Edmonton. Sundays, 4 p.m. Eastern; 15 people in three time zones, three families with kids, plus me, Grandma, in Peterborough. Attendance is optional but has been robust. The contributions have been interesting and varied. Megan, 17, spends Sundays on her horse at the stable. But she is a joiner. So we see video of the horse, Annie, and Megan riding off into the sunset. We get quite a few shots of hindquarters.

We hear Jack, 17, from Vancouver Island, tell us about his dreaded advanced placement economics exam.

Emma, 11, from Newmarket, prefers to repair to her room with her tablet and take part in the Family Zoom by Chat. "What's economics?" appears across our screens. Jack answers, "Money, markets, trade, income." "Oh," she writes knowingly.

Jack and his sister Jensa, 15, miss their island-level soccer so much they have taken to watching Bundesliga from Germany, playing without fans. Our favourite team is Bayern Munich, whose star player is Canadian Alphonso Davies. I'm simply telling you what there is to learn on a Family Zoom call.

Ava, 8, Newmarket, prepares carefully for Family Zoom. She brings her latest impressionist watercolours.

Me: "Is that a sunrise or a sunset?" She also brings a big bowl of popcorn and uses two hands to enjoy it. "Ava," says Uncle Jim," I can smell that popcorn. How about sharing?"

Then Ava announces politely, "I have to LEAVE MEETING now."

We'll miss her.

Thomas, 19, from Edmonton, has a job at the University of Alberta. He's a science guy. His job is in satellite development for forest fires. "That's socially useful," I say. "If it doesn't work out, pivot to vaccine research." He laughs. "I don't think I have the skill-set for that, Grandma."

Some folks look as if they have just gotten out of bed. There is a lot of discussion of hair styles. The girls demonstrate long braids, topknots, and flowing tresses. The men are just craggy, awaiting the reopening of barber shops. "Jensa does mine," Jim reports. "It was her first cut, but she feels underpaid."

Shots are shown of the new trampoline in Newmarket and the therapy pool going in on Vancouver Island. Seems Jill is doing most of the lugging. The pool will be a great boon to Jay, 11, who is a family favourite. "I need to put the potatoes on," says Belinda, mom in Edmonton. "I'm working on our front lawn," says Paul, in Newmarket. "Looks like scorched earth. But I also do my jiu jitsu online."

"With a dummy," adds Emma, helpfully.

Danielle, a teacher in Newmarket, regales the meeting with stories of a Ministry of Education inspection that took place even within the lockdown. I'm afraid to physically move around in fear of breaking the connection, but I've arranged my background to show a different wedding photo of a son and his bride. This has led to charges of favouritism, so now I have to remember to change the photo before Zooming. Time for Netflix recommendations.

"Outer Banks," says Megan, who loves all things Hawaiian. "Unorthodox," says Mike, ever globally minded. "The Climb," says Sarah, 16, from Edmonton. "We saw it in French class before school ended."

Jim, who is an English teacher, reminds me that American humour writer David Sedaris frequently "throws his relatives under the bus," so to speak, by mentioning them in his columns in order to get a laugh. I promise to be careful. This pandemic has actually let us into each other's lives more fully.

The Peterborough Public Mood
as of June 2020
June 11, 2020

How ARE you?

Are you, as I am, torn between sorrow and worry about America, and euphoria, when we see folks in Minneapolis clean up the streets, or a police chief take his hat off respectfully when speaking live with the bereaved family of George Floyd.

I watch with pain a video of African-American parents giving lessons on self-protection to their children, "Be careful that your hands can be seen at all times. Say my name is.....and I have nothing to hurt you."

But that didn't seem to help George Floyd. Submission can be fatal too.

What on earth is society to do with racist, rogue police? Swift action from police leaders and politicians, and from union leadership, I think. Public support for proper recruitment, testing and discipline.

Are we also ready to confront Canadian racism and prejudice? Here in Peterborough, an impressive, well-organized (with masks, distancing and sanitizer), Black Lives Matter rally took place at Millennium Park and on the main streets on June 2. The crowd was nearly 1,000.

Best of all, the speakers were all from the black community; the mood was respectful, and the crowd was almost entirely young. Peggy and Richard Abbott, Sheila Howlett and I felt like the token elders. Great feeling.

The Examiner featured a picture of our police leadership taking a knee. I walked over to thank Chief Scott Gilbert and Deputy Chief Tim Farquharson.

I had come across a remark which I put on my sign, drawn for me by my friend, Justin Laurie. It starts with recognition that a white person, even an ally, can never deeply know the feelings of a black person in a society that has racism lingering in it. It reads, "I understand that I can never fully understand. Nonetheless, I stand."

Events are happening quickly south of the border. It was stunning and shocking to see President Donald Trump and his enablers (how do they sleep at night?) march out of the White House, order troops to clear the street of protesters by using rubber bullets and tear gas, and then walk to the historic 200-year Episcopal church nearby, St John's, where Trump posed with a bible. "A crude photo op," said commentators. Was it in hopes of attracting his right-wing evangelical followers?

Quick and articulate, the Episcopal bishop, Rev. Mariann Budde, who administers that parish, went on TV to denounce this unscheduled visit and say that Trump's behaviour is "inimical to the gospel we preach."

Not to leave the Catholics out of his "outreach," Trump made an uninvited call next day to the museum of Pope John Paul II. It is run by the Knights of Columbus.

Washington's first black Catholic archbishop, Wilton Gregory, told the press it was "baffling and reprehensible" that "any Catholic facility would allow itself to be misused and manipulated in such a fashion that violates our religious principles."

Take that, newly pious President. There's more. Rev William Barber, a nationally known Protestant leader, said the bible stunt was "shameful and heretical, an act of idolatry. When you see people in the streets, that's democracy trying to breathe."

There was the scene of our P.M. pausing for 21 seconds before not answering the reporter's question, "Will Canada denounce?" It went round the world. And he "took a knee" at the Ottawa rally, June 5.

As the weeks wear on, we behave co-operatively when out and about, observing distance, wearing masks and so on. Though not sick, I got myself tested this week at the site at Kinsmen Centre. Good experience.

We are tired, tired, and lonely. We are sadly aware of the Canadian Forces' report of conditions in our seniors' homes, and the fact that 80 percent of COVID-19 deaths have been among this group. So, our moods swing wildly.

Me, I'm taking in another webinar on resilience tonight!

A Potpourri of Topics for a Sunny June Day in Peterborough
June 18, 2020

People with time on their hands sometimes look up words. Mine today is "potpourri," from the French for an assembly of spices and scents. This column is a potpourri of ideas. I won't even mention that there is an alternative meaning for the word, "pourri" - "rotten."

Item No. 1: I took advantage of the free, public testing for COVID-19 on June 6, driving into Kinsmen Centre parking lot, full of winter memories of delivering boys to hockey games at dawn. I found a quick and efficient team of paramedics, in two open tents, welcoming cars, and conducting simple tests with a cheery attitude. That was Tiffany. Greeter Aaron gave me the sheet which had been written up by medical officer of health Dr. Rosana Salvaterra, a user-friendly handout about what would happen with my results.

The New York Times has just featured a glowing story about Dr. Bonnie Henry of B.C, who has so expertly guided that province through COVID-19. Salvaterra deserves similar gratitude for her leadership here. On Mother's Day, her staff of nine, eight of whom are mothers, were hard at work on the phones, contact-tracing. She brought each of them a nosegay of flowers. Premier Doug Ford has mentioned Peterborough as a success story, too.

Item No. 2: The matter of middle-class people such as myself, receiving $300 from the Government of Canada in early July, just for being old. I am having fun considering the charities (Canada has 70,000 of these) to which I can donate this money. One must be Black Lives Matter-related. The Black Legal Action Fund, I think. One must be arts-related. These people among us make life worth living, so it will be Electric City Culture Council. The third must be in the progressive ideas sector: Canadian Centre for Policy Alternatives.

Small amounts but heartfelt.

The lockdown has meant multiple opportunities to learn online. Every Wednesday at noon, Trent University has free "Trent Talks," featuring two professors discussing an area of their expertise. On June 10, it was "Unmasking Racism in Canada" with professors Daion Taylor and David Firang of Social Work.

I lived a challenging and satisfying life for six years in two Black-majority countries, Jamaica and Tanzania. I studied their literatures at their universities and co-founded a small development organization which brought Caribbean culture to Peterborough, among its several goals.

But even with this background, I have needed updating and an examination of my own white assumptions. I need to become more intentionally anti-racist. I think my role might well be to amplify Black voices, especially Black feminist voices, through social media and column-writing.

I have discovered the very interesting voice of Andaiye, a Guyanese activist whose book, *The Point is to Change the World* is now being published in Canada by "Between the Lines." And there is the work of 35 year-old African-American scholar Ibram Kendi, who argues that love and education about Black history aren't going to fix racism.

Racism serves economic interests.

On the pressing topic of police and defunding police, I think we need a calm, rational discussion of just what variety of skills are needed to help build a healthy, multiracial community here. More and more, the social problems to which police are called are alcohol, drug, housing and mental health-related. More funds must be allocated to these, and to trained people who are not law enforcement.

A helpful leader we might call on should we decide to undertake this discussion would be Alok Mukherjee of Toronto, chair of the Toronto Police Services Board, 2005-2015, and a thinker with ideas and experience.

Peterborough's police budget is $26 million, with an additional $1 million for capital expenditures. We have 140 informed officers. The total city budget for 2020 is $287 million. We have one policeperson for every 714 citizens.

I hope this discussion soon gets underway, and is respectful and public.

What Reconstruction Would be Like if Green and Female-led
June 25, 2020

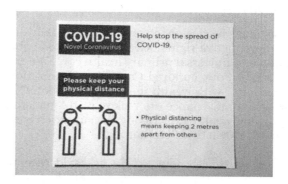

Time for blue skying.

While we have the time, many of us, let's ponder Big Thoughts: the kind of Canada we want. Without quitting the health practices we have developed, as pandemic restrictions ease, we can put all our best heads together and reimagine a global future.

We have many solid guides. I follow Katja Iversen of an NGO called "Women Deliver." Feminist, indefatigable and sensible, Iversen, a Dane, was named Danish Citizen of the Year in 2018. Her group, based in New York, delivered a terrific conference in June, 2019, in Vancouver. "Women Deliver" urges that reconstruction be "globally integrated." That makes sense. The pandemic has shown us in a powerful new way how related we are.

It must be woman-led. Decisions must be guided by a gender lens: How does this policy or program affect women and children? Access to education for girls must be ensured. Unpaid care and household work must be re-valued and distributed fairly. Education to promote gender equality must continue. And violence against women must stop. Violence against any identifiable group.

Nicholas Kristof, a widely read writer in the New York Times, said recently, "I crunched the numbers, and found that the death rate in female-led nations, that includes Taiwan, Germany and New Zealand, plus the province of British Columbia, was one-fifth of that in male-led nations. That's staggering. If the U.S. had the death rate of the female-led countries, the U.S. would have saved 102,000 lives.

The worst records have been those of male leaders who are authoritarian, blustering and no good at listening. Or maybe, it is simply that citizens willing to have a woman leader and those willing to follow guidelines from public health, are one and the same."

Women follow data, says he, men, egos.

Reconstruction must be designed, says "Women Deliver" to advance, not set back, reproductive rights: safe childbirth, safe abortion, access to contraception and universal primary health care. We can't go back to "business as usual." Four hundred Canadian organizations are calling for a "Just Recovery," with wealth inequity at its root. COVID-19 gives us a once-in-a-lifetime chance to reckon with inadequacies in our system; the growing wealth gap. Taxing the superrich is one important step, notes Dennis Howlett of Peterborough.

Pope Frances is worth listening to. He has said recently, "Fill your hearts with hope; focus on acts of respect and generosity. The pandemic may be nature's response to climate damage. Change lifestyles to more austere and humane lives. Find the antibodies of justice, charity and solidarity."

There are also many vital "green" voices. I listened to the webinar sponsored by Fair Vote Canada on June 21 with 10 candidates for the leadership of the Green party, who discussed a just and green recovery. It was hosted by Elizabeth May, who is stepping down. Greens report that 30 percent of Canadians now feel positive about their party.

Peterborough's climate activists urge us to contact Parliament with our recommendations. Reconstruction must include investment in green jobs such as retrofitting buildings, increasing renewable energy, training for displaced oil workers, more staff in seniors homes and prodigious efforts to meet our emission reduction goals. All are doable. If you believe, as I do, in making the effort to communicate with government, here is an opportunity to file a letter, a brief or a remark with the Standing Committee on Industry, Science and Technology (12 members, headed by Liberal MP Sherry Romanado) by June 19 (or just do it, and be late). That committee is preparing Canada's recovery plan.

Can we at last talk calmly about runaway capitalism, the economic system that has brought us to this? Not talking about small business here, but about huge corporations without conscience who exploit the Earth's resources, including its human ones.

Shifts in thinking are happening dramatically: Racism is exposed, health is under threat, democracy is vulnerable. All hands on deck this summer.

Dennis Howlett Brings Lessons in Tax Fairness to Peterborough
July 2, 2020

Dennis Howlett is one of those accomplished Canadians who has come to live in Peterborough for family reasons, and because he and his wife Elaine like the size of the community, and the access to culture, health and education (plus the ease of canoeing hereabouts).

We stand to benefit from their decision.

Now he is enriching local groups as a member of the board of the Kawartha World Issues Centre, and international ones, as treasurer of the Brussels-based NGO, "Global Alliance for Tax Justice." With modesty and patience, he gave me an education in taxation I had despaired of ever "getting."

After 25 years working for social justice in coalitions of civil society organizations, Dennis spent five years as co-ordinator of "Make Poverty History" and the last seven as executive director of "Canadians for Tax Fairness," based in Ottawa. These were fruitful years of research and policy formation, and then of advocacy as he got to know decision-makers in government and was closely listened to by House Finance Committees.

"I got to know PM Trudeau some years ago as a supporter of Make Poverty History when he was an MP. I am most proud of the reform of the child tax benefit which we worked for and which has lifted thousands of Canadian children out of poverty."

Howlett has a clear philosophy of taxes and he brought me to share the understanding. It was an American judge, Oliver Wendell Holmes, who said in 1927, "Taxes are the price we pay for civil society."

Taxes fund high-quality public services and programs required to meet our social, economic and environmental needs of the 21st century.

We moan and complain and dread income-tax time. But at our core, we know the remark to be true. We only ask that the tax system be fair and honest and transparent. In Canada, the CRA (Canadian Revenue Agency), delivers many of the social benefits which have done much to close the wide gap between rich and poor. Much remains to be done. Howlett is lobbying for northern and Indigenous peoples to get help in understanding and filing tax returns.

"In Scandinavia," he says, "a government agency does your tax return for you with all possible exemptions, and sends it to you to look over and approve."

What makes us enraged is knowing about tax havens which the wealthy use to avoid paying taxes. He agrees more must be done to uncover them and collect what is owed.

As to the $268 billion deficit we currently carry because of the economic supports issued during the pandemic, Howlett says, "Tax policy is crucial to the rebuilding of Canada. Austerity is not the way to go. Fair taxes and reinvestment is."

He uses the terms "progressive" and regressive" to describe taxes. "Value-added taxes" (the GST) are regressive, in that they hit the poor hardest, but the GST rebate is a help."

I am grateful that Howlett, a graduate in arts with a Masters in Adult Education, spends a lifetime examining tax systems from the point of view of the marginalized: a man of the common good.

His international work includes a project with Queen University and the country of Ghana. If Ghana had a fair and effective tax system, it would hardly need massive amounts of international assistance.

Activist, writer and media commentator, Dennis Howlett will benefit our city wherever he appears.

When I lived in Tanzania in the 1980's, a very poor country, but one blessed with a kind of social equality, my spouse, John, was most proud of a local NGO he helped start, the "Tanzanian Association of Internal Auditors." It gave young audit students confidence to go after the figures and report them to the public.

Hence, I am impressed with persons of integrity who pursue economic analysis from the bottom up.

What is the Influence of Canadian Catholic Bishops?
July 9, 2020

I'm a religion-watcher, particularly of my own. These powerful influencers in society are too seldom scrutinized in mainstream places. Seems only fair, after I criticized the American Catholic bishops a month ago for supporting Trump, that I have a look at the Canadians.

The Canadian Conference of Catholic Bishops (CCCB) founded in 1943, is the assembly of francophone and anglophone Catholic bishops of Canada, headquartered in Ottawa, with 79 active bishops and 40 staff. The president is Bishop Richard Gagnon of Winnipeg.

There are 12 million self-identifying Catholics in Canada, about 38 percent of the population. Two-thirds of our population describe themselves as Christian.

Bishops sometimes issue statements on the great questions of our time. Sexual questions have tended to predominate: what Sister Joan Chittister calls "pelvic preoccupations." I went to the website and saw a modest statement about the unrest in the USA, prayers for the pandemic, and an appreciation of the environment from 2017.

Our cultural context in Canada is more liberal and to my mind, enlightened, than the American one. But we too hunger for out-front leadership from spiritual sources.

The Catholic bishops have inherited several hard-to-defend sexual and gender policies. Still they would never dare, as certain American bishops have done, publicly refuse communion to a pro-choice Catholic politician. Amend that: in 2008, Archbishop Terrence Prendergast of Ottawa threatened such a move.

The prime minister, and several before him - Jean Chrétien, John Turner and Joe Clark for example, have been pro-choice Catholics.

I remember approaching the communion table at St. Michael's Cathedral in Toronto some years ago wearing a rainbow scarf as part of a demonstration in solidarity with LGBTQ people. We weren't refused, but we were looked on disapprovingly.

There are hints of an obsession (it must be global) with abortion. On the CCCB website, there is a letter to the prime minister assuring him that the Conference of Bishops is all in favour of a vaccine for COVID-19, but he must not authorize the use of fetal tissue in the research.

I am a fan of Melinda Gates, co-founder of the Gates Foundation. She had a Catholic upbringing in Dallas. The foundation supports women's and children's health, including family planning and access to abortion around the world. She says cheerfully, "My church and I just agree to disagree," and then gets on with what she knows is right and relevant.

In my years as a board member for Amnesty International Canada, 2007-2009, the Amnesty sections around the world were debating whether to include sexual and reproductive rights as human rights. As the only Catholic, I was turned to for advice. The Canadian bishops had issued a statement advising people to stop donating to Amnesty International. That got my dander up.

Ultimately, A.I. globally did adopt these important rights. I told my Amnesty colleagues not to pay too much attention to the bishops' letter. They spoke for so few.

I have another beef with the Canadian bishops. Five years ago, the important encyclical letter, "Laudato Si" was published by Pope Francis. It dealt with the most pressing issue of our time: the state of the earth, our common home.

The bishops by definition, are teachers, but I waited in vain for an effective campaign to teach this letter in schools, parishes, and seminaries. As far as I could see, only the Jesuit Centre in Toronto went all out to prepare tools. Asleep, is the kindest way to describe the bishops' efforts.

If women were involved in decision-making in this great institution, things would become a lot better. One archbishop, retired Rev. Sylvain Lavoie, wrote to the Pope in March, "I am finding when a space is created where it is safe to share, women open up with the pain they feel stifled by the church's patriarchal nature."

But most prefer prudence to prophesy. Lavoie: one lone voice. Feminists of this faith have so much work to do.

A Great Trip Doesn't Have
to Mean Travelling Far
July 16, 2020

Like you, from March to July, I went nowhere. From room to room, maybe. Around the block. Occasionally a bike ride through Jackson Park. The ultimate adventure was a ride to the trestle bridge near Omemee. That took two days recovery time.

I touched no one. I couldn't see my granddaughters in Newmarket. I went to church via Zoom. Every sock was mended, every drawer organized; the thrill of breadmaking gone. I was frankly going stir crazy by July 5.

Every day at 4 p.m., socially starved, I headed to the deck of one friend or another, taking turns, hoping for a glass of wine, until they were tired of me.

Then it came to me in a flash of light: I could perhaps drive two hours to a cabin the woods, carrying my copy of Thoreau's *Walden*, to an encampment of four well-spaced and roomy cabins operated by a dear and longtime friend, Jennifer Rowell Dailloux and her spouse, Jacques.

It is called Wolf Den Nature Retreat and Lodge, situated along the Oxtongue River, just nine kilometres west of the entrance to Algonquin Park. Jen and Jacques have had these cabins and a larger lodge across the highway for about six years. It is a Garden of Eden for their four-year-old, Tom, who in the winter goes to the public school in Dwight.

There is a great story in this family. When Jennifer Rowell was 16, a bright student at Adam Scott Collegiate, she came forward to volunteer with a youth team going to Kingston, Jamaica with Jamaican Self-Help.

She shone at the work, with the right attitude, lots of pluck and curiosity, an immense talent for friendship, and a solid analysis of conditions on the ground in poor communities.

Jen came again twice more as a youth team leader, including once with her mother Elaine Orgill, who is a gifted early childhood educator. Elaine went on to serve as president of JSH for five years.

It was no surprise to us that Jen went on to international studies at university and began to work for CARE U.K. In the next 17 years, she did development work among women in Peru, Chad, India and Afghanistan.

It was in Kabul at a tango dance class hosted by the Canadian embassy, that Jen met Jacques, a development worker from France. They married on Stoney Lake, at the Church on the Rock in 2010.

After experiencing many explosions in Kabul which were taking lives, Jen and Jacques decided to come "home," and not only home to Canada, but to deep rural, ecological, park-preserve Canada; to become hospitable to the world in a new way, by offering accommodation to as many as 60 outdoors-minded people at a time in a cordial atmosphere.

Elaine's partner Keith Dalton has been key in renovating the accommodations, and Elaine herself has, during the lockdown, stimulated Tom's learning, especially outdoor science.

With COVID-19, the lodge has not been able to be opened, but the cabins are fine and I felt lucky to have come along and found one. I kayaked and swam and read and hiked in the park, drinking in the silence and naturalness that has been so well-preserved there. Algonquin is Ontario's oldest park, from 1893, covering 3000 square miles and featuring six major rivers. Proudly, eight percent of Ontario is kept in protected parks.

Ever the conscientious citizens, Jen and Jacques have taken on public service. Jacques is a trained volunteer firefighter, and the fire hazard is high these days. Jen ran successfully for municipal council. She is one of five women on the Algonquin Highlands Township council, headquartered near Carnarvon, managing a budget of $8 million.

"My "ward' even extends into part of the park," she marvels. "If I can help save 40 lakes, maybe that's as important as any other piece of work."

With which this camper agrees.

With the End of Life in Sight: MAID in Peterborough
July 23, 2020

About a year ago, I was at the peaceful bedside of a close friend, Tony, who was being delivered from his excruciating and long-endured cancer pain by "MAID," Medical Assistance in Dying.

Tony was reconciled with his two daughters, from whom he had been estranged. He was 66 years old, a man alone. He had had a Catholic childhood. I asked him, "Would you like me to read you from the New Testament?" He smiled weakly. "No, thank you," he said, "from Richard Wagamese - *Embers* please."

The physician-provider of MAID arrived with an assistant, and asked Tony softly for his final consent. The family lit candles and sang. The implementation was moving and complete.

It must also be realized that the provision of MAID involves a complex human, emotional, spiritual and medical experience for the individual, for his or her family, and for the whole community.

In Peterborough, we are fortunate to have individuals and institutions who collaborate closely in offering a nuanced and flexible set of circumstances of choice, for people who are contemplating or planning MAID.

It was in June 2016 that the Parliament of Canada passed Bill C14, an act to amend the Criminal Code to satisfy the Charter of Rights and Freedoms. MAID providers, either a physician or a N.P., can provide assistance in dying to eligible adults, namely those of sound mind who have a grievous irremediable medical condition, whose natural death has become reasonably foreseeable, who have made a written request, and who have been independently assessed by two doctors.

By this new law, MAID providers were exempt from the criminal laws prohibiting the ending of human life. The request would have to be a signed one, with two independent witnesses who did not stand to benefit and who were not involved in the care. A ten-day reflection period was required. Doctors whose conscience prevented their taking part were excused. Counselling about other options was required.

This, of course, is a sensitive and complex area of ethics. Canadians have showed how much they care about the issue from all sides. Responding to an online invitation to comment, 300,000 Canadians did so. Some religious groups objected, believing life to be "sacred from conception to natural death." Disability advocates have sounded alarms. The debate has been passionate but respectful.

Careful statistics have been kept. Between 2016 and 2020, a little over 9000 Canadians have died by MAID, 5445 in Ontario. Sixty-four percent of those deaths were cancer-related, and 12 percent from neurodegenerative illness. Fifty-one percent were male and 49 percent female.

About 62 percent of those seeking MAID were over age 71. MAID accounted for 1.1 percent of all deaths in Canada over that period. There is an ever-growing public dialogue about end-of-life decision-making. Many Canadians are coming forward to share their stories.

Good palliative care and access to effective pain control are crucial factors in any fruitful discussion. Hospice in Peterborough, a stand-alone facility, has rooms for 10 people in palliative care. It does not provide MAID, but supports people in their journey and decision-making. It pays special attention to family members, left with the permanent loss of a loved one.

A group that also works to make end-of-life choices more available to Canadians is the advocacy group "Dying with Dignity," with 65,000 members. It has lobbied the government to amend the phrase, "reasonably foreseeable" death. The bill, C7, is before Parliament.

Peterborough Regional Health Centre has a co-ordinator of MAID, Jane Mark, RN. Since 2016, there have been 126 MAID deaths, 99 in hospital. Peterborough has enough medical providers, and a "robust, collaborative system" of care. The hospital also has a palliative care unit.

People can approach their family doctor or nurse-practitioner for more information.

The purpose is to help society more openly consider and act upon, all aspects of a "good death."

Many in Peterborough Go Thirsty
When There's Fresh Water All Around Us
August 27, 2020

In the dog days of July this year, temperatures were well over 30 degrees. I won't speak of the large issues of global warming hitting us with a heavy hand, but I will consider at the micro level the pain of many citizens, who make their home day-by-day on the streets of Peterborough or in shelters, already strapped by COVID-19.

A small group of alert citizens noticed a real and direct problem: downtowners, the homeless and marginalized, in addition to the people who walk and cycle, had few places to get free water to drink.

On the hottest of days. Members of a voluntary group, calling themselves "The Squeaky Wheel" became conscious of this deprivation, even as they personally had easy access to cold water in their homes.

The hardship was the result of the city providing five drinking water sources, only three of which are in the downtown. For two of those three sources, COVID-19 has drastically reduced hours: the library (only a few hours a week when book returns are open), One Roof Centre (9 a.m. to 3 p.m.), and the Lighthouse at the Marina.

The situation represents a real Canadian irony, considering that we have a lot of fresh water. Locally, we have the Otonabee River.

We also have the infrastructure to deliver clean water to almost everyone. Canada, with one-half of a percent of the world's population, has seven percent of the world's renewable fresh water. It comes from lakes, underground aquifers and glaciers. Half of our water drains northward to Hudson's Bay and the Arctic Ocean, so we do well to conserve water.

For 30 years, Canadian heroine Maude Barlow, now 73, has been a strong water warrior, educating, researching and writing. She has published 16 books, including *Blue Planet*, and the latest, *Whose Water is it Anyway?*

The difficulty is the lack of clean, public washrooms and water fountains. Every European city has them, part of sensible urban planning. Nurse Theresa Morris has researched safe designs. Such facilities need to be imagined first: then city council has to realize their importance and budget for them, and then Peterborough people have to respect and take care of them.

To apply pressure on decision-makers, the 12 or so "Squeaky Wheelers" led by Gord Halsey, organized a free water station.

Halsey is an engineer with considerable experience in risk management, who has lived in Peterborough for 6 years and has a social conscience formed in the Salvation Army. He set out to get water donated, and then give it out free downtown every day this summer.

The good news is that when the Squeaky Wheel asked groups in town to help, they got 42 volunteers from 8 organizations and faith groups to take one day a week. Rocky Ridge, Culligan and Greg's No Frills are donating five-gallon jugs: the DBIA loans a tent and donates gloves, and No Frills welcomes the tent to their parking lot under two trees.

Gord's figures show that since July 15, only two days have been rained out. So far, over 3000 thirsty people have been served. The volunteers are present six hours a day, 11 to 5, and have averaged 75 servings a day.

They would like it if those who come had a reusable bottle, and indeed one day, a car pulled up and a woman brought over ten of such reusables to give out. But no one is refused, and disposable bottles also figure in the handouts.

The plan is to continue daily until Labour Day.

I enjoy my shifts on Wednesdays: the sweetness of the recipients and the many blessings called down on us "Wheelers," the interesting conversations, the original appearances of some, and the comments of passersby who may drop off a bit of money.

That is the goodwill generated by the implementation of a good idea, which has a larger social and political purpose.

After all, water is a human right.

Canadians Would Feel the Impact of Another Trump Victory
September 3, 2020

If a Canadian election is sprung on us this fall, it will be vastly overshadowed by the American one on November 3.

Let's face it: We are transfixed by the desperate shenanigans down there, especially the profound denial of truth and fact in the Republican campaign. That tactic is called "gaslighting," after the 1944 movie in which a devious man convinces his wife she isn't living in reality, whereas she really is.

The performances the Republican convention, which was arrogantly staged without masks on the White House lawn, were for me, surreal. Example: Advisor Kellyanne Conway, who first uttered the wretched words "alternative facts," left her role after the convention when her 15-year-old daughter sent out a distress call on social media saying her mother was "ruining her life." Surreal.

I have a sense of disbelief that American public life has been so corrupted. Up is down, and down is up, if they say so. It's not a trivial matter, because the fate of that country and indeed the welfare of all on the globe, is at stake.

Do we Canadians live on the same planet? The same continent?

Can the Republican party spin the infection and death numbers of COVID- 19 for their faithful base and for the undecided voter, so that they believe the pandemic is over, or not so bad, or well-handled? Can the legitimate, nation-wide protests against the killing of Black people by police be dismissed as "violent, communist-inspired disorder?" Can Democratic candidate Joe Biden, a moderate politician of 47 years experience, be realistically called "socialist?"

Can the NBA, of which the Toronto Raptors are impassioned leaders who refuse to just "shut up and dribble," be called disloyal, or un-American?

How do advertisers continue to support the rabid rantings of Tucker Carlson and crew on Fox News? How can a prominent Catholic bishop open this charade of a convention with a prayer, and a Catholic nun in long black habit describe Donald Trump as the "most pro-life president in history?"

It's crazy-making.

But in any human situation, no matter how unpromising, there are the redemptive moments. Humour flows quickly from intelligent sources. Here is a good one, "When your convention features 12 speakers, and six have the same last name as the leader, we are moving into North Korean territory."

Then there's the joke referring to Canada's invasion of the States in 1814. We can always be asked to step in and save her.

I resonate with the moral outrage of CNN commentator Van Jones, who is an articulate Black man fearing for his son. He finds words to communicate his anguish. Then, because he is a seasoned debater, he flashes a wide, ironic smile.

Other hopeful signs include the sweet civility of Mark Shields and David Brooks (born Toronto, 1961) on NPR, Fridays; the calm clarity of CNN correspondent Abby Phillips, and the feisty delivery of Canada's own Daniel Dale, once of the Toronto Star, telling us in rapid-fire delivery that Trump has told 15,000 public lies in three and a half years in office, more than 20 in the speech on Thursday night at the convention. Dale gives us chapter and verse of the lies. He may well influence the election outcome in profound ways.

Hold on to your hats.

If you are a praying person, do that. Keep the border closed past September 21. Be alert for signs that these Republican strategies may take hold in our politics. Watch Erin O'Toole particularly. He courts the far right in order to take the Conservative leadership vote, but now is beholden to them.

Talk politics reasonably with others at every chance. Don't abandon it. It's all we got.

Believing as I do in the promise of America, and going way out on a limb, I predict a healthy Democratic win November 3.

On a Quest for Cannabis Oil in Peterborough
September 10, 2020

Nobody felt much like exercising outdoors during those steamy weeks of July and August, but I set out early one morning for downtown.

It is, as you, know a maze of signs, arrows, barriers and street repaving. Not attractive and somewhat confusing, but, one hopes, good for some businesses, those with outdoor seating and suitable beverages.

Still, I notice at street level many plaintive signs, hand-done by business owners not in the refreshment business, asking the city to restore the normal streetscape; that they are losing business.

Definitely a time of COVID-19 blues.

I have a mission: To enter a field of enterprise completely new to me. To learn about it.

I stop to ask three cool young people crouching on the sidewalk, with friendly faces, "Where is the pot shop?" They don't miss a beat at this query from a white-haired woman pushing her bike, an embroidered face mask hung on her wrist.

"Just down across from No Frills," they chime together.

Wishing my grandchildren were there to take a picture of me entering Growers Retail, or better yet, exiting with bag in hand, I walk into the newly decorated, air-cooled space. Lots of other customers are there, most of them 45 years younger than me. A vigorous staff in black T-shirts is giving advice, unlocking cabinets and making sales, everyone masked.

I stand and look. Then I hail Haley, and confess to her my ignorance of the scene, but my desire to try a hemp oil or a CBD oil, having rehearsed those terms before I left home. I would like a bit of help with insomnia. Insomnia? It's a COVID-19 thing.

Haley finds just the remedy, and writes out my instructions clearly: Three drops a day, see if it's effective, increase or decrease after a week. But there's more. On Aylmer Street, the GO bus now has a stop, since Simcoe Street is being resurfaced. I see the Greyhound terminal is for sale.

Then I join the lineup of book lovers who are retrieving their requested books from the Peterborough Public Library. Talk about pivoting. A staff member stands at a table for two hours speaking into a walkie-talkie; we are all distanced, and we show our card as librarians act like retrievers, hauling small piles of books out for patrons.

It is an edifying scene. I am seeking a children's story to read at a small gathering marking a 40th wedding anniversary which will have five children under the age of eight. The responsive children's librarian, Erin, has found five which are about love between grandparents and grandchildren.

Then, further up Aylmer, I sit at an outdoor table at Black Honey for what must be the best coffee in town. I wish Lisa Dixon had a good large permanent sign on Aylmer pointing to her shop.

Then there are Dave and Sue, the cheery and skilled proprietors of Spokes and Pedals, doing business. I remind them that my trusty Norco bike was acquired and has been serviced by them for eight years.

Aylmer Street becomes, some of my women friends are wont to say, a bit more "dicey" for a couple of blocks. Rooming houses, a rundown feeling, and passersby who may be muttering to themselves. It's all the more important for the privileged to walk those streets and be seen too.

I choose to shop at FreshCo on Brock, partly to be in touch with the "inner city," and partly because the veggies are so fresh.

I see that Bedford House has been sold. For some years, Rev. Allan Reeve and his spouse, Lynn Reeve-Smith, have been there hosting meaningful discussions among Peterborough's disadvantaged and its middle-class people seeking to understand each other and build bridges.

Awaiting me is the cool, treed trail starting at the bottom of Aylmer and emerging at Parkhill. Once, I could cycle up the Benson hill, but no more. Home again. And with my cannabis.

Biking, Walking and Active Transportation in Peterborough
September 17, 2020

I'm a fan of our local newspaper, and in June, I read about the Shifting Gears Bike Commuter Consult, whereby I could take my trusty Norco bike to B!KE on George Street, all COVID-19 compliant, leaving it at the door, and they would, for free, examine it and call me on Zoom to report on its condition for summer.

For my pains, I would receive a free bike accessory. I chose a light, though I seldom cycle at night. Lo and behold, the mechanic instructor was longtime acquaintance Jean Greig, a woman of many talents; writing and music to name two, who is working at the non-profit community-based shop. Jean found a few problems and gave me advice.

B!KE is a remarkable resource here in town. It is managed by the indefatigable Tegan Moss, and does all kinds of outreach, teaching "do-it-yourself" skills, keeping used parts and second-hand bikes, always mindful of economic barriers to widespread cycling. It has just acquired its charitable number and can issue receipts for donations.

Then, I met the impressive Lindsay Stroud, a Trent grad and one-time B!KE volunteer, who has for eight years organized programs at GreenUP, in schools ("Pedal Power") and the community ("Shifting Gears") to encourage active transportation for all ages.

We have 72 kilometres of bikeways within the city. There is a latent demand for more and safer infrastructure. From all appearances, COVID-19 has brought out increased numbers of people motoring under their own power.

There are many groups of enthusiastic cyclists, and the road cycling organization Peterborough Cycling Club, rides on county routes. There is also the Tandem Bike project for people with low or no vision. But for most of us, it will be cycling to errands and work and school. In that regard, wiser planning years ago would have put small grocery stores within better reach.

I chatted with Susan Sauve, the transportation demand planner at City Hall, a dedicated outdoors person. These four women work closely together in Peterborough to increase the percentage of us who cycle and walk to our destinations. That number is now about 10 percent, the highest percentage among communities in the GTA and Hamilton. Hurray for us.

In 2008, city council approved a plan to install more sidewalks where they are missing. We won't walk unless we are confident of the way. It is now 50 percent complete. I notice and am grateful for the sloped ends of sidewalks that makes transitioning at corners smooth.

In 2012, the city approved a Transportation Plan with a proposed cycling networks. The Transportation and the Cycling plans are under review and residents can offer input online at www.connectptbo.ca.

The coordination of four groups, the city, the county, public health and GreenUP, is impressive in making Peterborough bike-and walk-friendly. COVID-19 has changed the local landscape recently. Active transportation has increased about 20 percent. We see many more people walking and cycling, for something to do, and to increase good mood.

It is hardly necessary to itemize the fitness benefits of this activity. Nor the very desired reduction in greenhouse gases. But more subtle effects are also felt. At bike level, we're more likely to connect with driver of cars, and with pedestrians and other cyclists. It makes the city we occupy more friendly and comfortable and "lived-in." We may become a slowed-down place. There are now additional pages in the Ontario Driver Training manual about the cycling presence.

As for me and my newly-tuned bike, I am about to replace my cycling down George Street on a busy afternoon for some alternative route. In Chinese cities, for example, a whole lane is reserved for cyclists, sometimes an entire family on a bike.

I keep my bike under a tarp in the backyard, trying to see it first as I step out. I want to postpone those hip and knee replacements as long as possible. A salute to those people planning and encouraging us.

COVID-19 Doesn't Mean Our Lives Are On Hold

September 24, 2020

Each of us in our personal circumstances is being called on to give up, adjust, work twice as hard, and worry a lot more these days. The dilemmas facing young parents are extreme; whether to send kids to school, earning enough to live, watching for signs of illness, and caring for others in the family, are just some.

For me, alone, in my senior years, vigorous, and on a pension, life is outwardly easier than for many. Prolonged isolation has its challenges too. I've been thinking about my coping strategies.

I've cleaned my living space, drawers, closets, and files, and given away a lot of excess. Vinnie's is receiving donations again from Wednesday to Saturday. I've brought my will up-to-date and written out a page of bequests, those treasures acquired during 65 years of moving about, for cherished grandchildren: knick-knacks, jewelry, pictures and books.

I have attempted to improve myself; that always feels good. Cultural institutions have been generous during lockdown: the McMichael Gallery and the National Gallery in Ottawa have offered free tours and tutorials. The Metropolitan Opera in New York dug into its archives and presented some of their 500 opera performances. Then I got serious, and watched parts of 19 operas, having consulted the synopsis of the drama first. When the works began to run in together in my head, (something which happens when you don't have followup discussion), I gave the Met a rest.

I took a 90-minute course from, get this, Pandemic University, a startup in Calgary: on "Writing Opinion," with a fine freelancer, Max Fawcett.

Success has been had with the family Zoom calls each Sunday. The five teens have kept hanging in. I watch for signs of depression. They have so many reasons to get depressed. So far so good.

Jim, the son on Vancouver Island who has started keeping chickens, and built a coop he calls the Taj Mahen, has persuaded his 14 layers to produce an egg, even if it's blue. The project was partly sabotaged by their dog, Gracie, who shook one of the chickens to death. Bad dog.

I have watched an inordinate amount of pro sports on TV. So desperate was I for sports, I began following Bayern-Munich in the European Bundesliga. Couldn't find anyone in town to discuss it with. But there was a silver lining, seeing Edmonton soccer player Alfonso Davies, age 19, named rookie of the year in that league. I saw his dazzling footwork.

Then of course the Raptors returned, to our national delight. I wish announcers Matt and Jack would tell us the back story of that amazing player, O.G. Anunoby. Of course they are Americans and don't have our sensibility. He is a 23-year-old Nigerian, an orphan now, whose father, a professor, brought him to the U.K. and then the U.S., where he started playing basketball. His first name is Ogugua.

I walked a lot, especially pleasant on a warm day at Little Lake Cemetery, our treasure in the middle of the city, where the surroundings give rise to deep thoughts.

I learned Twitter, more or less, and completed my annual ambition to swim in Ontario lakes: Rosseau, Eagle Lake in north-eastern Ontario, and the Oxtongue River in Algonquin Park.

I followed politics, too closely. I regularized my drinking to one a day, Appleton rum or red wine. That was probably from following the politics.

Socially, at four o'clock, I made my way over to the deck of one of three couples: Joe Webster and Casey Ready, Peter Laurie and Cathy Bolan, or Colleen Crawley and Steve Brown. It was the conversations I craved.

For this long haul, it is psychospiritual resources we must draw on.

I'm rereading old Christian classics such as Teilhard de Chardin's *Le Milieu Divin*, and Teresa of Avila's *The Interior Castle*, finding them relevant to today's challenges.

Plus participating in prayer, and in two communal meditation groups, utter silence, via Zoom each week.

Villa in Cobourg is a Resource for the Planet
October 1, 2020

Our area has some amazing, often hidden, places, full of historical lore and modern relevance. One of these is the Villa St. Joseph Ecology and Spirituality Centre, on Lake Ontario in Cobourg.

It is a stately old building first constructed in 1844, on the north shore of the Lake, with a vast vista and ten acres of grassland and gardens, walkways, a beehive, a labyrinth, pollinator gardens and large areas of milkweed, making it an accredited monarch "way station," supporting butterflies on their flights.

It's a kind of a naturalist's Shangri-La, right close to urban areas.

In 1844, a Cobourg merchant named Winkworth Tremaine had the great home built. Then, late in the 19th century, the famous Civil War general who later became the 18th president of the United States, Ulysses S. Grant, bought the property for his daughter, Nellie Grant Sartoris, who lived there in the summers for about 20 years.

It was then the site of grand parties with prominent American guests. In fact, the present chapel of the Villa was once a stable, and later, a ballroom.

Bought by a community of nuns, the Sisters of St. Joseph of Peterborough in 1921, to serve as an orphanage for girls, it was renovated in 1974 to become a retreat centre now served by four Sisters. Several of the Sisters took advanced studies in environmental science and spirituality. This has led to the Villa assuming its present identity as an ecumenical centre for ecology and faith. As we face climate chaos, and wise voices are calling for deep cultural, ethical and religious conversion alongside crucial technical and scientific changes, the Villa seems to have been prophetic in discerning its mission for these times.

Its readiness and spiritual strengths have meshed with a renewed contemporary attachment to the natural world which is in distress, in a time of great threat, and in a time of COVID reassessment. As Sister Mary Rowell, CSJ said to me, "COVID-19 has its invitations."

With a full program of small-group gatherings, days of stillness and theology courses, and a vast library of books, magazines and tapes on the topics of creation, food, nature, water, growing things, wisdom from the past, simplicity and consumerism, the Villa is attracting people from all over Ontario and beyond, who are seeking reflection, purpose and hope.

In 2021, there will be a graduate course in eco-spirituality over four weekends.

I was happy to see that the Villa was partially open to visitors again, under COVID-19 protocols. My day in September was a facilitated one, led by Les Miller, a retired educator from Richmond Hill and a gifted photographer, who has just published a book entitled *Northern Light*, full of his stunning photos from all across Canada, our iconic scenes: the Confederation Bridge, the Gaspe, Peggy's Cove, the Rockies, the city of Toronto skyline and so on.

Les Miller's pictures are accompanied by reflections and prayers, all contemporary and agreeable to a modern consciousness.

We walked the grounds slowly, marvelling at the trees, the puff balls, the marigolds, goldenrod and snapdragons, the glistening lake with a distant sail boat, the lake birds, the fossil embedded rocks, the vegetables, and the 80 plots being tended by members of the Northumberland Community Gardens.

Miller speaks often of "spiritual curation." To "curate" is to look after and preserve, after selecting and organizing. It implies choice, decision and clear thinking. He is also seeking a specifically Canadian way of appreciating the world. We have become so dominated by the views and values of our southern neighbour, we risk having nothing to offer.

The Villa is full of delightful surprises. This visit introduced me to a wise fifth century Chinese philosopher, Lao Tzu, who is considered the founder of Taoism. There was a wall hanging that drew my attention:

"Say what you have to say fully, then be quiet."

Quiet and deepening is what the Villa offers tired souls.

Learn more at www.lesmiller.ca and www.villastjoseph.ca

Fresh Ideas for Climate Action:
A Good War
October 8, 2020

Seth Klein

The 1980's were a decade of nuclear dread in Peterborough, the Cold War era. Russia was seen as a great threat, and the Darlington nuclear plant near Port Hope a major target, which, if hit, would badly affect us. Peterborough has long had a group of conscientious people alert to signs of the times, thinking critically and taking non-violent action. Members still make waves, regarding poverty, racism and climate chaos. Then, they hosted SAGE.

Into town came four teenagers from Montreal, all of them 18 years old, with a youth group called "SAGE: Students Against Global Extermination." They were driving a rusty old station wagon, two boys and two girls, articulate and motivated, who had promised their parents that on a two-month-long, cross-Canada trek to show a documentary film and organize youth groups for peace, there would be "no funny business."

We had a call asking us if we could billet two of these youth. Gladly.

We took in Seth Klein, the son of filmmaker Bonnie Sherr Klein and physician Michael Klein. This couple had fled the United States for Canada as part of the Vietnam War resistance movement.

The kids did a great job, showing "If You Love This Planet," and conducting vigorous discussions with high schoolers here. Next morning, the front-page story in the Globe and Mail was the SAGE tour.

More than three decades later, Seth Klein, now in Vancouver, has worked for 20 years as British Columbia co-ordinator for the Canadian Center for Policy Alternatives, a think tank which turns out the Alternative Federal Budget each year.

Seth, married to a Vancouver city councillor, has written his first book, *A Good War: Mobilizing Canada for the Climate Emergency*.

Like his sister, Naomi Klein (of *The Shock Doctrine* and *No Logo*), he is shaping Canadian opinion and policy formation.

He was the first to note the irony of his title. The child of "peaceniks," he was reluctant to adopt the metaphor of war for his thesis, but when he researched how Canada behaved in the Second World War he realized it was fitting to describe the scope, scale and speed of what was needed then, which Canadians rose to, and what is needed now.

It is bracing to recall that our small country of 11 million people, in a six-year span, produced 16,000 aircraft and 800,000 military vehicles.

We sacrificed 45,000 lives overseas.

He turns to climate chaos and our dismal record. But Klein's attitude is, we did it then, we can do it now. From 2000 to 2018, our high greenhouse gas emissions were flatlined at 700 megatonnes.

Yet the world has just until 2050 to reach the decarbonization of the atmosphere.

Klein writes strongly and clearly and with good nature. He assumes we have already grasped the science; the dire calculations of climate scientists around the world. He focuses on political and cultural necessities with many ideas: a Youth Climate Corps, national resolve to spend what is necessary to win this "good war," because if we lose, nothing else matters; new taxes on the wealthy and the sale of Green Victory Bonds.

He calls for new Crown corporations, to "get the job done," and for the leadership of creative people.

"Determine the conversion needs," he says, "just as C.D. Howe did in 1940."

How many heat pumps, solar panels, wind turbines, electric buses and so on? Invoke the War Measures Act. Match workers to needed jobs, lower the voting age and prepare to receive tens of thousands of climate-displaced people annually. Mandate the end of gas-powered vehicles by 2025; mandate the end of fossil-fueled homes by 2040.

Canadians are deeply anxious about the threats upon us, so Klein's ideas do not seem so drastic.

The American Election: Shock and Horror
October 15, 2020

I've been gently chided for commenting too often on the looming election in the republic to the south of us.

However, I make bold with another piece because I am persuaded that that great, shuddering democracy, now at 244 years of age, is either awakening at last to its imminent peril, or succumbing to incipient fascism. That is too ominous for any of us to ignore.

The first presidential debate was debased by the behaviour of the sitting president. He ran roughshod over his opponent, the moderator and us, so that all semblance of civility was surrendered in a flurry of fact-free, personal insult. The 90-minute exposure became an ordeal: A classic case of abuse, shown to 71 million voters in the US and several hundred thousand Canadians.

A brutal man attempted to overpower another, in the absence of rational argument, heckling and shouting at a rate of 128 loud interruptions per hour (some people keep track of these numbers), in the face of a moderator out of his depth.

Wrote American Sherry Peters Wafford on Twitter, "Canadians probably feel like they live in the apartment above a meth lab right about now."

A favourite cartoon showed a large split-screen TV. One half, the presidential face, is covered by a tea towel, and the caption says, "Grandma has had enough."

And for Canada? Here we have, once again in our living rooms, an object lesson in citizenship and politics. We have been granted the dubious privilege of being involved watchers.

We must learn, and quickly, how a poorly-educated, and unreflective electorate, fed vicious lies on social media and other platforms, unable to face its racist past or come to terms with its inequalities, is on the brink of destroying its own noble experiment in living together.

I took part recently in a Zoom call with 45 American feminists. They wanted to know why Canada is so far ahead in progressive policies and views. I started with the two original notions: The American, "Life, liberty and the pursuit of happiness," and the Canadian, "Peace, order and good government."

The first is confident and startlingly self-centred; the second, modest and communal. The second underlies our halting but real attempts to put flesh on the idea of the common good: equality, universal services, a fair tax system, inclusion of all and, more recently, making amends with Indigenous people. The first glorifies the individual and his tribe before all.

The searing divisions and threats of violence in the run-up to election in the U.S. are revealed, none more so than by the assiduous work of CNN fact-checker Daniel Dale.

He wrote, "Trump lies about every conceivable subject, but voting and the election might be the single subject on which he is most thoroughly dishonest." Ah, the value of good journalists. The New York Times revealed that the "Midas touch" man owes more than $400 million to unknown creditors. This gives them leverage over him.

A Peterborough friend, an American scholar, tells me has mailed in his ballot, giving it four weeks to arrive. He has two friends who have done the same. "Peterborough," he laughed, "based on three votes, is solidly Biden-Harris."

For my part, I hear the U.N. may be seeking volunteers to be election monitors. I will sign up.

Finally, from American journalist Anand Giridharadas, "He hosted a superspreader event to honour a justice who would have the government control your body and refuse the duty of care for it, and when the virus he helped go around, comes around, he avails of the health care he would deny others, financed by the taxes he refuses to pay."

That, to me, is a perfectly crafted sentence. It rings with reality.

We hope for a massive rejection of this American administration, for all our sakes. And the complete exit of its dominant player.

A Canadian Speaks on Resisting this Supreme Court Nominee

October 22, 2020

What Canadian cares about an appointment to the U.S. Supreme Court? It seems a lot of us do, mindful as we are of the multiple breaches of law, precedent and civil norms committed by the president and his administration on a daily basis in the last four years. Mindful too, of the immense power of that high court, sitting in Washington with nine members, two of whom are women, in lifetime positions.

It involves an unfortunate death, an unseemly, hasty process to fill the seat by the Republicans before the election, a questionable nominee and an insult to the legacy of the recently departed feminist justice, Ruth Bader Ginsburg.

It also changes the composition of the nine-member court from the present 4-4 liberal-conservative split, with Chief Justice John Roberts, a question mark in any decision, usually siding with the conservatives. If this nominee, a person who is deeply conservative, with only two years on a bench of any kind is confirmed later this month, a 6-3 majority for the right-wing will be established.

Talk about culture wars. Such a majority would cast America to the far-right of the spectrum for decades to come. On health care, on immigration, on climate, on reproductive rights.

A friend said to me this morning "Trumpy things seep over the border no matter what." So I pay attention, not only because I proudly share the same initials as Ruth Bader Ginsburg (RBG). This week I was relieved to have an opportunity to speak out against the whole sham, along with a number of American leaders, in a statement deploring the nomination of Amy Coney Barrett.

Since much has been made of her Catholic identity, we spoke as Catholics, of very different positions from her on issues.

The statement will go out to the media and to all 100 Senators. My name and nationality will no doubt grab the attention of the senators from Montana or Alabama. But seriously, other signatories will attract attention, I am sure.

The coalition issuing the declaration is "Women-Church Convergence," a coalition of 30 Catholic-rooted women's organizations in the states including Dignity, the Women's Ordination Conference, Catholics for Choice and several orders of nuns.

It says, "We urge the Senate to stop the process before it further erodes our democracy. We suggest that Judge Barrett signal her unwillingness to participate in such a charade. After the November election, the duly-elected chief executive can resubmit her name or begin again with another candidate. A clean process is in everyone's best interest."

It continues, "The current nomination is tainted by a flawed process that will forever affix an asterisk to any justice nominated under such circumstances: an election already underway, and a rush to install, with clear implications for Post-election cases."

"We have serious concerns about the judgment of any nominee who would collaborate in material ways in such a morally dubious enterprise. To collaborate in the public corruption of the judicial system is to create scandal."

The Women-Church letter goes on, "Judge Barrett is a moral agent capable and responsible for making her own choices. But even an appearance of willingness to put her own agency and integrity in service of a long-standing, conservative, and parochial agenda is deeply troubling to us. We cry foul here, not simply because we disagree with her on many substantive issues to which she has the right to her opinions, but because the process diminishes and demeans all involved. We state the obvious when we say that Amy Coney Barrett does not represent us or legions of Catholics who find the agenda of the current administration morally repugnant. We are pro-choice and pro-family; pro-LGBTQTI rights and pro-marriage-equality. Systemic racism and climate change are not matters of opinion. Facts must ground judicial decisions."

Women-Church Convergence, to which I happily belong, amplifies diverse feminist, faith-filled voices. We raise our voices to call a halt to this pernicious process and return to fair and honourable bipartisan practices.

Hate Speech and Disinformation Find a New Platform Online
October 29, 2020

Sophocles, the great Greek playwright who wrote tragedies around 500 BC, said something that reverberates today. "Nothing vast enters the life of mortals without a curse."

In this century, we are trying to cope with both the blessing and the curse of the World Wide Web. It entered our lives only 20 years ago, and has become dominant in the age of COVID-19. Anyone who cares about our culture and our kids must analyze both its good effects, and its dreadful ones.

The web can find an organ donor for a needy patient, offer up urgent news or show an inspiring poem. At another time, it can empower hate groups or depress a teenager who is being bullied online. We must reduce and regulate its damage, at the same time acknowledging its positive effects. Every country is struggling to understand the communications revolution in its awesome power and reach.

Then there is the additional question of guarding free speech.

In a recent New Yorker magazine article, writer Andrew Marantz said bluntly, "Facebook is overrun with hate speech and disinformation." And conspiracy theories, I would add. Although it has policies against their spread, the corporate giant inadequately moderates the input, too rarely takes down an ugly post, and seems to exempt certain toxic politicians. White supremacists and ISIS use the networks it to recruit members and spread hate.

Facebook has three billion monthly posts, and several thousand moderators all over the world look them over. Many seek mental health counselling after viewing a day of them.

But Facebook maintains it is not a publisher of content, since true publishers are subject to hate and libel laws, but is merely a platform for "user-generated content." These are weasel words from tech giants disavowing responsibility for giving a megaphone to those enabling child abuse, incitement to suicide, pornography and other evils. Meantime, the social fabric frays and erodes.

There is a new documentary called "The Social Dilemma" on Netflix (and who among us doesn't know Netflix now, because of the isolations of COVID-19). It is an important 90 minutes of watching and listening to fine-looking young men from Silicon Valley in California, all white, almost all aged 20 to 35, who have been former innovators and employees of the internet giants, Facebook, Google, Twitter, Apple and Pinterest.

They are bright and they have consciences. They speak about their worries regarding the technology they helped develop. They have left their jobs because of ethical concerns. So they warn us and equip us with some harm-sniffing awareness. Several keep devices away entirely from their children; others keep strict rules about their use such as time limits, storage outside bedrooms and the like.

"They become 'digital pacifiers,'" one said.

I watched "The Social Dilemma" because I am a grandmother concerned about the dependence of my grandchildren, and to a lesser extent, my grown-up children, on their devices. There is a cartoon around showing a gleaming phone attached by a strong chain to a heavy ball.

Teachers makes rules about students dropping phones into a box on entering class, lecturers refuse to teach to a room full of undergraduates looking attentive but focusing on Facebook, and pedestrians bumping into others, oblivious to everything and everyone around them, so plugged-in are they.

The young people on "The Social Dilemma" say that the big corporations are selling our eyeballs to advertisers. It's lucrative. The internet companies are the richest in human history.

"Only tech companies and the drug industry call customers 'users,'" says one interviewee wryly. "It is a drug, and dopamine is released," says another. "We all become more afraid and more anxious."

I will soon comment on a thoughtful response to this dilemma in Canada, written by Daniel Bernhard of "Friends of Canadian Broadcasting."

Enjoy Those Little Moments
in the Midst of All This News
November 5, 2020

How's it going, eh? Just routine trivia today.

That may be a relief from the apocalyptic happenings down south. My American sisters are in distress at the appointment of that judge. The Supreme Court now has six right-wing Catholic justices. Out of nine. Doesn't seem balanced or representative to me. I take no pleasure in that. I stand with AOC on the principles of faith and politics.

The Founding Fathers from 1776 are not looking too good these days either. Politicians of the machiavellian sort are using and abusing the Constitution for their partisan purposes, and the Republican campaign tricks break all rules.

America may need an amendment to the 25th Amendment, strengthening the section about the mental capacity of a sitting president.

Overall, it will be so good to return from CNN (I know all the hosts now) to CBC news and commentary.

We've had 30 family Zoom calls on Sundays since lockdown, so that's how long this ordeal is lasting. The turnout continues to be fairly solid and we end up laughing. Emma, age 11, is a voracious reader and holds up her latest book. The family is riddled with English teachers so there is always someone to comment on the book.

Grandson Jack, 17, on Vancouver Island, had to give an inspirational talk of one and a half minutes to his school assembly. He told the story of flunking his driver's test.

Cousin Megan in Edmonton shared her woe at the same outcome. Those western roads may be safer as our young drivers try again.

Jack ended up telling his audience that the good news was his braces were coming off.

There's snow today. I got myself long underwear, grey of course, and registered for the local Winter Wheels program, whereby I pledge to cycle at least once a week from November to March. In exchange I fill in surveys and have winter tires put on my bike.

In other news, there is the story of the lost-and-found hearing aid. You know what they cost. This year, with hat, eyeglasses, mask and hearing aid, it is all too much for the back of the ear. Yesterday I plunked myself down in the driver's seat of the car, ripped off the mask, and heard a slight noise. Hearing aid had disappeared. A lot of unladylike minutes were spent searching with flashlight, to no avail.

At the Honda dealer, Cindy Lester, Tony Minicola et al, bless them, said "Bring'er in." There, two lads, Eddie, and another pleasant chap in a hoodie, used a magnet to find the heading aid and save me big bucks.

Father Leo Coughlin, old friend, has published a coil-bound *Daily Reflections* book and distributed 300 from his back door. He is a pastor for all.

For Halloween, my engineering-student grandson built a chute for candy. His siblings urge a catapult. Me, I used tongs, and Pringles in small packets. The government of Ontario left it up to us to decide how to mark Halloween. I printed off an orange-and-black sign saying, "Halloween Here." The other choice was "See you next year."

There were a few kids out on our street, all protocols observed.

I have two friends who have adopted the routine of asking, "Who needs cheering up?" and "Who can a give a cheering-up today?" I met John Martyn, our finest housing advocate, and he told me, "Here's a cheery story: we at the Mount just opened five new apartments for people in need." I met him as we both were picking up a copy of Pope Francis' recent letter on friendship and social solidarity.

My book club met on Zoom and dealt with being cut off after 45 minutes. Then we rejoined, tech wizards, all. We were reading Seth Klein. All liked it.

So ends the trivia stories. Maybe they are as important in meaning as the breaking news. It will break Tuesday. We will stand.

Protecting Canadians Means
Getting Control of the Media Giants
November 12, 2020

Recently, my column discussed the harmful effects of huge web corporations. The data came from revelations from inside the industry, former employees in Silicon Valley, disgusted at the harm being done. They charged their bosses with inadequate policing and infrequent withdrawal of hateful content.

Now, I praise a made-in-Canada analysis from Friends of Canadian Broadcasting executive director Daniel Bernhard. It is an impressive report of 48 pages. Not a lawyer but an informed social critic, Bernhard spent the summer thinking about Michael Enright's rousing sign-off after 50 years of dedication to public broadcasting. Enright hosted "The Sunday Edition" for 30 years on CBC radio.

He said, "The first thing a tyrant does is shut down the public broadcaster."

I believe that part of the reason we in Canada have not gone down the dark path of the U.S, in its threatening divisions seen so clearly, is that we have had the enormous benefit, since the 1940s, of an arms-length, adequately funded public broadcaster, informing us, assimilating our differences, telling our stories and showing us each other, in a fair and positive light.

The strongest democracies around the world do likewise. But the U.S. is riven by private, for-profit broadcasters. Imagine being subject to the biased, inflammatory Fox News as your daily source of information. Or to the hateful posts on Twitter, which have so contributed to Mr. Trump's ascendancy, at the same time as they plunge American values lower.

Presenting extremist positions and driven by ratings and profits, such networks undermine communal feelings, increase grievance and betray truth. Is Facebook, for example, to be permitted to pollute our democracy and pit us against each other? Will Netflix be allowed to take billions in ad money out of our country with no obligation to invest in our stories?

Bernard researched and wrote a 48-page paper intended, he says, to educate MPs and other decision-makers. And us citizens, too. Called "Platforms for Harm," it was launched on a webinar a month ago which featured former Environment Minister Catherine McKenna of Ottawa speaking of the terrible abuse she endured online. It led to the trashing of her office.

As Bernard says, "The early internet held out promises of Eden, but it delivered anarchy instead." It is the greatest tool for informational exchange since the printing press. But double-edged it is. It increases global connectivity while being overshadowed by hate speech, bullying, disinformation, and other illegal content.

The companies, he argues, not only disseminate harmful content to millions, but, having learned of our tastes through data collection, proactively recommend harmful content to users. Bernard holds that present Canadian law "while certainly imperfect, is decently equipped to beat back the online harms."

Can we use our current laws? In our courts? Can we lift the burden of complaint from the individual citizen who, when harmed, has only the option of taking a giant corporation to court in a "titanic imbalance of power," that is, certainly a "barrier to justice."

The Canadian government through an agency such as the privacy commissioner must do the suing, and hold those who threaten the public good responsible for the harms they inflict. Do it urgently, argues Bernhard. Courts must learn and fast. And impose big fines.

There are two rights at stake here: One, the right to free speech and two, the right to be protected against defamation and hate. A line between acceptable and unlawful speech does exist in our common law tradition and must be invoked, in a court before a judge. We must build up a number of decided cases with appropriate penalties assessed.

Then we can show the world we are leading in confronting this great modern challenge to civic and personal well-being. Bernhard's paper should get us thinking and talking.

As well as supporting his group, "Friends of Canadian Broadcasting."

The U.S. Voting is Over, But the Division Remains
November 19, 2020

In the reams of posts, cartoons and opinions which I looked at over the torturous few days of the American election, I most often clicked "save" on a poem. Poetry is the mode of expression adequate for these soul-sized times. Here is one I clicked.

"We need to sit on the rim of the well of darkness/and fish for fallen light/with patience," by Pablo Neruda, the Nobel-winning poet from Chile.

Fishing for fallen light is what America must do now and for some time to come. More than 70 million voters, knowing all about children in cages, about 230,000 fellow citizens dead from COVID-19, about insults to minorities, the disabled and soldiers, about gloats regarding conquests of women, about the cultivation of white supremacists, and about 20,000 documented lies uttered while in office, still voted for this president. "That is what hurts," said Van Jones, an African-American commentator on CNN, in tears.

On Twitter, I follow Gerald Butts, the smart Cape Bretoner and friend of the prime minister who served as his principal secretary. Butts writes succinctly and wittily. He said early on election night, "We think of ourselves and the Americans as being very much alike. We are not alike." Another poster said, "I don't ever again want to hear someone say, "This is not who we are. This is clearly who half of us are."

How that must sting conscientious Americans. Who dares say that he or she understands these voters? We know the arsonist-in-chief lights flames of grievance and calls for violence when he is cornered, but what is motivating them?

White guys we get, but Latino men and African-American men too? Catholics? Evangelicals? What is it in them that Trump speaks to?

I really wish I had studied more abnormal psychology. Failing that, I turn to poetry, whose very ambiguity gives me some insight. In 1933, as Stalin was opening his gulags, a Jewish-Russian poet, Osip Mandelstam, wrote, "We live without sensing the country beneath us. Our speech is inaudible at ten paces."

That resonates with us today through our masks and our deep sense that we don't "get" America any more. The dogs of war were unleashed by this immoral man, but we didn't know such hate was hidden there. A lot of reflection and investigation must follow if America is to come together with the slightest sense of renewed understanding of itself. And work to reform its outdated electoral system which so baffles the world and did not serve this election well.

At McGill, American-born professor Jason Opal savaged this electoral system. Set up in 1787, it endows the states with 538 "electors," nameless people who must vote as directed by the voters in their States. He said, "Today we have hyper-partisan hatred. America is an outlier among democracies. We need a Canada-like, national, non-partisan commission, such as Elections Canada, running the show, evenly, across the country."

I have a thoughtful friend here in Peterborough, John, who says, "I am a 70-year old liberal dismayed by their unhealthy views of God, their belief in a prosperity gospel, their juvenile understanding of socialism and its benefits, and the corruption of their political system with big money, gerrymandering and voter suppression." A glimmer of hope, indeed a bright light, has been President-elect Joe Biden's behaviour, highlighted by a masterful speech in which he dared to quote biblical sources (Ecclesiastes), a beloved hymn by Minnesota priest Michael Joncas called "On Eagles Wings," and poetry by Irish poet Seamus Heaney.

"History says 'Don't hope
this side of the grave.'
But then, once in a lifetime,
the longed-for tidal wave
of justice can rise up,
And hope and history rhyme."

For those Canadians galvanized by the efforts of one Stacey Abrams to mobilize voters in Georgia for their January 5 runoffs for two Senate spots, there is the website "New Georgia Project." I don't think we can donate money but we can send cheer.

"Progressive" Pontiff Falls Short in Some Areas
November 26, 2020

It's a hard thing to be in a position such as I am today: a fan in many respects of the leadership shown by Pope Francis, the Argentine pastor and a brainy Jesuit too, who has been head of the Roman Catholic Church for seven years.

At the same time, I am a sharp critic of his major blind spot, which is really a big one, regarding gender, women and sexuality.

The man is, as we say in Jamaica, very vexing, all taken together.

One's head spins. Last week, he was quoted in a film called "Francesco" as accepting "civil unions" for LGBTQ2 people, a huge progressive step forward. It is getting a thunderous rejection from traditionalists, even among his own bishops. But it is completely the right thing to do and shows his profound pastoral side.

Yet the Vatican, which perhaps has him trapped, is "walking the statement back" in a letter to the world's bishops.

I also applaud his two important letters; the one five years ago entitled "Laudato Si (Praise to You)," a quote from his favourite saint, Francis of Assisi. That work was hailed by scientists all over the world. The respected environmentalist Bill McKibben of 350.org recently quoted it again.

Based on solid scientific evidence, which the Pope acquired from scientists he brought in to advise him, it focused on the cultural, ethical and spiritual aspects of the climate crisis, appropriate for a religious leader. He used the term "integral ecology" because he wanted to jointly hold up the earth and the human, both in distress.

"Laudato Si" remains a key modern exhortation, widely hailed around the "secular" world as timely, preceptive and profound. To the everlasting shame of the middle management of his church of 1.2 billion people, it never got the exposure at the grassroots which it should have. A faithful parish member shouldn't have to go online to www.vatican.va and dig up important statements from the supreme leader. These gentlemen-bishops should never assume their posts without teacher education in their resumes.

Now comes his long letter, October 3, about social friendship and the deep divisions in societies, called "Fratelli Tutti," in Italian, "Dear brothers."

Oh dear, the exclusively masculine language again: he could so easily have added "Sorori" (sisters), too. A few good women in his circle would have helped him avoid such an error, which deeply offends modern sensibilities. He quoted no women at all.

It is a long letter, fully 40,000 words and easily readable. No country is mentioned by name, but the slide of America toward authoritarianism was clearly on the Pope's mind. He feels the pandemic has laid bare the inequalities and injustices of our world.

Francis has developed a remarkable friendship with the grand Imam of the mosque in Cairo, and it is this inter-spiritual context he speaks from. "Laudato Si" taught that everything is connected, and this letter asserts that everyone is connected too.

Interestingly, the letter condemns capital punishment and does away with the long Catholic tradition of the "just war."

Then in a small but significant step on October 26, Pope Francis announced 13 new cardinals the men who will elect his successor. The bishop of Washington, a Black man named Wilton Gregory, was named to the group. He stood up to criticize Donald Trump after that photo op in front of a church when the president awkwardly held a bible.

But virtue begins at home, and the Vatican is rife with rivalries, power struggles, financial funny business, unresolved pedophilia scandals and obtuseness in regard to the needs of its members.

One sympathetic critic, the Franciscan Sister Ilia Delio, wrote with sorrow that the Pope speaks to the world because he is not heard at home.

He could, before his end, appoint women cardinals, rescind several damaging teachings about human sexuality and let some fresh air in.

Peterborough's Camp Kawartha, the Environment, Straw Bales and Influence
December 3, 2020

It has been fully eight years since I last visited Camp Kawartha, our district's own 100-year-old, non-profit camp for kids and adults on Clear Lake. Back then, in 2012, with Jamaican Self-Help, I brought 20 teenage volunteers who were on their way to Kingston, Jamaica to the camp for a weekend briefing on cross-cultural learning. Then later, we came back to integrate the formidable experience in the global south into their lives.

But I found out recently I am very much behind on the remarkable achievements at two sites: the camp itself and its second site, the Camp Kawartha Environment Centre, built in 2009 on Pioneer Road on 200 acres of wetland at Trent University. So I made busy to get up to speed.

Experience and education about the natural world is creatively offered in the two locations. Perhaps just in the nick of time. We all have a sense of peril at the state of the earth, damaged by overconsumption and bad practices. But most of us are left without entry points, or consistent ways of changing our habits and our politics. Enter these two places and the people who have created them.

Jacob Rodenburg is the visionary director of Camp Kawartha. He grew up in Ottawa, roaming the outdoors, "a feral child," he says with a grin. But he followed that childhood with degrees at Queen's including a Masters in Education, and leadership in the Katimavik program. A national leader in environmental education, Rodenburg says that advocacy begins with caring, moves to commitment and culminates in action.

The overall goal is to inspire a new generation of environmental leaders in Canada.

First founded by the Rotary Club in 1921, as a summer camp for Peterborough kids to get into nature, Camp Kawartha now hosts some 1000 children and teens each summer.

But it has become year-round, at both the original and the second site at Trent. In a normal school year, the camp offers more than 80 outdoor programs linked to the Ontario Ministry of Education curriculum, from kindergarten to Grade 12, and eco-certification to student teachers. Some 10,000 people come to the places each year.

In this COVID-19 year, it has nimbly pivoted to offer a Forest School, which is a European model: a school day spent outdoors. Partnerships are all important in the development of the vision here. They include Trent and Fleming, the Rotary Club, the Gainey Foundation, the school boards, Green Up and others. There are "green" entrepreneurs such as Chris Magwood and Jen Feighen of Endeavour Centre, and Deidre McGahern of Straworks, experts in doing and teaching straw-bale building.

Camp Kawartha's fourth straw-bale building, a health centre, is underway, to be ready in June 2021. It is "net zero," a 1400 square-foot building with straw bales as insulation. These are acquired from a farmer near Port Hope at $6 a bale. Net zero" means zero carbon, zero water and zero toxins.

Deirdre McGahern, a Mount Allison university graduate in fine arts and a construction technologist, has been in business since 2004 in Peterborough. "We have a triple bottom line," she says, "the dollars, the carbon footprint and how well it fosters connection."

I don't need convincing that mental health is connected to regular and sustained contact with nature. I'm even winter biking, wobbly but willing. Another principle of the camp is "regeneration," doing less harm for sure, but also creating places that are healthy for both people and the planet.

Camp Kawartha is fundraising for financial help with this building, led by volunteer David Goyette. The website is www.campkawartha.ca/health-centre. It would be investing in a better future.

A teacher said recently, "We have been growing a society of learned helplessness about the outdoors. We need Camp Kawarthas all the more." On Wednesday, I joined those hardy youth in Cam Douglas' "Youth Leadership in Sustainability" class, hoisting a straw bale myself.

These thought leaders and activists could very well change the future.

Lease for Life, Lease on Life at The Mount Community Centre in Peterborough
December 10, 2020

Housing is once again on everybody's mind. We are distressed by the pictures of the homeless being moved off their "squats" by authorities, and are constantly concerned by the numbers of poor and confused persons begging downtown.

Our society needs all kinds of housing; all price levels, all densities, all possible designs and with the health of the environment in mind.

Here in Peterborough we have a very successful and highly-regarded model of an integrated community, achieved in just eight years, The Mount Community Centre (TMCC).

As of 2020, it has 63 affordable apartment rentals, and several significant non-residential tenants who share the vision and values of the Mount, and provide a revenue stream. These tenants include St. Paul's Presbyterian Church, the Rowan Tree School, the Kawartha Land Trust and the Victorian Order of Nurses.

It has a state-of-the-art food centre which provides training and education in food preparation, and delivers meals as part of the Meals on Wheels service to seniors in the city. It has a community garden nestled in its attractive green space.

Now, the visionary board of The Mount Community Centre, led by chair Steve Kylie, is considering a new project. It is to build and sell market-value, life-leases, for 15 units which would be renovated in the oldest wing of the former convent.

The purposes are twofold, says Kylie.

"First, life-leases will attract a broader diversity of people to live in the Mount spaces. Second, they will provide upfront funding for reinvesting in social housing. Life-lease holders would pay the total amount for their unit upfront. This capital can be used to build more affordable housing units."

The "life lease" concept is not common in Peterborough. The life-lease holders purchase a condo-style unit and have a right to live in the unit for the balance of their lifetime, although they do not actually own the unit.

For this reason, units will likely be somewhat cheaper in price than other condo developments in town. The owners of TMCC life-leases can sell and bequeath their unit. They do not pay rent, since they have bought outright, but they will pay a monthly maintenance fee, as happens in other condo arrangements. In addition, they can sell their unit.

Government looks kindly on such arrangements since they increase housing stock, and therefore it does not charge land-transfer taxes on the purchase of a life-lease, provided it is the principal residence of the buyer and it is sponsored by a non-profit organization such as The Mount Community Centre.

It is a new concept that offers housing for people not in high need, but who wish to live in an integrated type of neighbourhood and who have a fondness for the Mount.

They may wish to contribute more fully to the social good that is created when housing for more low-income people is provided.

Potential buyers may also be impressed by the Mount's long history of good works. They may appreciate the location on Monaghan Road.

"We need to consider the long-term sustainability of our projects," says Kylie.

He knows of other successful housing life-lease development including one in Lindsay. Usually they are initiated by a non-profit group, often a faith group.

"For me," says board member John Martyn, "It is profit with a purpose."

Profit with a purpose is a strategy gaining steam globally. It accepts that non-profits seek out profit opportunities to ensure the sustainability of their works.

Aid Group Continues Honduras Relief During Pandemic
December 17, 2020

With an air of hope and determination even in a difficult COVID-19 year, the board and supporters of the local international aid group, Friends of Honduran Children met virtually in November.

With Zoom technology, they were able to bring in their Honduran partner Carolina Aguero of Sociedad Amigos de los Ninos, who reported on conditions in the Central American country, especially in the children's village, called "Nuevo Paraiso" that Friends has supported since 1980. It has 150 children and teens living in homes of 12 with a woman (a "tia"or "aunt") in charge.

Aguero said that the country, with a population of 9 million people and a poverty rate of 60 percent, has experienced severe food shortages, and has an inflation rate of 4 percent, but no reported surge in the crime rate. The difference in the per capita annual income between Canada and Honduras is staggering: $47,000 to $5000.

"Spirituality and solidarity have been our main supports," she said.

Hunger has increased in the pandemic, especially in the aftermath of two hurricanes. Earlier in the summer, Friends organized a special drive for funds for food baskets in the capital city of Tegucigalpa itself. The food packages included cornmeal, beans, oil, rice and pasta for several weeks.

Just as a measure of the hardship in Honduras, the U.S. State Department and the Canadian government advise no travel to the country, but that message is for tourists. For Friends, courage and tenacity lead their work. For the brigades of volunteers, educational, medical and construction, extra security is arranged.

Finance chair Peter White reported that although donations in 2020 had decreased, Friends was still able to transfer more than half a million dollars to Honduras. A registered charity with an office on Clonsilla Avenue at Westmount Plaza, and two employees, Friends has more than 1,000 donors.

It is a remarkable story of quiet Peterborough philanthropy. Started by Dr. Jim McCallum and his wife Anne McCallum in 1993, FoHC's parent organization had been Horizons of Friendship in Cobourg. When Horizons expanded into other Central American countries, the local supporters decided to intensify their support of Sister Maria Rosa Leggol, an inspirational Honduran nun.

Sr. Maria Rosa died in October at age 93. She had instilled in scores of Honduran youth, teachers and social workers and international volunteers a deep commitment to aid their society. Libby Dalrymple, who teaches Spanish at Lakefield College School, reported via video with ESL teacher, Luis, about his work with the children at the Village. Skills in English and Spanish will help them in later education and employment. The village has a technical high school, and Friends offers scholarships for impoverished students in the surrounding area to attend.

Retired Peterborough teacher Dan Durst has long been interested in the children as they become young adults. He was instrumental in bringing two sisters, Fanny and Evin, to Fleming College in 2017. They graduated with honours and went on to Cleveland to John Carroll University, sponsored by a professor there. For several years, Grace United Church, led by minister Lyle Horn, has given volunteers and funds to Friends. They organize building teams. and small schools in seven villages near Nuevo have been constructed. Jane Bleecker of Grace Church has volunteered nine years in a row.

Medical teams led by Dr. Kathy Chapman of Lindsay take personnel and supplies to remote villages around Nuevo Paraiso, often facing challenging terrain. Volunteers raise funds to finance their brigade.

The meeting announced its Volunteer of the Year award, to the Life Team at Trinity United Church. It was accepted by Chris and Dave Freeman. Trinity's congregation has sponsored two children since 2009. Also Installed at the meeting were two new directors, Steve Bark and Gary Lister. Friends continue to be one of those valuable strands in Peterborough consciousness that contributes to international understanding, and leads back to good work at home.

President Anne Morawetz and team deserve thanks and recognition. More details are at www.friendsofhonduranchildren.org.

Almost Too Much Good News Lately. Really.
December 24, 2020

How much good news can a girl take in one day? For me, that day was December 11, 2020. It was news from the public realm, the private realm and the one in between, the sports world.

All together, a day to remember.

First off, the Supreme Court of the United States, politicized and distrusted since DJT packed it with three right-winging judges, Kavanaugh, Gorsuch and Coney-Barrett, and amid fears that that court would side with him on every bizarre thing, issued a prompt rebuke of the wacky Texas-initiated motion to invalidate the election results in four American states.

The court said no, based largely on the hallowed American belief in states' rights, with no interference from other states. Wars have been fought on that matter.

So, good on you, SCOTUS for upholding the law. I saw a good joke, "When will we come to the place where Corona is a beer, and Donald is a duck?"

Maybe that will happen before long, patient Canadian readers. We will watch closely other cases before that court, because their record on cultural matters is not a good one.

And take a break, Anderson Cooper, Daniel Dale, Chris Cuomo and Abby Phillip, those intrepid CNN warriors, who have educated their viewers and expressed their moral outrage for months over the ex-president and his threat to the integrity of the country. Good for you, Joe Biden, for holding your fire with such discipline, trusting, against many odds, in the process.

Good news No. 2.

On December 11, the same day, the federal government of Canada announced a meaty climate action plan that is "really courageous," said Adam Radwanski in the Globe and Mail.

It is five years since we signed the Paris Accord and promised to cut our carbon emissions by 30 percent by the year 2030. Environment minister Jonathan Wilkinson announced an ambitious, 10-year plan whereby carbon price is to go up by $15 a tonne each year after 2022 till it reaches $170 a tonne in 2030.

It will enable us to achieve our goal but it is a "market mechanism" and will garner heavy opposition from Conservative premiers. However, the rebate part of the increase in costs is scheduled to go to Canadians quarterly.

Mark Jaccard of Simon Fraser University urged Canadian to rally behind the plan. I tweeted Jaccard, asking him for bullet points I could publish. There is going to be some pain in rising prices at the pumps, but there is going to be a whole lot of gain, say environmentalists. Not here at home but in other parts of the world, climate heat is making living impossible.

Perhaps the environmental minister has been reading Canada's best popularizer of solid environmental information, Drew Monkman, who writes exclusively in The Examiner. I am proud to share pages with him. Let the Liberals go to the polls on this climate change plan. We are sufficiently worried about global warming that we will support them.

Good new three: same day, we got word that vaccines for COVID-19 had been approved and were being shipped to locations all over the world. The first injection was to an Englishwoman, who said it made her "feel great." Two vaccines require freezing temperatures; the third can be at room temperature. I'll wait my turn and wear my mask and turn down all invitations to parties.

Adding to all this good news, I watched my two teenage grandchildren in B.C. speak at a school assembly (Brentwood has in-person classes) in "cohorts," and tell their peers about their handicapped 11 year-old-brother and the appropriate way to include him.

The icing on the Christmas cake: the Raptors, many new and lively, started playing again. What's not to love about a brown-skinned guy with reddish hair named Malachi Flynn, who can pot three-pointers?

I'll spend tomorrow reading Yuval Harari's *21 Ideas for the 21st Century*, having my Swiss Chalet and attending a Zoom mass. Then, Merlot.

Ringing in the New Year
the Scots Way in Peterborough
December 31, 2020

About a year ago, I sent off my sample of saliva and $80 to Ancestry.ca for an analysis of my ethnic heritage. The company then tried to upsell me. For more money, I could find out names and places of my ancestors. I declined this kind offer, since I was afraid of finding out more about sheep thieves, or worse.

The report about who I really am came back promptly. I am 80 percent Celtic, that is, Scots and Irish, though no breakdown between them was given. I am also 15 percent Nordic. One son laughed. "That'll never get you a Norwegian passport, Mom."

In my growing up years, the Irish part was pretty well present. I knew about poetry, holy wells, St Brigid's cloak, little people, the Great Famine of the 1840's, those English oppressors, religious wars, the Easter Uprising of 1916, Kilmainham Jail and so on. But the Scottish part not so much.

So this year, the Year of the Pandemic, I set out to remedy that situation. I started with Google, and then, providentially, went to Miriam McFadyen of Aylmer Street, a true Scottish lass. Miriam, a nurse, came to Canada in 1990, recruited by St. Michael's Hospital in Toronto and has made a full and generously-lived life since. I decided to order a Hogmanay meal ("with or without haggis?" They asked), which I saw mentioned in the Examiner, cooked at Hutchison House, our Brock Street treasure which recreates the early days of Scottish settlers in Peterborough.

I ordered the take-away meal for December 31. Who could resist tatties and neeps, oatcakes, Scotch eggs and potted salmon? And clootie dumpling? Not I.

One supplies one's own whisky.

In 1836, Peterborough's first doctor, John Hutchison, needed a home for his family of five children. Community members rallied with materials and labour to build it. The cost was $244. Dr Hutchison went on to host his 18 year-old cousin, Sandford Fleming for two years. The latter went on to great fame. Hutchison House is tenderly kept as a living museum by the Peterborough Historical Society. It is busy with tours, teas, and educational programs even in this stripped-down pandemic year.

Hogmanay, (stress on the third syllable) puts New Year's well ahead of Christmas in importance. Christmas was for a time viewed as the domain of Roman Catholics. There are traditions such as the "first foot," meaning that your first visitor of the new year brings good luck. There is the greeting "Lang may yer lum reek" (long may your chimney smoke). Poet Robert Burns wrote "Auld Lang Syne." And some people take a dip in the Firth of Forth.

I am ready to read A History of Scotland for Dummies. It is a turbulent and complex story, beginning in 843, full of battles and intrigues and a thirst for independence, continuing until 1703 when the Scots, Irish and English signed the Act of Union and put their flags together to make the Union Jack.

The Scots, or Caledonians, had turned back the Romans 2000 years before and although they voted "Yes" to staying in the UK in 2014, they voted to stay in the European Union in 2016, against England's wishes.

It is a harsh, beautiful, mostly mountainous terrain. Many Canadian viewers have been enjoying the television drama series "Outlander" now entering its sixth season. It is a kind of time-traveler story of an English nurse in 1945 who is transported back to the Highlands in 1745.

Today modern Scotland, with 6 million people, thrives. Its First Minister is Nicola Sturgeon of the Scottish National Party. North Sea Oil has helped Scottish prosperity.

It has always had many significant thinkers - Thomas Hobbes, James Watt, Adam Smith, David Hume, Sir Walter Scott to name a few. Even J.K. Rowling. It has a famous university, St. Andrew's.

Glasgow will host the United Nations conference on the climate emergency in late 2021. This will be the most crucial meeting since the world signed the Paris Accord in 2015.

Aye to Scotland.

Monsef Looks Back at a Year of Challenges and Successes
January 7, 2021

Peterborough's Member of Parliament is marking six years in both the House of Commons in Ottawa and in the cabinet. And what a year 2020 has been.

So I decided to try to speak with her, see how she was and write a column. In late December, I called her office and spoke to her communications person, Ryan Young.

"Well, yes," he said, "Minister Monsef is doing 'media availabilities' tomorrow." That's me. He could squeeze me in with 15 minutes. Probably, I mused, between CTV and CBC. She'll have to keep her Rosemarys straight, Barton or Ganley. I took it. I'm an old schoolteacher: I can cram a lot into 15 minutes.

After all, she and I used to chat at Black Honey seven years ago, when she, so loaded with promise, was trying to decide whether to run for mayor. She has always been good at consulting others before making a decision. Good at a lot of things.

Now at the cabinet table, Monsef is one of several members speaking up for women and children, for COVID-19 relief, for the rural sector, and for Peterborough, always Peterborough.

"I headed to Ottawa with the goal of refurbishing the reputation of Peterborough-Kawartha as a thoughtful and progressive place." she says. "Ideas generated by people here make it to federal policy."

"What were your worst moments," I ask, "in this very difficult year?"

"My worst moments were personal ones," she answers. "The day my grandmother died. That was a great grief for us all. Shortly thereafter, my 'godmother,' Sr. Ruth Hennessey, in whose home on Downie Street we lived after coming to Canada as refugees when I was 11, died also. Two great women in my life gone."

And your best moments?

"There were many. The election of the 100th woman to the House of Commons (it has 338 members) was one. The leadership of the prime minister when he said there will be no cuts to services, no new taxes. We will chip away at this large deficit by green growth and investment." People know that eight out of $10 spent on COVID-19 relief have come from the federal government.

"Another great moment was hearing Finance Minister Chrystia Freeland start her fall financial update with the words 'I am a mother.'" Women have been 80 percent of health care workers, have been laid off, and have had extra care-giving and tutoring at home. Some have suffered from an increase in male violence. We need to make sure that we aren't sliding back on progress for women.

"Another good moment was seeing the way the Syrian refugees are being integrated in my riding. Yet another was the news about the earlier-than-hoped arrival of vaccines. People are recognizing our steady handling of the pandemic."

"Then there was my ability to get some needed new funds into Peterborough-Kawartha: $4.7 million for the Causeway reconstruction, $6 million toward the composting facility, almost a million dollars for 50 local organizations caring for others, almost $2 million for the police service to develop a mobile overdose response, which will divert people who use drugs away from the criminal justice system and into harm-reduction services. Plus job support in the Clean Tech sector."

"There was some money injected here in housing, $2 million for the Curve Lake water treatment system, and help for the city to get new buses. There was a substantial climate action announcement on December 12, which reflected Peterborough hopes."

Altogether in 2020, new federal funds here came to $36 million. That is in addition to the Child Tax Benefit (about $75 million) and Old Age Security and annual funding agreements already in place.

"We are in a minority position in the House, and we have the pandemic yet to defeat, but working together, locally and globally, we can prevail," Monsef concluded. Gave me new hope.

America is Now a Tarnished Model of Democracy
January 21, 2021

Millions of words have been written about America's brush with fascism this month. There is a national reckoning going on, cries of anguish and disbelief, and attempts to grasp the magnitude of what just happened. A sober undertaking, perhaps even a turning point.

Here are 650 words more, from a Canadian.

We watched, some of us too much, as events unfolded and the turpitude of certain leaders emerged. As did the heroism of a few.

Tattered and torn, the U.S. system, designed so that one branch of government (legislative, executive and judicial) can interrupt the madness and evil of another, staggered to an end, leaving a bloodied battlefield. Arrests, trials and evidence will reveal to Americans the identity of the insurrectionists, and expose any insidious co-operation from within, whether from politicians or police.

American racism, stupidity, misogyny and hatred was seen in all its nakedness. Somebody called that siege of the Capitol a "slob coup." Those white-men-galoots could be seen as tragically hilarious except for the bloodshed they caused and the foreboding they instilled. Who can ever forget the sight of the officer being crushed between doors?

But not only the confused men-babies, living in their mothers' basements, the ruffians and the enraged, were there. The polished Yale and Stanford grads were there too: Sen. Josh Hawley, who was once a law clerk for Chief Justice John Roberts and ex-mayor Rudy Giuliani.

They are much worse because they know better.

The world is disabused of any vestiges of awe about America. A newspaper in Kenya headlined, "Who is the banana republic now?" The Pope said "I am astonished. They have been the symbol of democracy and freedom around the world for two centuries."

Peggy Noonan in the Wall Street Journal said, "I have resisted Nazi comparisons for five years. But that is what is happening; the same kind of spirit Hitler had. At the end he intended to blow up Germany, since his people had let him down."

Another American commentator, Michael Sean Winters, wrote, "We do not know, and God willing will never be forced to find out, the lengths to which Donald Trump would have gone to preserve his power." Winters finds a closer comparison between Trump and Mussolini.

What is the antidote to such mass delusion? That is the question. Courts have ruled that the election was indeed free and fair. That has failed to convince the hard core of conspiracy people. "How now to reattach 60 million trumpers to reality?" asked former evangelical Frank Shaeffer.

Humour, dark as it was, helped us all through the days. A cartoon showed a cat on his hind legs, in a heavy sweater, peering over a wall of snow, southward. "What are they doing over there?" In salty Maritime language, even funnier. Another Twitter post said, "What is the good of a liberal arts degree? Oh, I don't know. Not be brainwashed by a death cult or storm the Capitol?"

Another, "We spend $750 billion annually on defence, and the centre of government is taken over in two hours by a duck dynasty and a guy in a Chewbacca bikini."

Almost as ironic was the fact that two California billionaires, Jack Dorsey of Twitter and Mark Zuckerberg of Facebook, finally stopped Trumpian power by flicking a switch.

Janette Platana, a Peterborough writer, posted a picture of the three louts in the Capitol rotunda and announced a contest. "All wrong answers, please. Name this rock band." Peterborough wit was sparkling. Here's some of what came in, "The Aryan Monkeys," "The Ungrateful Living," "Public Enema," "KKKurt Vile," and "FU2."

The United States is a severely tarnished model now, and every friend of the country is sorrowing. Maybe it was inevitable, after four years of unrelenting demagoguery. America will have to be reimagined. And we do well to see to our own delusions and incivilities.

How a Peterborough Man Shines Through a National Tragedy
January 28, 2021

Just a year ago, on January 7, 2020, we woke to the awful news that a civilian airliner, more than two-thirds full of Canadians, had been shot down in those troubled skies over Iran, and 176 lives had been lost, 158 of them either Canadian citizens, permanent residents or people coming to Canada to study.

Ukrainian Airlines Flight PS752 had been shot down by two missiles launched by the Iranian military toward American bases in Iraq, Iran's western neighbour.

The previous few days in that conflicted area had been alarming: The U.S. had assassinated by drone an Iranian general, Quassem Soleimani, in Iraq. Iran was retaliating by firing missiles into Iraq, aiming at American bases there.

Still, civilian aircraft were being allowed to enter and leave Tehran's airspace. The doomed flight was headed for Kyiv, the capital of Ukraine, from where 158 passengers would board flights to Canada.

In the aftermath, Iran denied responsibility, then admitted it, then said it was a low-lever error. Then it kept the black box for eight months.

The sad loss of life demanded a co-ordinated Canadian response. The Prime Minister's Office, Global Affairs Canada, the Minister of Transport, the immigration department, the RCMP and civil aviation authorities organized to help the bereaved families, and seek information from Iranian authorities.

In March, Prime Minister Trudeau asked Ralph Goodale of Regina, a respected parliamentarian who had been in the House of Commons for 31 years, to undertake a full inquiry into the incident.

Now, in fewer than 11 months, we have a government report that deals with a sorrowful and enraging episode, but is so clearly written, with passion and anger, so well-documented and enlivened with pictures, names and data, it becomes an important read.

The report, entitled "Flight PS752: The Long Road to Transparency, Accountability and Justice" has a strong, local connection. At 62 pages in length, it singles out Peterborough's Greg Dempsey, a Canadian foreign service officer for the past 12 years, who had stints in Afghanistan, Geneva and New York, as one deserving of "special thanks for his skill, judgment and hard work."

Dempsey, who grew up in Peterborough, attended Edmison Heights School and Adam Scott Collegiate, researched and led the writing of the report. It is a model of clear narrative, and a significant contribution to international discussion. It honours the lives lost, and shows our public service at its best. It is of some comfort to the bereaved, and outlines the prevention of such air disasters.

Goodale, even in the pandemic, had co-operation from many government sectors, Global Affairs Canada, the Transportation and Safety Board and the RCMP. Since Canada closed its embassy in Iran in 2012, travellers have had to go to Turkey for their paperwork and then fly out of Tehran on one of a limited number of airlines. Goodale says It was "the toughest and most moving assignment I have ever undertaken." He praised the poise and courage of the families here in Canada, while they seek answers and grieve loved ones.

Global Affairs Canada had sent members of its Standing Rapid Deployment Team to Iran, regarding the issuing of death certificates, and then to five cities in Canada which had suffered the most casualties: Vancouver, Edmonton. Toronto, Montreal and Winnipeg. Poignant quotes from those people highlight the document. In receiving it, the prime minister pledged to institute a National Day of Remembrance for victims of military attacks on civilian aircraft, and a commitment of promote a "Safer Skies" pledge by all nations.

Says Greg Dempsey, "Although I have represented Canada in some of the toughest places in the world, and have worked to end all manner of human rights abuses, the tragic senselessness of flight PS752 is difficult to bear. The families of the victims have been incredible in the face of the tragedy. I hope this report and the commitment it expresses bring them some comfort and closure."

Exploring Greenland through the Arts
February 4, 2021

Aluu! (That's "hello" in Greenlandic.)

A chance encounter a few months ago when I went downtown to see Public Energy stage some unique, site-specific performances, led to watching eminent Canadian dancer Bill Coleman dance on the rail line, literally on the four-inch rail itself, in Millennium Park.

I ran into actor-director Patti Shaughnessy, whom I had known in the '90s when I was a teacher and she a student at St. Peter's. She was on her way to the red dress installation held in the park to honour Missing and Murdered Indigenous Women in our country.

Patti told me she and Coleman, her partner, were going shortly to Nuuk, the capital of Greenland, to create a play for its National Theatre. A whole new world was opening up to me. But first, I needed a map.

Greenland, situated entirely above 60 degrees north latitude, is the world's largest island, located in the Arctic and the Atlantic oceans. It has 56,000 people, mostly of Inuit heritage, and is an autonomous territory within the Kingdom of Denmark.

It has two official languages: Greenlandic and Danish. It is the least populated country in the world, and "the air quality," says Patti, "is the world's best." The size is stupendous, at 2 million square kilometres, and its mountainous beauty, with hundreds of coastal fjords, is staggering.

There have been 30 cases of COVID-19 since the outbreak, and precautions regarding visitors are in effect. The fishing industry dominates the economy, and there is rising interest in its rare minerals and in the new pathways in the North Atlantic.

Patti says, "In my 10 years of coming to Greenland, I have witnessed more ice in the fjords, the result of melting glaciers."

Tourists come for the northern lights, for whale watching, and to see to see snow hares and reindeer. And the friendly Inuit people.

Denmark sends an annual financial contribution to Greenland, and has devolved some government responsibilities to its leaders.

Greenland has self-government. Although Denmark maintains control over foreign and justice affairs, it benefits greatly from GL. It made a deal with the U.S. for Thule Air Base in the north.

Eighty percent of Greenland is permanently covered in a massive ice sheet. People live along the coast in settlements. Transportation around Greenland is by dogsled, a few cars in its 16 towns, airplanes and coastal vessels. Nuuk, with a population of 16,000, boasts the National Museum, an art gallery and the Katuaq Cultural Centre. To get to Greenland, one flies from Iqaluit in Nunavut, or from Iceland or Copenhagen.

Patti lives creatively out of her dual heritage, Irish and Anishnaabe. Both cultures are rich with storytellers. She grew up in Ennismore with her Irish-Canadian father and Anishnaabe mother and two brothers. "We were good at keeping life imaginative," she says. "We listened to my grandparents, Muriland and Ila Knott, telling stories in English or in Nishnaabemowin. And with grandparents Rita and John Shaughnessy on Highland Road, often singing and dancing."

Her family moved to Curve Lake when Patti was 14, and she worked in Whetung's Art Gallery, absorbing the art of Daphne Odjig and Norval Morrisseau. Teacher Patricia Young recalls Patti's warmth and humility. In 1992, the 500-year anniversary of the arrival of Europeans in Turtle Island, Young called together the Indigenous students at the school to produce a play using the words of Chief Dan George. Later, at Trent, Patti was influenced by elder Edna Manitowabi. "She helped me find my voice," Patti says.

Then she went to CIT, the Centre for Indigenous Theatre in Toronto where she met Makka Kleist, an actor from Greenland. An invitation to come to the great island followed. Patti has worked some months each year in Nuuk, this year directing "Angakkussaq: To Become a Shaman."

"My identity comes from my family and ancestors. They are with me wherever I go."

"Qujanaq" (thank you).

Pope's Book Offers a Message of Hope and Sharing
February 11, 2021

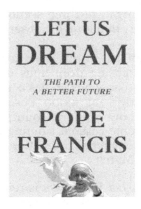

These days, early 2021, we are weary and dispirited, I think it safe to say. We are looking for leadership from anywhere, and leadership of the broadly spiritual kind, as well as the political.

I've been finding some in Pope Francis's recent letter to the world, written during the pandemic since last March, and published speedily by Simon and Schuster in only two languages, Spanish and English.

It is down-to-earth and accessible, almost folksy, with many personal examples of change of heart. It is called *Let Us Dream*. I am astonished at its frankness and self-revelation.

My writing over 40 years shows a frequent focus on the church of my formation, Roman Catholicism, and its supreme leaders. I've been enthusiastic about John XXIII, disappointed by the next two, John Paul II and Benedict, and now, although with deep feminist reservations, positive about Francis.

The organizational church is vast, both very flawed and at the same time, important in the lives of many people in the world. In a global pandemic, a climate crisis, and rising populism threatening democracy, Francis's behaviour and his words are worth considering.

Elected pope in 2013, he is 84 years of age, an Argentinian, the son of Italian immigrants, a Jesuit priest, and celibate. He is the 266th Pope of the church. I downloaded this short book to my Kindle, and I have been uplifted.

Five years ago, I rejoiced when he issued "Laudato Si" about the climate emergency. It brimmed with science, good sense and an ecumenical ethic that led to its being hailed around the world. Just as we locked down, the Pope called his good friend, British journalist Austen Ivereigh, to come and chat. Francis wanted to speak to the world, and Ivereigh guided him to organize three sections, following the format used by liberation theology in the 1970s: observe, judge and act.

It is clear that we are not "all in this crisis together." It is a class and race-based pandemic, exposing deep lines of inequality around the world. I heard today that Israel, which has control over the Palestinian territories, has reluctantly sent 5,000 doses of vaccine there. UN Women is crying out about western countries buying up available vaccines at any price. People without running water and crowded into slums have little chance to practise precautions. Francis notices all this. He plans a trip to Iraq in March.

Only 149 pages in length, *Let Us Dream* is remarkably open. The Pope says he has had three "COVID moments," including serious lung disease in his 20s, a feeling of desolation when sent to Spain to study, and a sense of inadequacy as bishop in Buenos Aires in the 1990s. "They were a purification, giving me greater ability to forgive and a fresh empathy for the powerless."

He pleads again and again that priority attention be given the poor and the natural world. No return to old ways. Rather, new growth after a harsh pruning. He is ever astute. "When people lose a sense of the common good, we are left with anarchy or authoritarianism in a violent, unstable society."

He warns of pessimism, narcissism and discouragement "Be an island of mercy in a sea of indifference" he says. "The economy is not the stock market: it is the well-being of a society."

"I am at the end of my life," he says, "overwhelmed but not hopeless. Go to the margins, to the saints next door, offer every person access to a dignified life, while regenerating the natural world."

This Pope shows a broad grasp of modern culture, mentioning poets, musicians and women economists. He refers to the "MeToo" movement, to George Floyd, to the Rohingya and Yazidis.

He is fiercely critical of the global economy, obsessed with profit but heedless of people and the environment. "We are being sifted," he says.

Altogether *Let us Dream* is a pleasure to read and an affirmation for these days. I'm tempted to call Francis a global spiritual director.

A Year's Worth of COVID-19 has Meant a Learning Explosion
February 18, 2021

The Sankofa Bird

Just think back a year. A difficult, worrisome year. For those of us securely housed and adequately incomed, (that's a new word "incomed," but you know what I mean), the lockdown has been full of trials and deprivations, mostly psychological and social. I find myself easily irritated and must strive daily not to let it show.

For the harder hit, the impoverished, the sick, the jobless, the bereaved, ever so much more pain. One pauses in respect. The one overwhelming privilege for the "comfortable" is the time to learn, really learn. Not only formally, but informally, as in reflection on our world and its travails.

Formally, I registered early on for a 90- minute course ($10) on writing, given by a cheeky startup in Calgary calling itself "Pandemic University." I await my certificate to be framed and put on the wall. My granddaughter takes virtual singing lessons, something she's longed for, and she gets full feedback from her teacher, Jen. She will sing at every invitation, mostly numbers from "Hamilton."

On family Zoom calls, we have played "Geoguessr," in which a location somewhere in the world is offered up, thanks to Google Earth, and the players have to guess where it is, from the visible landscape and language and other clues. We once failed to get Kentville, N.S. to our chagrin.

I respect all the teachers who have mastered the technology, even though most don't love it, in order to continue teaching online. That is beyond me, colleagues.

And the students shutting themselves in bedrooms with their computers, and emerging, bleary-eyed, in their pyjamas. Then they write exams at home under a kind of a technical surveillance thing. How awful is that?

One son takes up cooking. He is the unlikely, sports-minded one. He asks me for old family recipes, "That classic chili with sausage?" If finding sticky cards in a box marked "Mother's Favourites" is learning, then learning I am doing. How can one throw out cards in one's mother's handwriting?

Then there has been the loud return of essential humour. I think it played a large part in bringing Trump down. More witty people are drawing and posting clever pictures and jokes than ever. Stephen Colbert is a treasure on CBS if you can stay awake that late, and I laughed out loud at the "Colonoscopy Journal" written by Miami Herald humour writer Dave Barry. We have Michael de Adder in Halifax and John Fewings at the Examiner.

Some have learned to slow down and appreciate the outdoors. Trails and rinks are full of warmly-dressed people. Kawartha Nordic has almost doubled its membership. Some are honing their advocacy skills and writing persuasive letters to the editor. Some are exercising their basic altruism in caring for others, supporting the marginal, increasing their donations. We all sense a solidarity with others in fresh ways. Young people move off the sidewalk and let me pass unimpeded. Kind of like a leper to be avoided, but no, out of concern for me.

On one of our recent "Feminist Forum" webinars, I was struck with more new learning. A panelist, the eminent Jean Augustine, the same woman who, born in Grenada, was the first Black person elected to the House of Commons, and made the motion to declare Black History Month 25 years ago, turned our attention to the mythic Ghanaian bird, the Sankofa, which uniquely walks forward with her head turned backwards, while holding an egg in her beak.

It is a dramatic symbol of the importance of remembering the past while moving into the future. I've suggested that my family find me a tea towel or a painting of the Sankofa for my birthday.

My reading group is now into Robin Wall Kimmerer's 2013 book *Braiding Sweetgrass*, and for the first time, I feel that I'm learning something of the Indigenous worldview. When we chuck Adam and Eve as our only creation story, we see new things.

A quiet explosion of learning; let's look at lockdown that way.

Filmmaker James Cullingham Now Calls Peterborough Home
February 25, 2021

We've scored yet again, Peterborough! In our ongoing, unofficial project to attract talented and accomplished people in the arts, our middle-sized city continues to draw people of achievement to reside here.

Sometimes they arrive quietly, as James Cullingham and his spouse did two years ago. Sometimes it is to live closer to family. Often it is because we have a supportive and vibrant arts sector here. And our size, plus the access to the out-of-doors is appealing. Sometimes too, it is Trent University with its long arm beckoning return.

They usually come without fanfare, not overwhelming us with all they have done elsewhere. Into the fabric of Peterborough they weave their commitment and their work, to all our benefit.

Here is a shining example. James Cullingham is a Toronto-born, award-winning documentary filmmaker, who graduated from Trent and went on to work for CBC as executive producer of "As It Happens," and later to earn his PhD in Canadian and Latin American history, and launch his documentary film company, Tamarack Productions.

Here in Peterborough, Cullingham has joined the board of the Peterborough Historical Society.

He made "As Long as the River Flows" in 1991, a five-part series on Indigenous rights in Canada. Cullingham's longtime passion has been social justice topics. He teaches occasional courses at Seneca College, and serves as adjunct professor at Trent, all the while continuing to make documentary films, even in COVID-19 times.

Having served on the board of the Canadian Association of Journalists, he has long been concerned about the harassment and threats endured by journalists in other countries, suffered because of their work telling the truth about people in power. Hence his present project producing a one-hour documentary on 3 refugee journalists, from Syria, Turkey and Mexico, who have been granted refugee status in Canada, and live now in the Toronto area.

All his subjects, whom he now knows well, are brave, conscientious and well-educated citizens of their troubled countries. All three, Abdulrahman Matar from Syria, Arzu Yildiz from Turkey and Luis Najera from Mexico make their homes in the Greater Toronto Area, seek to be reunited with loved ones from home and either have attained or are seeking Canadian citizenship. That they have fled their native countries is harrowing, and James Cullingham wants to tell their stories. They themselves are storytellers whose lives have been threatened for such acts.

Canada, as a liberal democracy where freedom of speech and expression are protected, owes it to fellow practitioners of journalism to speak up for those who are threatened for truth-telling by tyrannical regimes. Canada must welcome and help to resettle such people.

And we do love our documentaries. Seventeen years of Reframe Film Festival have created a discerning audience in Peterborough for fact-based filmmaking. Cullingham found a local film company started by Rob Viscardis, called Paradigm Films to work with. Viscardis is the associate producer and post-production co-ordinator of "The Cost of Freedom." Hoping to have it out by fall, the team is seeking local and national financial support.

Rob was born here, attended Holy Cross and PCVS and made music for a while with a group called "Charming Ruins." He then went on to filmmaking, and works with cinematographer Pawel Dwulit. Cullingham says, "Many of my journalist colleagues in other countries do not enjoy the democratic rights and personal safety that I do. Each has paid a dreadful price professionally and personally for fleeing their countries for fear of their lives."

Local support for "The Cost of Freedom" has come from Gzowski College, the Symons Trust for Canadian Studies, the Kawartha World Issues Centre and the New Canadians Centre. In a nice small touch, I was at an Amnesty International Group 46 virtual meeting last week where the group voted that, from its present bank balance of $174, one hundred dollars would happily be donated to this project. That's what we do. For further information about the project, contact: www.tamarack productions .com

Wit and Worry After a Year of COVID-19 in Peterborough
March 3, 2021

Let's start with three jokes. That's how we should start each day. That and meditation. Laugh heartily, then go on to the serious stuff. Look in any direction and you'll see the worrying stuff. But with the laughter and the silence, you'll be the stronger.

First the funny from Twitter, "Looks as if Colin Kaepernick, Dr. Fauci and Hillary Clinton were right all along."

From Facebook, "I haven't been out in a while. Does anyone know if Eaton's, Consumers Distributing and Blockbuster still have the same hours?" Another wit responds, "Same hours as Zellers." Finally, don't, whatever you do, miss James Corden and celebrity cook Gordon Ramsay conducting their Master Chef contest for Seniors. On YouTube.

Next, the worrying. We are still absorbing what just happened to threaten democracy in the U.S. What a close call. How off-balance are those millions of Americans who have accepted the lies spun by amoral leaders and amplified by amoral media?

New York Times columnist Nicholas Kristof writes that when Donald Trump is charged with conspiracy to subvert the Constitution, Fox News should be charged as a co-conspirator, so harmful has this "news" channel become.

In Canada, voices of alarm are being raised about some Conservative members (Derek Sloan), and now Cheryl Gallant (Pembroke-Renfrew), who make outrageous charges about their political opponents. There is the National Post newspaper, celebrating nonsensical writers such as Conrad Black, and now Rex Murphy. There is Rebel Media. The Proud Boys are labelled a terrorist organization. There is Lifesite News. All ours.

I took part in a webinar on this problem recently, sponsored by the voluntary group Friends of Canadian Broadcasting, and convened by its able director, Daniel Bernhard.

It was about Canadian delusion and nastiness. Two UBC professors, Heidi Tworek and Chris Denove, reported on their study of Twitter posts over a two-month period during the federal election of 2019. The messages were directed at the five national leaders. The researchers examined one million of these posts and found only 7 percent were positive. Sixteen percent were abusive and the rest, highly negative. Prime Minister Justin Trudeau was mentioned 51,000 times and Andrew Scheer 23,000.

A few were "probably illegal, really poisonous," said Denove. "Most were antagonistic. We need to realize that these messages are not just a platform problem, but reflect the wider Canadian society."

If we slide down this path of ugly public speech, by which anonymous, online haters discourage good people from entering politics, we will be poorer in every way. Most of the vile messages have to do with one's identity. Many are sexist and many racist. Another dangerous effect of them is that they trigger off-kilter people, to be inspired to act out their hate for others.

Yet, 64 percent of Canadians agree that online harassment and threats are a threat to democracy. The challenge is to curb them: to get the algorithms under control. Governments everywhere are pondering what rules to bring in. MP Iqra Khalid, chair of the House of Commons Committee on Justice, said that the dilemma is to find the balance between "free speech and safe space." America clearly hasn't got that balance yet. Charlie Angus, the thoughtful NDP member from northern Ontario, spoke of the breakdown of public conversation and his own experience bringing in police to curb a stalker. He fears some dreadful future event such as the murder of British MP Jo Cox, in 2016.

There is a difference between "awful but lawful" remarks, he said, and illegal calls for violence. Bob Zimmer, an MP from B.C. works on designing mechanisms for enforcement.

I looked up "algorithms." It comes from mathematics and computer science, "a set of rules, well-defined instructions; like a recipe." When we click on a social media platform, an algorithm calculates our action so that advertisers can pitch products to us according to our interests. Clicking is "a political act," says Susan Brooks Thistlethwaite, a public theologian and columnist. We need to take that in, and praise and practice civil speech.

This is a Troubling, Difficult time for Post-Secondary Students
March 11, 2021

The word "enwayaang" is an Anishinabe term meaning "the way we speak together." It is pronounced "en-why-ing," and describes the weekly Zoom chats and other activities going on these days organized by Gzowski College, for its students particularly, but open and advertised to everyone.

Gzowski College, led by its dynamic principal, Dr Melanie Buddle and her creative college assistants, Stephanie Curtin and Alison Peek, is at the moment host to about 80 percent of its usual first-year campus population. In these days of community indignation about COVID-19 infections on campuses, it must be remembered that the vast majority of students respectfully abide by protocols and are equally embarrassed by the situation that has developed.

How does leadership support and strengthen these students during a very hard time of their lives? After all, a recent Globe and Mail story describes this group as "bored, lonely and stuck." Some of their classes are "synchronous," which means beamed out online by their professors at a specific, announced time. Others are "asynchronous" or taped for watching anytime. For a young person at university, that's usually at 2 a.m.

All groups have had life turned upside down, but for the young it is dreams gone awry and key events gone forever. Into the breach, step educators resolved to make life more bearable. Lead them outdoors for one thing. At Gzowski, there are weekly "Tipi Treks" to the First Peoples House of Learning grounds where a Firekeeper will speak, and "Wellness Walks" with the principal, sometimes on snowshoes.

Weekly zoom chats take place on a subject the students are interested in. A speaker, either a professor or a community member who is passionate about a subject, will come on and chat for an hour.

These enwayaang meetings have featured Joel Baetz on comic books, Jenna Pilgrim on safeguarding one's reputation on the internet, Drew Hayden Taylor on Indigenous storytelling, Cam Douglas on his high school class on sustainability, and yours truly on growing a global mind.

Since its beginning in the 1960s under the leadership of the visionary late Thomas Symons, Trent University has sought to serve the larger community of Peterborough. This is just the latest project. I have been enriched by hearing Stephen Lewis, former ambassador to the U.N. who spoke at the Athletic Centre, and world-famous journalist, Gwynne Dyer at Gzowski.

I do treadmill, when we aren't locked down, at the Athletic Centre and enjoy soups from Planet Bakery. So at home am I at Trent, that it pains me to hear about citizens, those who have never attended a post-secondary place and have a feeling of intimidation, or a fear of not understanding what goes on.

I spoke to a young woman recently, a college graduate, the first in her family. Her grandparents, who had raised her, were intimidated coming to her graduation, feeling they had no right to be there. Universities owe a lot to the cities and towns they are located in. Relationships matter. They are expensive institutions to build and to maintain. Trent seems to understand this. Its fundamental responsibility is to research, high scholarship and teaching.

But it will also cooperate fully with the community, providing lands and sports facilities and access to a library. I delighted a year ago to attend the World Women's Field Hockey tournament at Trent. I always take in the annual rowing regatta.

Recently I spoke with Trent's chancellor, a graduate from the sixties and an arts producer, Stephen Stohn. He himself has been busy during the pandemic hosting weekly "Trent Talks," online conversations with two professors each week about their interests. It's another link between "town" and "gown."

So, a salute to Trent and Gzowski and Buddle, who, I hasten to add, is a "local girl," the daughter of science teacher Bill Buddle and his wife Liz Buddle, a yoga teacher, in Lakefield. Years ago, I was motivated towards fitness by Liz Buddle.

Now it's about continuing my education at our university. Miigwetch.

Rosemary Ganley in Scotland, October 2019

Epilogue

At this time of publication, we are slowly emerging, battered but not broken, from the long global COVID-19 pandemic. The stories of human and earth resilience and creativity are still there to be told. More necessary than ever. I hope to tell some of those stories, now and in the future.

Rosemary Ganley

About Rosemary Ganley

Rosemary Ganley is a Peterborough-based writer and journalist. Born in Kirkland Lake, Ontario, she studied English and philosophy at the University of Toronto, and taught secondary school for many years in Cornwall, ON, Dorval, PQ, and Peterborough, ON in public, separate and independent schools.

In 1975, she and her spouse John Ganley and their three young boys accepted a teaching assignment in Kingston, Jamaica through the Canadian International Development Agency. Their lives were changed. In 1977, the Ganleys returned to Peterborough and began to draw people interested in supporting poor people's projects in Jamaica, both urban and rural.

The Ganleys were then off to Dar-es-Salaam, Tanzania on another CIDA posting from 1978-1981, but the seed of Jamaican Self-Help had been planted, and it became incorporated as a registered charity and NGO in 1980. In 1985, the YWCA of Peterborough named Rosemary Ganley "Woman of the Year."

To her delight, the award was presented by her favorite Canadian writer, Margaret Laurence. The two women shared a deep admiration for Caribbean literature, and for peace and justice activism. Rosemary studied Caribbean literature at the University of the West Indies, and African literature later at the University of Dar-es-Salaam, Tanzania.

Rosemary's interest were broad - internationalism and the role of religions from a feminist perspective were among them. She attended the United Nations Fourth World Conference on Women in Beijing in 1995. She and her colleague Linda Slavin founded the first "Person's Day Breakfast" in Peterborough in 1991.

Rosemary and John Ganley made frequent trips to Jamaica to strengthen links, monitor projects and encourage partners. They moved back to Jamaica in 1998 to rural Highgate, St. Mary, and lived there part of each year for three years. Rosemary taught feminist theology at the University of the West Indies.

The writing continued. Coming back to live in Canada, Rosemary commuted to Toronto from 2001 to 2006 as co-editor of the independent newspaper, Catholic New Times. Her volunteer work with Jamaican Self-Help was onging, and she accompanied some 600 youth to Jamaica on awareness trips from 1984-2012. In 2011, the Ganleys were added to the Peterborough Pathway of Fame, and in 2012 Rosemary was named a "Woman of Distinction" by the Red Pashmina Campaign.

Rosemary currently writes a weekly column for the Peterborough Examiner. Most recently, Rosemary Ganley was named by Prime Minster Trudeau to the Gender Equality Advisory Council for the G7 meetings in Canada in June, 2018.

Rosemary's email address is **rganley2016@gmail.com**

For updates and to purchase books online, please go to ~
www.yellowdragonflypress.ca